D1406710

READER'S GUIDE
TO THE BIBLE

Chronological Reading Plan

GEORGE H. GUTHRIE

LifeWay Press®
Nashville, Tennessee

Published by LifeWay Press®
© 2011 George H. Guthrie

No part of this book may be reproduced or transmitted in any form or by any means, electronic or mechanical, including photocopying and recording, or by any information storage or retrieval system, except as may be expressly permitted in writing by the publisher. Requests for permission should be addressed in writing to LifeWay Press®; One LifeWay Plaza; Nashville, TN 37234-0175.

ISBN 978-1-4158-7105-8

Item 005414497

Dewey decimal classification: 220.07
Subject headings: BIBLE—STUDY AND TEACHING \ CHRISTIAN LIFE \ BIBLE—READING

All Scripture quotations are taken from the Holman Christian Standard Bible®, Copyright © 1999, 2000, 2002, 2003, 2009 by Holman Bible Publishers. Used by permission. Holman Christian Standard Bible®, Holman CSB®, and HCSB® are federally registered trademarks of Holman Bible Publishers.

To order additional copies of this resource: write to LifeWay Church Resources Customer Service; One LifeWay Plaza; Nashville, TN 37234-0113; fax (615) 251-5933; phone toll free (800) 458-2772; order online at www.lifeway.com; e-mail orderentry@ lifeway.com; or visit the LifeWay Christian Store serving you.

Printed in the United States of America

Leadership and Adult Publishing
LifeWay Church Resources
One LifeWay Plaza
Nashville, TN 37234-0175

Contents

The Author 4

Foreword 5

Introduction 6

Act 1: God's Plan for All People 7
  Scene 1: Creation 8
  Scene 2: The Fall 9
  Scene 3: The Flood 10

Act 2: God's Covenant People 13
  Scene 1: The People 14
  Scene 2: Deliverance 28
  Scene 3: Covenant and Law 32
  Scene 4: The Land 51
  Scene 5: Kings and Prophets: God Shapes
           a Kingdom People 62
  Scene 6: Kings and Prophets: God Divides
           the Kingdom People 103
  Scene 7: Kings and Prophets:
           The Southern Kingdom
           as God's People 120
  Scene 8: Exile 140
  Scene 9: Return 158

Act 3: God's New-Covenant People 167
  Scene 1: Christ's Coming 169
  Scene 2: Christ's Ministry 170
  Scene 3: Christ's Deliverance
           of His People 185
  Scene 4: Christ's Church 192
  Scene 5: Christ's Second Coming
           and Reign 221

The Author

George H. Guthrie serves as the Benjamin W. Perry Professor of Bible at Union University in Jackson, Tennessee. A respected New Testament scholar and a deeply committed churchman, he is the author of numerous articles and several books, including Hebrews in The NIV Application Commentary (Zondervan, 1998) and "James" in Hebrews–Revelation, The Expositor's Bible Commentary (Zondervan, 2006).

As the architect of the Read the Bible for Life biblical-literacy initiative, Guthrie has written or edited four tools, including this reader's guide (LifeWay, 2011), the small-group study Read the Bible for Life (LifeWay, 2010), Read the Bible for Life: Your Guide to Understanding and Living God's Word (B&H, 2011), and Reading God's Story: A Chronological Daily Bible (B&H, 2011). Guthrie has participated in translation projects, such as the revision of the New Living Translation, and has served as a consultant on the Holman Christian Standard Bible, the New Century Version, and the English Standard Version. At Union University he led in the establishment of and serves as Senior Fellow in the Ryan Center for Biblical Studies, which is committed to promoting sound Bible reading, study, and interpretation in local churches.

Guthrie holds PhD and MDiv degrees from Southwestern Baptist Theological Seminary and a ThM from Trinity Evangelical Divinity School. He and his wife, Pat, live with their two children, Joshua and Anna, near Jackson, Tennessee. The family attends Northbrook Church, which Guthrie and his wife helped plant and which he copastored for 10 years.

Foreword

I was sitting across the lunch table from George Guthrie. "I'm considering leading our church to read through the Bible together next year," I said.

"It's interesting that you say that," Dr. Guthrie responded. "I'm developing a plan to help people and entire churches walk through redemptive history chronologically so that they can see the power of God's Word and understand how their individual stories fit in God's story."

By the next week we were finalizing details for how our church could field-test what you now hold in your hand, *Reader's Guide to the Bible*, an intentional, devotional, systematic journey through the history of redemption in Scripture. During the next year, starting at Genesis 1, the members of our church journeyed from creation to new creation. For the first time many of them saw how the different books of the Bible come together to form one story. This journey through God's Word dramatically transformed the lives of individual followers of Christ and radically revolutionized our church.

Indeed, the Bible contains one grand story of one global God who is saving His people through one glorious gospel. *We need to know this story.* We need to see, understand, and comprehend how all of the pages of Scripture come together in one overarching plot. Such knowledge, penetrating both our hearts and our minds, is essential for growing in Christlikeness.

We need to experience this story. It's not just about people thousands of years ago. It's about you, me, and the people God is drawing to Himself all around us.

We need to tell this story. When we know and experience this story, we are compelled to give our lives to proclaiming this story to the ends of the earth.

Reader's Guide is an invaluable tool for individual followers of Christ, small groups of Christians, and entire churches. Let this guide lead you to discover the boundless treasures contained in the Bible, God's story, and let His Word change your life and your church for your great good and His great glory.

David Platt, Pastor
The Church at Brook Hills
Birmingham, Alabama

Introduction

Reader's Guide to the Bible gives you step-by-step guidance as you walk through the pages of God's Word day by day. This guide is laid out in a chronological reading plan and provides personal coaching in how to read the portion of Scripture suggested for each day. As you read, this guide will help you keep track of where you are in the story of Scripture and will provide help for reading the different kinds of literature found in the Bible. It will also help you understand especially difficult passages and will point to the significance of people, places, and events as they relate to the grand story of Scripture.

Here are some suggestions for getting the most from *Reader's Guide.*
1. *Read at a specific time and place each day until it becomes a habit.* If you miss a day, make it up and keep going.
2. *As you start each week, read the introduction to that week.* Then read the brief commentary for that day before reading the passages from the Bible.
3. *Always keep the big story in view.* Reader's Guide is laid out in three acts and 17 scenes to familiarize you with the framework of the Bible's story. The headings at the top of each page remind you where you are in the story. You can use *Reader's Guide* with any Bible translation, but you might want to consider *Reading God's Story: A Chronological Daily Bible* (HCSB translation).
4. *Fill in the names of important characters on the timelines each week.* Three biblical timelines are inserted in *Reader's Guide.* As you work your way through *Reader's Guide* each week, you will find directions for writing on the timelines the names of key people who appear in the Bible readings that week.
5. *Read in community with others.* Small-group discussion questions are provided at the end of each week.
6. *Acquire tools to help you read the Bible better.* You can find free study tools at the Web site *www.mystudybible.com.* A sound study Bible would also be helpful. Other support materials are available at *www.lifeway.com/readthebibleforlife.*

I want to thank David Platt and The Church at Brook Hills in Birmingham, Alabama, who field-tested *Reader's Guide* and wrote the small-group discussion questions you will find at the end of each week. Also, in addition to many good study tools, I found special help in *How to Read the Bible Book by Book* (Zondervan, 2002) by Gordon Fee and Douglas Stuart.

I pray that as you work your way through *Reader's Guide to the Bible,* you will understand God's Word better and be changed by it forever.

God's Plan for All People

t way in thes
om e has appointe en of
univ rse. e is th radiance
re, d H sus ins in
catie for sin , e sat down at th
h. He eca e h ar
erited is superior eirs. for to which of the angels did e eve
ou are My Son; today ave become Your Father," or again, "I w
His Father, and He will be My Son?'" When He again brings His
n into the world, He says: "And all God's angels must worship H

WEEK I

In our first week of readings, we will cover all of act I in the story of the Bible. This act consists of three scenes:

1. The creation of the world, with human beings as the pinnacle of that creation
2. The fall into sin and its consequences
3. The flood, the first expression of God's judgment on the human race as a whole, as well as His desire to preserve the life He created

Act I is very brief in comparison to the other two acts in the biblical story, but theologically, it is very important. In numerous ways act I lays the foundation for the rest of the Bible. In addition to the main events, we will see many expressions of God's desire to have a relationship with people and His grace when people sin. As you read, slow down and notice the details, including moments of tension and crisis, and how these are resolved. This segment of Scripture is packed with important themes that will continue throughout all of Scripture, including the central theme of covenant. As you read Genesis I and Psalms, allow the music of these passages to touch you and teach you things about God.

 SCENE I: CREATION: THE GOD OF ALL LIFE

DAY 1 Genesis 1–2

Notice ways the days of creation relate to each other: day 1 to day 4, day 2 to day 5, and day 3 to day 6. Days 1, 2, and 3 tell of God's creation of settings to be inhabited, while days 4, 5, and 6 introduce the characters that inhabit those settings. God built both beauty and order into His creation. There was also a progression in creation, a process climaxing in the creation of human beings. According to Genesis 2:2-3, God rested on the seventh day, blessed that day, and declared it holy. In declaring one day of the week special, God built order and rhythm into the weekly human routine.

Identify the order and rhythm of rest in your weekly patterns.

In Genesis 2 the author took one aspect of the creation account in Genesis 1—the creation of man and woman—and expanded on it. When you read narrative passages in Scripture, remember that God is the hero of the story.

How is God the hero in Genesis 2?

What does the passage say about the nature and beauty of marriage as God designed it?

TIMELINE
Old Testament Timeline, Part 1: write *Adam* on line 1 and *Eve* on line 2 in act 1, scene 1.

10/16/11

DAY 2 Psalms 8; 104; John 1:1-3

Psalm 8, a reflection on Genesis 1–2, describes our worth and responsibility as human beings. Think about what this psalm means for us as modern believers. Notice the first and last verses of the psalm; God is the real focus here.

Meditate on the description of God in Psalm 104:1-9 and notice how the psalmist responds to God in verses 33-35. The psalms often use rich word pictures to communicate truth.

How did the author paint a picture using word pictures?

Notice how the words of John 1:1-3, which speak of Jesus as the Word, echo Genesis 1:1.

Read Genesis 1:1 again in light of John 1:1-3 and take a moment to worship Jesus as the Creator of all that is.

 ## SCENE 2: THE FALL: REJECTING GOD'S VISION FOR LIFE

10/17/11

DAY 3 Genesis 3–5

Watch for the patterns of human sin depicted in Genesis 3–4:
• Temptation to question God's Word: "Did God really say … ?" (3:1).
• The false promise of desire
• The experience of shame and consequences of sin

Also notice the attempt to blame others for sin, the refusal to take responsibility for sinful actions. Finally, notice that in chapter 4 the problem was not just with Cain's offering but with Cain himself; this is a key to understanding the story.

How do these stories reflect your own battle with temptation?

TIMELINE
Old Testament Timeline, Part 1: write *Cain* on line 1 and *Abel* on line 2 in act 1, scene 2.

SCENE 3: THE FLOOD: GOD JUDGES AND MAKES A COVENANT TO PRESERVE LIFE

DAY 4 Genesis 6–7

10/16"

Watch for details as you read today. Also keep the big picture in mind: the pervasiveness of sin and its devastating consequences. Notice what we learn about God in the first eight verses of Genesis 6, keeping in mind that He is the main actor in the story. Watch for expressions of God's grace and His desire to preserve life in the midst of judgment. Also notice what we learn about Noah as the story continues: he was a righteous man and walked with God. Noah's responses called for a great deal of trust in God in the face of cataclysmic events, yet at times it is difficult for us to trust God in minor events of everyday life. Perhaps Noah's walk with God was the key.

How might you express your trust in God today and learn to walk with God every day?

TIMELINE
Old Testament Timeline, Part I: write **Noah** on line I in act I, scene 3.

DAY 5 Genesis 8–9; Psalm 12

10/19"

Read Genesis 8:15–9:7, discerning how these verses echo the first three chapters of Genesis.

Why might the author have included these echoes?

Now read chapter 9 and notice the differences from Genesis 1–3.

How do these differences develop the overall story of Genesis?

A covenant with God is often at the heart of the story of the Old Testament. A covenant is basically an agreement between two parties. God established a covenant with the Jewish people, first through Abraham, and then renewed it with various leaders throughout the Old Testament. The covenant stated that if the people kept God's law, He would be their God, and they would be His people.

What role does the covenant play in Genesis 9?

Reflect especially on verse 5 of Psalm 12. Worship God as One who rises up to help those burdened by evil people, providing a safe place for them. If you are being hurt by wickedness, cry out to God for help even as you worship.

10/24/11

DAY 6 Genesis 10–11

Genealogies in the Bible strike some readers as uninteresting. However, these are part of God's Word, and we can learn from them. Among other things, the genealogies give us a sense of the passing of time, moving the story along. We also get a picture of the connectedness of people and events in the Bible's narrative. This is not a patchwork of loosely connected stories but one story God is writing on the world. Meditate on the contrasts you find in Genesis 11:1-9. Now read the passage in light of Acts 2:1-21, noticing both the contrasts and the parallels with that passage. One problem reflected in Genesis 11 is that these people had an arrogant disregard for God's mandate to "fill the earth" (Gen. 9:1). Think about how that mandate was ultimately fulfilled through the church in Acts as it advanced the kingdom of God in the world.

How are you called to participate in God's mandate to "fill the earth" by sharing the good news with others?

SMALL-GROUP DISCUSSION QUESTIONS

1. List several big stories of the Old Testament that are often taught to children.

2. Describe a time you began to watch a movie in the middle. How did it affect the way you understood the plot? How might a lack of information about the beginning of God's story affect how we understand Scripture?

3. List all God created in the six days of creation. What does that account reveal about God's character? How should that revelation affect the way we live each day?

4. Read Genesis 2:15-17; 3:1-7. How is God's authority acknowledged and rejected in these events? Why did God bring judgment on Adam and Eve?

5. How does North American culture try to convince us that we have no judge? How do we think and act as if we were our own judges?

6. How did God show both judgment and compassion to Adam and Eve?

7. How do our need for redemption and God's compassion toward His people through Adam and Eve's story set the stage for God's acts throughout history?

8. Why is God's plan to redeem humanity the only one that has power to work?

ACT 2

God's Covenant People

WEEK 2

It would be hard to overstate the importance of this moment in biblical history. This week's readings take us halfway through act 2, scene 1 in the story of the Bible. This scene introduces Abraham as the father of the Jewish people and the patriarch with whom God made a foundational agreement (covenant). In the Old Testament stories, covenant is often at the heart of what is going on. Notice how God advanced and developed the covenant through Abraham's son, Isaac, and his grandson, Jacob, and how God challenged each man's faith through moments of crisis that defined who he would be as God's representative. As you read, also notice the prominent role God played in the developing story. He was the main actor, moving the story along according to His grand design.

SCENE 1: THE PEOPLE: GOD CALLS A COVENANT PEOPLE

DAY 1 Genesis 12–13

Genesis 12 tells the story of God's calling Abram (whose name would eventually be changed to Abraham). Abram was born during a violent time in which nations constantly fought with their enemies. The aspects of God's promise to Abram in Genesis 12:1-3 seem very countercultural for that time: God's people would be a blessing to other people groups!

> *How might this promise lay a foundation for the biblical emphasis on the way God's people should treat their enemies, a theme developed in both the Old and New Testaments?*

> *Whom might you bless today? How will you do so?*

Notice the movement from place to place and the importance of geography. Abram's relocation lays a foundation for the importance of the land of Canaan in the Bible's story. Look at a map in your Bible or in a Bible dictionary to trace Abram's journey.

DAY 2 Genesis 14–16

Genesis 14 recounts the rescue of Lot and the blessing given to Abram by Melchizedek. Notice that when the covenant with Abram was established in chapter 15, this encounter with God placed a greater emphasis on Abram's children and faith than we saw in chapter 12. Yet the story of the birth of Ishmael in chapter 16 showed the results of a lack of trust in God when Abram faced a delay in God's fulfillment of His promise. Rather than affirming polygamy and the sexual use of concubines, God subverted these institutions in the Book of Genesis, showing that they are not the divine pattern. Nevertheless, God was gracious to Hagar and Ishmael, and He worked through the cultural patterns of the Ancient Near East.

With what delay are you presently trusting God?

Worship God for His grace as you struggle to trust Him with your wait.

DAY 3 Genesis 17–19

In Genesis 17 God reiterated the covenant, changing Abram's name to Abraham, meaning *father of a multitude*, and giving him the sign of circumcision. Genesis 18:19 emphasizes that God would fulfill the promises He had made to Abraham as Abraham's children lived out God's commands (see Gen. 12:1-3). Meditate on the fact that today God also uses circumcision as a sign of covenant (see Rom. 2:28-29), and God uses our obedience to His commands to fulfill certain promises to us today. In other words, God blesses us as we live according to His ways.

Is there any situation in your life now for which you are requesting God's blessings although you are not living according to His ways?

The destruction of Sodom and Gomorrah in Genesis 19 presents a clear picture of God's judgment on sin, while His rescue of Lot depicts God's compassion and desire to rescue.

Do you grasp the seriousness of sin? What evidence supports your answer?

TIMELINE
Old Testament Timeline, Part I: write **Abraham** on line I in act 2, scene I.

DAY 4 Genesis 20–23

One subplot in the Book of Genesis is the choosing of the younger son instead of the older. In the Ancient Near East honoring the rights of the firstborn son was a dominant cultural practice. In Genesis God subverted this aspect of the culture by consistently blessing the younger son. God traced His covenant promise through Isaac instead of Ishmael because Isaac was the son of God's promise; Ishmael, on the other hand, was the product of human ingenuity. Notice the expressions of faith in God that are found in Genesis 22:3-10.

With what sacrifice are you currently being asked to trust God?

15

How does this part of the story of the Bible underscore God as the hero?

What details of the story seem most significant to you?

TIMELINE

Old Testament Timeline, Part 1: write *Isaac* on line 2 in act 2, scene 1.

DAY 5 Genesis 24–26

A new character enters the story today: Rebekah, who would become Isaac's wife. Chapter 24 presents a beautiful story of God's providence. Notice that the story of Rebekah focuses on God's sure guidance and Rebekah's willingness to follow God's lead. This was a significant moment in the development of God's people. At the end of chapter 25, Esau sold Jacob his birthright, which was the right of the firstborn son to a double portion of the inheritance from the father. Consider what this tells us about Esau (see Heb. 12:14-17): he was oriented to physical wants, undervaluing spiritual realities. Perhaps this is the reason God planned for His people to come through Jacob.

How might you demonstrate that you value the truly important things or people in your life?

TIMELINE

Old Testament Timeline, Part 1: write *Jacob* on line 3 in act 2, scene 1.

DAY 6 Genesis 27–29

Biblical families sometimes provide prime examples of dysfunctionality, showing us that God works with and through very imperfect people and their imperfect cultures. Read Genesis 27:5-13, about Rebekah's role in Jacob's theft of Esau's blessing, in light of the broader context of today's reading (especially Gen. 25:19-27).

How does the context help you understand Rebekah's actions?

Take a moment to praise God for your family, warts and all, and to pray that God will work in and through you as a family in spite of your weaknesses and problems.

SMALL-GROUP DISCUSSION QUESTIONS

1. Abraham took a risk to obey God. Discuss a situation in which you were forced to make an important decision without much information. How did you feel trying to make this decision? How did you feel about the final decision?

2. Read Genesis 12:1-9. How did God's call disrupt Abram's life? What securities did Abram leave behind? How did God's call lead Abram to fully rely on God?

3. Why is relying on God difficult for us? Why is it scary?

4. How do we ignore God's call on our lives when we claim not to have enough information? What things or people are we not willing to leave in order to obey God?

5. Which areas of life are the most difficult in which to obey God? How does our obedience testify to our relationship with Him?

6. What was God's purpose in blessing Abram and calling this nation to Himself as His chosen people? How is God's heart for the nations revealed in this covenant?

7. Read Genesis 15:1-6. How did Abram respond to this covenant reminder?

8. Summarize the story of Abraham and Isaac in Genesis 22. How did God provide for Abraham? How did God later provide a sacrifice for us?

9. Look at God's covenant promises to Isaac in Genesis 26:23-25 and to Jacob in Genesis 28:10-17. How do you see God continuing to fulfill the covenant promise that He first made to Abraham?

WEEK 3

This week we will cover the last half of act 2, scene 1 in the biblical story, taking us through the remainder of Jacob's story and focusing especially on the story of Joseph's travails and triumphs in Egypt. This week look for recurring themes in the narratives about Jacob and Joseph. We have seen that Jacob's life was marked by deception. Yet notice the great integrity of Joseph's life; in his integrity he confronted and forgave the lack of it in his own brothers. Finally, this story is one of deliverance (from famine), but it also sets up the story of the great deliverance, the exodus, by moving Jacob's family to Egypt.

DAY 1 Genesis 30–33

Notice the progression of the story in today's reading.

1. In Genesis 30 both the resources and the sons of Jacob multiplied; he became rich in sons and material wealth.
2. Jacob then separated from Laban and moved his family back toward the land promised by God.
3. A crisis arose. Genesis 32:24-32 is a difficult passage, but we have clues about what was going on. Remember to watch for details when reading Old Testament stories. Jacob's name, the name of the tributary he crossed (Jabbok; see v. 22), and the word *wrestle* in Hebrew all sound very similar, so this was obviously a significant crossroads moment in Jacob's life. Jacob's wrestling with the angelic being, who was there representing God, had to do with who Jacob would be in the future; notice the change of his name to Israel, which means *God strives*. He had lived as a deceiver but was humbled here by the striking of his hip; he was blessed in this moment of struggle. Read this story as a turning point in Jacob's life and experience with God.

> *What does this passage teach you about a relationship with God and how blessing often comes from struggle?*

DAY 2 Genesis 34–37

As you read the narratives in today's chapters, notice several dynamics. In the story of the rape of Dinah, watch for the motives of the various characters and how the craftiness of Jacob's sons defeated the craftiness of the local inhabitants of the area. The sons of Jacob took after their father, whose name means *deceiver*. Remember that covenant often lies at the heart of Old Testament stories. Genesis 35 is built around the renewal of the covenant with

Jacob and the confirmation of his new name, Israel. He was to chart a new course in life. The family dynamics in Genesis 37 echo earlier dynamics seen in Genesis. A father's loving one child more than his other children led to problems. Yet God worked through even the dysfunctionality of this family. Think about the fact that God uses less-than-perfect people and less-than-perfect families to accomplish His purposes. He can use you and your family if you will yield to Him.

How might God want to use you and your family?

DAY 3 Genesis 38–40

The story of Genesis 38 shows that the Israelites were beginning to assimilate the practices of the people of Canaan. This explains why God sent them down to Egypt, where their identity was maintained and refined. The practice depicted here is the law of levirate marriage (see Deut. 25:5-10), by which the brother or close relative of a childless husband who died would marry the dead brother's widow and have children with her. The story underlines that Judah was beginning to incorporate patterns of behavior into his life that were destructive and unrighteous.

Look for several statements about Joseph that are repeated in Genesis 39. They will tip you off to main themes in Joseph's story.

How can Joseph serve as an example to you today?

TIMELINE
Old Testament Timeline, Part 1: write *Joseph* on line 4 in act 2, scene 1.

DAY 4 Genesis 41–43

A dominant theme in the story of Joseph is the sovereignty of God as He orchestrates events in the lives of individuals and nations. He is the main actor or hero in these stories. Watch for key verses that emphasize this theme.

Also notice the emphasis on justice in these chapters. Joseph's brothers saw their treatment by this administrator of Egypt as an expression of God's judgment. Ironically, it was really an expression of God's grace as He prepared a way to preserve their lives.

Finally, identify the temporal setting of this section of Genesis—the time when the events took place.

Why might God have waited until this point to exalt Joseph?

How might God's purpose in Joseph's waiting relate to God's timing of events in your life?

Think about the fact that timing is of the Lord. God works out the timing of His work in the lives of His people.

DAY 5 Genesis 44–46

Today the story comes to a dramatic climax.

What elements of tension are built into the story?

How is the tension resolved?

We also see in this passage the grand means of God's fulfilling His promises to His people. Jacob and his whole family were preserved by the move to Egypt, and Joseph paved the way. As you read this section, look for various expressions of God's grace. Worship God today as a God of great grace for you.

DAY 6 Genesis 47–50

Because the Lord worked through Joseph on behalf of Egypt, the powers of the world (Pharaoh in Egypt) worked on behalf of God's people. Notice that Joseph worked as a force of blessing all the way to the end of the Book of Genesis.

Another key theme in Genesis is the blessing of children as a father was about to die. Notice ways Jacob's blessing of Joseph's children (see Gen. 48:13-20) was both similar to and different from Isaac's blessing of Jacob in Genesis 27.

How might you bless people around you today?

SMALL-GROUP DISCUSSION QUESTIONS

1. Describe events that make people question God's goodness. Why is it easy to question God in these situations?

2. How might Joseph's unjust treatment have seemed horrible and unfair to him even though his life was spared?

3. Think about the decisions of Joseph's brothers, Potiphar's wife, and Potiphar. How do their actions seem to contradict God's plans?

4. What was God's purpose for Joseph's life?

5. How did Joseph's faithfulness allow God to use him?

6. In what ways is it easy to miss God's work in our circumstances? How is God's love for His people evident through His actions?

7. Why is it easier to see God's hand in our lives as we look to the past?

8. Why do we desire to place blame on someone for our circumstances?

9. How does it make you feel to know that you or anyone else cannot keep God's purposes from being accomplished?

10. What is most often our attitude toward God when our plans are thwarted?

11. How should we view our circumstances when our plans don't turn out as we expected?

WEEK 4

The Book of Job attacks the idea that good things happen to good people, and bad things happen to bad people. Think of ways Job's story is both similar to and different from the story of Joseph you read last week.

Instead of focusing on the Book of Job's position in the grand story of Scripture (scholars debate where it fits), we will explore the great, timeless question posed by this masterpiece of religious literature: how should God's people respond to evil and suffering? Primarily, the book challenges us not to give simplistic answers in the face of suffering.

As you read this week, notice Job's constant cry for answers and his false friends' constant supply of answers. Yet the book is not really about answers or how to understand suffering. It is about how to appropriately respond to suffering and especially how to respond to God in our suffering. As you read, enter the emotions expressed by Job, often in figurative language, and see if you can identify the fallacies and truths embedded in the speeches of his friends.

DAY 1 Job 1–5

Notice what God said about Job's character in Job 1. Think about ways the problem of suffering is treated differently than in the story of Joseph we read last week. In both stories a righteous person suffers. Yet the Joseph story clearly reveals the reason Joseph had to suffer: to deliver his family. In contrast, Job was offered no answers. This book teaches us about moments in life when our suffering seems meaningless.

> **If you are suffering today, express to God your trust in Him in the midst of your suffering. If you know someone who is suffering, pray that this person will trust God and draw closer to Him in their suffering.**

DAY 2 Job 6–9

Much of the Book of Job is Job's lament, in which he expressed deep anguish to God about his suffering. Notice in Job 6:1-4 the emotions expressed through word pictures (as heavy as sand, as piercing and poisonous as arrows, and so on).

> **Do you sometimes feel such emotions when you are suffering?**

> **Do you feel free to be honest with God about such feelings?**

If you are suffering now, use Job's words as a prayer to God and then thank Him for the ability to approach Him honestly in prayer, even in your pain. If you are not in a time of suffering, use the words of Job to cry out to God on behalf of those who are suffering, praying earnestly for them.

DAY 3 Job 10–13

In Job 1:9 Satan asked a key question for this book: "Does Job fear God for nothing?" In other words, Satan suggested that people love God only for the benefits and blessings God gives them; they do not love God just for Himself. Notice what Job said in Job 13:15: he would hope in God no matter what.

How do you respond to God when things get difficult?

DAY 4 Job 14–17

In light of what you know about Job's suffering (review Job 1–2), notice in chapter 16 that Job had misunderstood both God's role in his suffering and God's attitude about his suffering. With our limited perspective, it is also possible for us to misunderstand God when we suffer.

Pray that God will help you respond to suffering with trust even when you don't understand God's ways.

DAY 5 Job 18–21

The speeches of Bildad in chapter 18 and of Zophar in chapter 20 are basically the same: wicked people come to ruin. The implication is "Job has experienced ruin; therefore, Job has been wicked." Job answered them in two very different ways. In chapter 19 he lamented his suffering but expressed hope in God, suggesting that he was suffering innocently. Carefully read his response in chapter 21.

Examine how you think about God's justice. Like Bildad and Zophar, do you assume that justice means good things happen to good people, and bad things happen to bad people? If so, how do you need to change your thinking in light of the Book of Job?

DAY 6 Job 22–24

In chapter 22 Eliphaz made a lot of assumptions about Job's wickedness (see, for example, vv. 5-9), adding insult to injury. All suffering is not physical; some suffering is intensely emotional, as when we are falsely accused by others. Notice the emotions Job experienced.

Have you ever felt any of the emotions Job experienced? Do you feel free to express these emotions to God in prayer?

SMALL-GROUP DISCUSSION QUESTIONS

1. Share a time when you experienced suffering. What questions did you ask? What was your attitude toward God? Did you gain any long-term benefit through your suffering?

2. Why did Satan notice Job? Why did God point out Job to Satan?

3. List the various categories of loss and suffering that Job experienced. How did Job respond to the disasters in his life? Why did Job praise God?

4. Why does our culture often feel that believers who are faithful do not deserve to suffer? Is that a biblical perspective? Why or why not?

5. Why should we faithfully serve God if we may encounter the same, if not greater, hardships as everyone else?

6. Would suffering be easier if we understood the reason? Why does it matter?

7. How does suffering often help us know God more deeply than times of peace?

8. Summarize Job's interaction with his "friends." What did these men assume about God and about Job?

9. How can we be true friends to those who are suffering?

WEEK 5

This week we will finish the Book of Job. Notice that two new witnesses on suffering entered the story. Elihu (day 2) was a young person who thought he knew more than he actually did. His speech extends for more than five chapters! Yet no one else in the book even acknowledged his presence except, perhaps, the Lord in Job 38:2. The other witness was God Himself, who pointed to the glories and mysteries of His creation. Notice especially how the Book of Job ends. Job didn't get answers; he just got God, who vindicated Job in the end.

This week we will also start another story of suffering. Act 2, scene 2 in the biblical narrative leads us through the deliverance of God's people from slavery in Egypt. We will read the way God raised up a savior to address slavery and will recognize ways Moses was both like and unlike Jesus, who would bring about a different kind of deliverance.

DAY 1 Job 25–28

Job is filled with eloquent poetry. In Hebrew poetry one primary feature is repetition, especially parallelism, two lines communicating the same or a contrasting thought. Another device is the use of word pictures.

Identify examples of parallelism and word pictures in the reading for today.

Job 28 is a wonderful hymn about wisdom. Read this chapter and think about the source and nature of true wisdom.

For what areas of life do you need wisdom today?

DAY 2 Job 29–32

In chapter 29 Job remembered the good old days when things were going well. This chapter contrasts greatly with the next.

What are the most striking word pictures to you in chapters 29–30?

In chapter 31 Job gave a long list of unrighteous actions or attitudes proclaiming his innocence.

How do you respond when you feel falsely accused?

Identify the transition that takes place in chapter 32.

DAY 3 Job 33–36

Elihu personified overconfident youth. He repeated much of what his elders, Job's accusers, said, but he also spoke of the disciplinary nature of suffering. His words mixed what is true with what is false.

Find one thing in your reading today you believe is true and one thing you believe is false.

DAY 4 Job 37:1–40:5; Psalm 19

After Job had asked for God's response throughout the whole book, the Lord finally spoke, beginning in chapter 38. Yet God neither vindicated Job nor sided with his accusers. Rather, He hushed all human wisdom by pointing to His creation—His work of creating and sustaining the universe and the creatures in it. Notice the parts of creation on which God focused in this passage.

As you read Psalm 19, think of ways nature declares God's glory. Worship God in light of His creation.

DAY 5 Job 40:6–42:17; Psalm 29

Chapter 42 concludes Job's story. Think about Job's response and notice God's response to Job. In his suffering Job never got answers, but he got God.

How does this conclusion to the Book of Job affect your view of suffering?

As you read Psalm 29, think of the great miracle represented by the fact that God has spoken to human beings at all and how powerful God's words are.

Use the words of Psalm 29 to worship the Lord today.

SCENE 2: DELIVERANCE: GOD RESCUES HIS PEOPLE

DAY 6 Exodus 1–4

In this passage God tells the story of the deliverer he raised up to lead His people out of captivity in Egypt. Watch for important details as you read.

What did you learn about Moses in these chapters?

Here we also learn more about God. He identified Himself as I AM (see Ex. 3:14), which means something like the Self-Existent One; that is, God depends on no one for His existence.

Read John 8:58 and think about the significance of Jesus' words in that passage.

Exodus 4:21-23 shows God's adoption of the people of Israel as His son. Immediately afterward we have the strange story in Exodus 4:24-26. Circumcision is the clue here.

Where have we seen this practice before, and why would it have been so important for Moses, through his wife, to perform the procedure on his son?

What are the spiritual marks of your relationship with God?

TIMELINE

Old Testament Timeline, Part 1: write *Moses* on line 1 in act 2, scene 2.

SMALL-GROUP DISCUSSION QUESTIONS

1. Recall Job's suffering and difficulties. Read Job 19:25-27. Where did Job place his trust? How should we respond in our suffering and difficulties?

2. How did God respond to Job's request for vindication in Job 38–39? Describe the picture God painted of Himself to Job.

3. How did Job respond to God's conversation in Job 42:1-6?

4. How can it be comforting to rest in the truth that we do not understand God's ways? How can it be scary or unsettling? Why?

5. Why should we trust and take comfort in the God who is supreme in all matters?

6. Describe a time in life when you thought God was silent or had forgotten you. How did it feel? What happened to break the silence? How do you view that time of waiting now? What was God up to?

7. Describe the factors that came together for the baby Moses to be protected and ultimately saved. What are the results of the other characters' radical obedience in Moses' early story?

8. How can God's trustworthiness give us hope in difficult circumstances?

9. Recall Moses' story. Does God give up on His people when they fail and sin? How does God demonstrate patience with us? What are the results of our disobedience? What are the results of our obedience?

10. Do you believe God has plans to use you? Why or why not? What do you think are some of those plans? What are some of the plans for God's people that are revealed in His Word?

11. Read Exodus 3:14. How does the name "I AM WHO I AM" give us insight into God's view of time? Into His greatness?

12. Who is our Deliverer? What has He delivered us from? How did Moses foreshadow Christ?

WEEK 6

This week we will move further into act 2, scene 2 in the story of Scripture, and we will begin scene 3. Here again we find vitally important foundational elements for the rest of the Bible. Be attentive to the characteristics that marked Moses as a leader, for he would come to be greatly venerated by Jews during the time of Jesus. Read about the establishment of the Passover, grasping the purpose of this special celebration and meditating on the fact that Jesus would become our Passover Lamb. This week's readings will also include the Ten Commandments and other laws that were to govern God's people as they moved into the land of Canaan. Notice the emphasis on the Lord's presence among His people, for this will be a major theme in much of the remainder of Exodus. God was the main hero in this story, moving the events to His desired ends. Yet we also see clearly the consequences of human actions as people interacted with a holy God. Finally, remember that the concept of covenant is central to the Old Testament stories, and vitally important covenant moments are found in the readings for this week.

DAY 1 Exodus 5–9

Several times in this passage Moses told God why he was ill equipped to lead the Israelites out of Egypt. Notice Moses' excuses.

What excuses are you most likely to give when you are asked to do something for God's cause in the world?

Watch for the importance of identity in these chapters. The genealogy of chapter 6 established the identity of Moses and Aaron as the leaders of the people. Circle their names, found in the center of this genealogy. Verses like Exodus 6:2 also emphasize God's identity.

Notice various kinds of tension in the story today. For example, there is the promise of freedom for an enslaved people. There is a power encounter, a display of God's power overwhelming worldly powers as God began to send the plagues. Each plague in some way attacked the gods of Egypt.

What do you learn about God from Exodus 5–9?

How might God address the tension in your personal story today?

DAY 2 Exodus 10–13

The plagues continue and climax in the chapters for today.

In what way is God the hero of this story?

In what ways do you see a heightening of tension, an escalation of the action as you move through these chapters?

A moment of crisis was coming that would cause a major shift in the story. Can you identify that crisis? It was the death of the firstborn, which led to the exodus itself, perhaps the most celebrated event of Jewish history. The Jewish people celebrate Passover every year.

What is the significance of the name Passover, according to Exodus 12?

Praise God for Jesus, who is the Passover Lamb for those who believe.

DAY 3 Exodus 14–18

It is interesting that God's deliverance of His people was followed by a series of crises, several of them brought about by the people themselves as they grumbled against God. Notice the pattern of crisis, then answer, then celebration in this section.

Here we see the *Shekinah* glory of God for the first time (see Ex. 16:10), God's glory manifesting His presence among His people. God wants to be present among His people, even when they grumble!

Exodus 16 explains at least two reasons God gave the Israelites manna:

1. So that they would have food to eat
2. To see whether they would carefully follow God's instructions

Meditate today on how the provisions God has given you can be a context for discipleship, teaching you to follow the ways of God carefully.

Also learn from the negative example of the Israelites. How might you be tempted to grumble about your circumstances today?

SCENE 3: COVENANT AND LAW: GOD EMBRACES AND INSTRUCTS HIS PEOPLE

DAY 4 Exodus 19–21

Much of the account in this passage drove home to the Israelites the holiness of God. Just after the Ten Commandments were given (see Ex. 20:1-17), Moses explained why God appeared in these terrible ways.

Identify forces in your culture that fight against a clear-eyed view of the holiness, the awesomeness of God.

DAY 5 Exodus 22–24

Remember that when we read the stories and the laws of the Old Testament, covenant (a meaningful relationship with God) is often at the heart of what is going on. Exodus 22–23 gives various laws for how the people were to live for God under the covenant they were making with Him, and chapter 24 presents the covenant ceremony. Both the laws and the ceremony show us what God values. Watch for those things as you read.

Identify ways your values today should reflect these values of God.

DAY 6 Exodus 25–28

One great theme of the Bible is God's desire to be with His people. We know God is everywhere (see Ps. 139:7-12), but He desires to be actively involved in the lives of people. The passage today begins with the building of the tabernacle. Notice the places in Exodus 25 that indicate God's desire to be present among His people.

Do you desire to actively experience God's presence with you today?

Notice the great care and cost that were involved in building the tabernacle and in preparing the priests to worship. Whereas the focus in this Old Testament context is on a physical place of worship, followers of Jesus are the tabernacle of the New Testament (see 1 Cor. 3:16; 1 Pet. 2:5).

How can you and the members of your church carefully prepare for worship each day in your personal times with the Lord? Each week in your worship services?

What price are you willing to pay to have focused, meaningful time in meeting God face-to-face?

SMALL-GROUP DISCUSSION QUESTIONS

1. Think about Pharaoh's rebellion. Why do people rage against God and continue in wickedness? What is their ultimate end?

2. Why do you think God took Pharaoh through a process of 10 plagues instead of showing His superior power in one event?

3. How did God provide for His people in the Passover? How is Jesus our Passover Lamb?

4. Read Exodus 14:31. What was the Israelites' response to God's powerful deliverance?

5. How does the story of the exodus relate to Christ's deliverance of us? What were we enslaved by and freed from?

6. How can the story of the exodus encourage and comfort God's people today?

7. Share a time when God delivered you from evil or difficulty. How did God show you His power and faithfulness? What did you learn about yourself and about God as you went through this experience?

8. How did God provide for His people after they left Egypt? Why do you think the people kept complaining?

9. How do the laws in Exodus 20:1-17 reflect God's perfect character and His perfect plan for His people? Are these laws relevant for us today?

10. Read Exodus 24:3. What did God require for the people to fulfill the covenant?

WEEK 7

As we continue this week with act 2, scene 3, we will finish Exodus and move into Leviticus, a book that takes its name from the tribe of Levi, who served as God's priests. All of the readings for this week surround the topic of worship. Watch for aspects of the presence of God, the place of worship, appropriate practices in true worship, the people who led worship, and preparation for worship. Also reflect deeply on your worship of the Lord. What do you learn from these passages of Scripture that has relevance for worship today?

DAY 1 Exodus 29–32

As you examine the details of the tabernacle and priesthood, keep in mind the main purpose for which they were created. That purpose is found in Exodus 29:43-46. Notice how that purpose was tragically violated in the events of Exodus 32.

What in your life has the most potential to draw your heart away from God?

DAY 2 Exodus 33–36

Because of the golden-calf incident in chapter 32, God said He would not go into the promised land with the Israelites. As you read, notice the reasons Moses was urgent about God's going into the land with the people.

Think about how God's going with us in our daily lives makes us distinct from those around us who do not know Him. How do you need to live distinctly today?

As you read Exodus 34, notice how God described Himself. He again laid out covenant obligations for the people to follow. God's presence is related to those covenant obligations. Also notice the effect of God's presence on Moses' face. Acts 2:3 and 2 Corinthians 3:18 show that in the new covenant God's glorious presence rests on every believer.

How is God's presence seen in your life today?

DAY 3 Exodus 37–40

Exodus ends with building the furniture for the tabernacle, making the priests' clothes, and setting up the tabernacle. All of this culminates in Exodus 40:34-38. The importance of the special place and special people to lead worship highlights the presence of God. Meditate on the fact that in the new covenant God has made believers the special place (God lives in us) and special people designed for worship. First Corinthians 3:16 says, "Don't you yourselves know that you are God's sanctuary and that the Spirit of God lives in you?"

Praise God that He not only dwells in the midst of His people but also lives in each one of us.

DAY 4 Leviticus 1–4

Keep in mind that the sacrifices described here were part of God's guidelines for how the Israelites would live in covenant with God, so the emphasis is on a relationship with God.

Think about sins in your life. Thank God for the sacrifice provided in Jesus' death and for His forgiveness of sins.

DAY 5 Leviticus 5–7

At least two ideas lie at the heart of the instructions on sacrifice in these chapters:

1. Sin is costly, always having consequences.
2. A price must be paid to restore broken relationships.

Think of ways you have seen these two realities in your life.

DAY 6 Leviticus 8–10

Today's reading describes the ordination, inauguration, and regulations surrounding the priesthood of Aaron and his sons. They were representatives of the Israelites before God, and they presented sacrifices both for themselves and for the people. Notice especially the emphasis on making a distinction between what is common and what is set apart as holy.

How is your life set apart to God today?

TIMELINE
Old Testament Timeline, Part 1: write *Aaron* on line 1 in act 2, scene 3.

SMALL-GROUP DISCUSSION QUESTIONS

1. Read Exodus 34:1-14. How did God describe Himself to Moses? Why do you think He revealed Himself to Moses this way?

2. What were Moses' three requests of the Lord in Exodus 34:9? Why do you think he made these requests?

3. What was the Lord's response to Moses' request? What does His response reveal about Him?

4. What was the intent of God's action, as shown in verses 10 and 14?

5. Do we rely on God to lead us today? How? How do we sometimes reject God's leading?

6. How is the awesome work of the Lord shown among the nations today?

7. What does it mean for God to be a jealous God (see v. 14)? What does it mean for us to be jealous for God's name?

8. How were the people instructed to treat the tabernacle as holy (set apart)? Why do you think God wanted the tabernacle to be treated in a special manner? Why did He prescribe so much care in the preparations?

9. Do we follow God's commands for worship with the same intensity that the Israelites did? How do we prepare ourselves for worship? Do we worship in spirit and in truth? Do we lift up Christ above all in our worship?

10. How does God dwell with His people today? How does His presence comfort us? Convict us? Why do you think our lives are not always characterized by His power?

11. Share a time when you experienced God's presence in an especially intimate way. How did it feel?

12. Read John 1:15-18. How was Christ's incarnation similar but superior to the tabernacle?

13. Christ died once for sin, in contrast to the repeated sacrifices required of the Israelites. How should a full grasp of Christ's atoning death affect our view of our sin? How does it increase our gratitude and love for Christ? How does it reject any possibility of salvation by works?

WEEK 8

This week we will continue with act 2, scene 3. As you read this week, watch for an emphasis on the holiness of God and for ways holiness shapes the behavior of God's people toward Him and toward one another. Meditate this week on the need for holiness in keeping covenant with God. First Peter 1:15 says, "As the One who called you is holy, you also are to be holy in all your conduct." Think about our need for holiness and appropriate patterns of holiness as God's people today. We do not keep all of the same laws the Israelites were commanded to keep in Leviticus and Numbers, but our attention to holiness is to be just as vigilant. How do we pursue holiness today?

DAY 1 Leviticus 11–14

It is important to understand that the word *clean* in these chapters means *able to approach God in worship*, and *unclean* means *unable to approach God in worship*. Laws about food and skin diseases partly addressed hygiene and partly symbolized the unique relationship Israel had with God, depicting His holiness and the care needed when coming to Him in worship.

Identify laws that emphasize Israel's separation to God.

DAY 2 Leviticus 15–18

Read Mark 5:24-34 in light of Leviticus 15:25-30. Think about the terrible social and religious implications for a woman who had this kind of physical illness. According to the law, what happened when the unclean woman touched Jesus? Yet power went out from Jesus, cleansing the woman and reversing the curse. Rather than being made unclean, Jesus made the woman clean.

What does this incident tell us about Jesus?

What are the implications for your life?

DAY 3 Leviticus 19–22

Leviticus 19 is one of the most practical chapters in the Old Testament. Prescribing ways God's people were to treat one another, these guidelines set the Israelites apart as very distinct from the pagan peoples of the land of Canaan and showed that they had a special covenant with God. God shapes the way His people live in relationship with others.

In what specific ways is God shaping your life through your relationship with Him?

DAY 4 Leviticus 23–25

This passage establishes "appointed times" (Lev. 23:2), including Sabbath days (see 23:3), one of which was the Day of Atonement (see 23:26-32); festivals (see 23:4-44); and Sabbath years (see 25:1-7), among which was the Year of Jubilee (25:8-55). The Sabbath days and years provided rest for the people and the land. Jubilee highlighted freedom and restoration. As you read, reflect on the role rest and celebration play in a healthy life.

How are you experiencing rest, liberation, and celebration in your life?

What patterns in your life and the lives of those around you discourage rest, freedom, and celebration?

DAY 5 Leviticus 26–27; Numbers 1–2

Leviticus 26 begins to conclude the explanation of the covenant God made with the Israelites at Mount Sinai. Notice the progression of God's discipline if the people hardened their hearts. Notice especially the culmination of God's discipline. This judgment occurred half a millennium later when the Babylonians drove the Israelites into exile at the beginning of the sixth century B.C. Meditate on the consequences of an increasingly hardened heart.

Do you have a hardened heart in any area of your life?

Do you know someone who is hardening his or her heart toward God? Pray for yourself and that person, asking God to grant the grace of a softened heart toward Him.

DAY 6 Numbers 3–5

Much of the Book of Numbers shows that God's presence among His people demanded careful attention. Because He is holy, they were to do things a certain way. A passage like Numbers 5:11-31 can seem strange to us. We might be tempted to read this teaching as harsh or unfair, asking, "What about the man committing adultery?" Yet the passage assumes at least three things about the Lord:

1. He is holy and demands holiness.
2. He is all-knowing.
3. He is completely fair and will bring about a just outcome.

Trust God today with the portions of the Bible that seem odd to you. Focus on principles that are clear in light of the broader testimony of Scripture.

Worship God today in light of His attributes revealed in Numbers 5:11-31.

SMALL-GROUP DISCUSSION QUESTIONS

1. Read Leviticus 10:1-3; 16:1-5. What was the consequence of entering the presence of God in an inappropriate manner?

2. How did God tell Aaron to prepare to enter the holy place? How was purity or holiness represented?

3. How do we prepare or not prepare for corporate worship today? What should be the emphasis of our preparation for worship—internal or external or both?

4. What sacrifice paves the way for us to have fellowship with God? Compare Romans 3:25.

5. What offerings can we bring to God in worship as a church and as individuals as a response to having been forgiven?

6. Read Leviticus 16:6-19. For whom did Aaron sacrifice first? For whom did he sacrifice next? What was the scope of his sacrifice? Read Hebrews 7:27; 9:12. Why didn't Jesus need to sacrifice for Himself? What did Jesus offer instead of the blood of goats and bulls? What is the scope of Jesus' sacrifice?

7. Can anyone atone for his or her sins apart from trusting in the work of Jesus Christ? How should Jesus' perfect sacrifice give us perfect assurance of our forgiveness?

8. Read Leviticus 16:20-28. How many sins did the live goat representatively take on itself? How does verse 22 represent the forgiveness and removal of sins? Read Psalm 103:12. As forgiven saints, how should we view our past sins?

9. Read Hebrews 13:14-16. How should we now live in response to Christ's sacrifice? In relation to God? In relation to others?

10. Read Leviticus 16:29-34. How often did the Day of Atonement occur? How many people were involved? Who was the one person who could enter the tabernacle before the mercy seat? How is Jesus our High Priest? How is Jesus our perfect Sacrifice?

11. How were the people supposed to observe the Day of Atonement? How are repentance and rest connected? In whom were the Israelites to put their faith?

12. Read Hebrews 9:25-26; 10:11-14. How is Christ's sacrifice better than all others? How can we rest in Christ's sacrifice on our behalf?

WEEK 9

This week our readings we take us into the second year of Israel's time in the wilderness, and already we will begin to see preparations for entering the land of Canaan. Yet the Israelites' progress is hampered by problems of various kinds. As you read this week, notice this mix of preparation and problems in the development of the story. How is God still very much at the center of the story? What role does the covenant with God play in this part of the story? What details of the story seem most surprising? What details do you find most encouraging?

DAY 1 Numbers 6–9

This passage describes the Israelites' preparations to leave Sinai, especially the consecration of the priests and the final steps in setting up the tabernacle. The conclusion in Numbers 9:15-23 emphasizes God's presence among the Israelites and His guidance of them. Think about the importance of preparation even in small tasks but especially in key transitions in life. Recognize how vital it is to walk with God in times of preparation and transition.

Are there life events or transitions for which you are preparing at present?

What principles from this section of Numbers can guide you at this time?

DAY 2 Numbers 10–13; Psalm 90

It is now the beginning of the second year since God brought the Israelites out of slavery in Egypt. The passage today from Numbers shows them moving out toward the land of Canaan. Yet notice that progress was accompanied by problems—with resources, leadership, and courage. Note how these problems can negatively affect God's people even when He is working among them, especially when their hearts are spiritually dull.

What are some current problems in your family, church, or community?

How can you encourage yourself and others to look to God in a fresh way?

Bring your problems to God today, softening your heart toward Him.

How does Psalm 90 put in perspective who God is and who we are as His people?

Pray the words of Psalm 90.

DAY 3 Numbers 14–16; Psalm 95

The reading from Numbers today begins and ends with accounts of rebellion against God. The refusal to enter the land and Korah's rebellion are key turning points in the story. Notice that the rebellion was against the Lord, but the people focused their anger on the Lord's leaders, Moses and Aaron. Korah accuses "a very humble man, more so than any man on the face of the earth" (Num. 12:3) of seeing himself as greater than anyone else (see 16:3)!

Notice the emotions driving those who rebel. Reflect on the effects of emotions in our relationship with God and others. Notice ways Psalm 95 contrasts a life of worship with a life of rebellion.

How do patterns of worship work against rebellion in our lives?

DAY 4 Numbers 17–20

The passage today continues to make distinctions between what is clean and what is unclean, between the leaders and the people, and between the priests and the people. Think about the roles these distinctions play in the developing story.

How is the distinction between clean and unclean revealed in your life as a Christ follower? For part of the answer, read the instructions on the sacrifice of the red cow (see Num. 19:1-10) in light of Hebrews 9:13-14.

As the Israelites finally came to the end of the 40 years in the wilderness and moved toward the occupation of the land, they began to battle people groups on the outskirts of the land. Our conflicts today are different. In Ephesians 6:10-13 Paul said our battle is not against flesh and blood but rather against spiritual forces that fight against God's cause in the world.

What are the ways we fight this battle, according to Ephesians 6:14-17?

DAY 5 Numbers 21–24

Several times in the Pentateuch (with Jacob and then with Moses), God sent someone on a journey, only to confront that person along the way. In Numbers 22:20-22 God told Balaam to do exactly what He had told him. Perhaps when God was angry in verse 22, He was responding to specific actions or intentions of which the reader is not told. The story as a whole drives home that our sovereign God in heaven overrides the superstitious schemes of people.

In the story look for humor (a talking donkey) and irony: God used a pagan prophet to bless His people even as they were about to participate in pagan worship (see Num. 25)!

Praise God today for ways He is working in your life, even through people who are not His followers.

DAY 6 Numbers 25–28

As you read this passage, notice details that point to preparation for entering the land: the census, the commissioning of a new leader, the struggle against paganism, and so forth.

It is difficult to read about the harshness of judgment on those who mixed with other people and embraced their religion, but meditate on what this reality must say about the horrible nature of sin and God's zeal for holiness.

Notice that God said Phinehas was zealous for holiness "with My zeal" (Num. 25:11). Ultimately, God would pay for sin by the death of His own Son in place of sinners, demonstrating both the unimaginable cost of sin and the unfathomable depths of His grace.

What would it look like for you to be zealous for holiness in your life with God's zeal?

SMALL-GROUP DISCUSSION QUESTIONS

1. What similarities do you see between the report from the spies and God's description of the land in Exodus 3:8? What examples of faith and faithlessness are clear in this story?

2. Is it more common in the Scriptures for men and women to stand against the crowds or to follow the behavior of masses? What kinds of people follow the masses? What kinds of people take a stand against them? Which kind of person are you?

3. Read Numbers 14:13-19. In what ways was Moses a precursor of Jesus Christ?

4. What is your typical response to the leading of the Lord? Describe a time when you could discern clear leading from God. How did you respond? What were the short-term and long-term results?

5. What is your typical response to the Lord's correction? Have you thought of the discipline you have received as negative or positive? What were the reasons for discipline? Did God want to harm you or prosper you?

6. What can you do to be more prepared to respond like Joshua or Caleb? In the little things? In the big things?

7. What can you do to be a Joshua or Caleb to the people around you, helping them honor God and avoid the need for discipline?

8. What does the story of Phinehas in Numbers 25:6-15 tell you about the life of holiness God desired for His people?

WEEK 10

This week we will finish Numbers and move into Deuteronomy, where Israel is finally poised to enter the land of promise. Deuteronomy, meaning *second law*, is Moses' retelling of Israel's short history and especially a recounting of its covenant with God, told to a new generation during the final weeks before crossing into the land. As you read, watch for emphases on God's uniqueness (He is one and the one true God), God's covenant love for Israel, the call for obedience so that the covenant people would reflect God's character and be blessed in their relationship with Him, and the dangers of disobedience. Watch for ways God's people were to model His righteousness as they related to God and to one another and for ways they should care for foreigners, widows, and orphans.

Keep in mind where we are in the story of Scripture. The laws of God make sense only in the context of the grand story of God.

DAY 1 Numbers 29–32

The holy war described in this passage can be disturbing to modern readers. How should we, followers of the Prince of Peace, read such passages?

1. Remember that the Midianites had attacked Israel and played a part in seducing the nation to worship Baal. The people who lived in Canaan at this time were violent and worshiped a fertility god.
2. This is God's war, and thus the holy war served not only to protect God's people but also to judge the Midianites. God's judgment against sin is violent because sin subverts God's relationship with people. God would judge Israel similarly at points in its history (though not to the point of annihilation).
3. God would eventually war against sin and Satan, providing deliverance for all people through the violent death of His Son.

> **How did God's instructions to kill the Midianite men and burn their cities reflect His larger purposes for the Hebrew people?**

DAY 2 Numbers 33–36

As Numbers concludes, the primary focus is on the division of the land. Think about the fact that God has gifts of inheritance for His people, a place for them to live.

In John 14:2 Jesus said, "I am going to prepare a place for you." What is the inheritance God has provided you?

Two special situations are mentioned in today's verses.

1. God provided for the Levites in a way that is different from the other tribes, in accordance with their unique role among the Israelites.
2. God established cities of refuge among the Levites' cities. Read about these cities with an eye for God's concern for justice—punishment of the guilty and protection of the innocent.

In what ways should we be concerned for justice today?

DAY 3 Deuteronomy 1–3

As we move into the Book of Deuteronomy, Moses, standing on the brink of the promised land, recounted the beginning of Israel's time in the wilderness. Notice why Israel was not to destroy Edom, Moab, and Ammon: they were Israel's relatives, and God had given them their land. These other nations had already done what Israel was poised to do, having taken possession of the land from the pagan people.

When Israel defeated Sihon and Og, God again instructed them to destroy the people. If Israel did not destroy the idolatrous people, idolatry would destroy Israel's purpose for existence.

Do you understand God's purpose for your life?

Do you recognize the importance of your obedience in staying faithful to God's purpose?

DAY 4 Deuteronomy 4–7

Notice today the emphasis on the Word of God. God's commands and instructions laid the foundation for the nation as it entered the land. Pay careful attention to why God gave the nation these words.

Evaluate your own commitment to the Word of God. Renew your commitment to read the Word daily, seeking to understand it and apply it to your life.

DAY 5 Deuteronomy 8–11

Notice the centrality of God's Word in the Book of Deuteronomy. God could have given the people many things as they entered the land—riches, power, miracles—and these accompanied the Israelites in some ways. Yet He primarily gave them His words.

Track all of God's purposes for the Word as expressed in these chapters.

Read Jesus' temptation in the wilderness concerning bread (see Matt. 4:1-4) against the backdrop of Deuteronomy 8:1-5. Jesus, the Son, succeeded where Israel, the "son," failed. Worship Him today.

DAY 6 Deuteronomy 12–15

Today's reading begins a brief section on laws for worship practices. Notice the central place, both in location and in importance, of the tabernacle, "the place Yahweh your God chooses from all your tribes to put His name for His dwelling" (Deut. 12:5). Right worship lays the foundation for right living. God's people were to live differently from others in the world by whom they worshiped; by the way they worshiped; by the way they ate; and by the way they treated the poor, the debtor, and the slave.

How might you, as one of God's people, live distinctly in the world today?

SMALL-GROUP DISCUSSION QUESTIONS

1. God commanded the Israelites to uphold and obey His Word in thought and deed in order to receive His blessing. How and why does God bless His followers today? What does the blessing of God look like for you? Why do we receive God's blessing even though we fail to uphold God's commands in word and deed?

2. Read 1 Peter 2:22 and 1 John 3:5. How did Jesus' obedience pave the way for God's blessing us?

3. The Israelites were to affirm the uniqueness of God in the midst of a pagan culture. False gods were in great supply. What false gods are prevalent in our society today? What idols do believers need to destroy today in order to walk in obedience to God?

4. What did total devotion look like for the Israelites? What does it look like in your life? Is total devotion possible for us?

5. Read Deuteronomy 6:6-9. How were the people instructed to teach God's Word to their children? How do we do that today?

6. The Israelites developed a pattern of forgetting God's faithfulness and sliding into idolatry. How do we see that tendency in our own lives? How do we avoid this?

7. How do you rehearse God's grace in your life?

8. What inheritance has God planned for us as followers of Christ?

WEEK 11

This week we will finish the Pentateuch, the first five books of the Bible, by completing act 2, scene 3, which deals with covenant and law. At the end of the week we will move into act 2, scene 4, "The Land: God's Place for His People." As you read the final chapters of Deuteronomy, watch for a continued emphasis on being committed to and living out the covenant with God and notice the transitions that begin to take place. Then, as you begin the Book of Joshua, watch for ways the beginning of this book both builds on and develops the story presented in the Pentateuch. Also look for new themes or emphases.

DAY 1 Deuteronomy 16–19

Today's reading presents a variety of guidelines. We find instructions for special celebration times, idolatry, the appointment of a king, provisions for the Levites, dealing with occult practices, how to recognize a true prophet, cities of refuge, boundary markers, and witnesses in court. Continue to read in light of how these laws relate to settling in the land.

Which one of these guidelines is most relevant for your life today?

DAY 2 Deuteronomy 20–23

Notice today the emphasis on fairness and justice. Remember that some of the dynamics in these chapters must be understood in their historical and cultural context of the Ancient Near East. Penalties at times were very harsh, but God continued to emphasize being set apart as His unique people.

How can you express fairness and justice toward people with whom you interact today?

DAY 3 Deuteronomy 24–27

As you read today, continue to watch for attributes that should characterize God's people: concern for the poor and disadvantaged, fairness in business practices, and thoughtfulness toward those who are going through transitions.

How might you be involved in living out these principles today?

A summary of the covenant begins in Deuteronomy 26:16 and continues through chapter 27 and beyond.

How does the commitment to the covenant by the whole community reinforce the covenant in powerful ways?

DAY 4 Deuteronomy 28–30

We are drawing near to the end of act 2, scene 3 on the covenant and the law. Today's reading describes a moment when Moses called for the people to renew the covenant. The section on the blessings and curses is powerful, graphic, and comprehensive. The underlying message is "Faithfulness to the covenant with God is the only way to live, the only pattern of life that promises a future."

Notice that in Deuteronomy 29:4 Moses said the people didn't have "eyes to see, or ears to hear." Centuries later Jesus, the author of a new covenant, often said, "Anyone who has ears should listen" (Matt. 11:15; 13:9).

Are you listening to Jesus today?

DAY 5 Deuteronomy 31–34

With today's reading we come to the end of the Pentateuch, the first five books of the Bible. Congratulations on finishing the first major section of Scripture. Today notice again the strong emphasis on the Word of God and the balance between promised blessings for obedience and curses for disobedience. In Deuteronomy 34 the story of Moses, which started in Exodus 1, comes to a close. Carefully read the description given of this great leader in the final paragraph of the book.

How can Moses be an example for you?

SCENE 4: THE LAND: GOD'S PLACE FOR HIS PEOPLE

DAY 6 Joshua 1–2; Psalm 105

Today we begin act 2, scene 4, "The Land: God's Place for His People." Joshua 1 focuses on the transition to Joshua as the leader of the Hebrew people, who would take them into the land. Certainly, Joshua must have been nervous when the people said, "We will obey you, just as we obeyed Moses in everything" (Josh. 1:17). Yet Joshua served as a great leader, guiding the people to settle the land of Canaan. Joshua's name means "The Lord is salvation," and this is Jesus' name in Hebrew.

Joshua 2 tells the story of Rahab. Notice especially verse 11 and Rahab's confession of faith (see Heb. 11:31; Jas. 2:25). Rahab, King David's great-great-grandmother (see Matt. 1:5) and an ancestor of Jesus, portrays God's grace.

Psalm 105 is a hymn about God's faithfulness to His people. It culminates with a celebration of God's giving the promised land to His people.

What is the reason God gave the Israelites the land, mentioned at the very end of the psalm?

Use the words of Psalm 105 to worship God today.

TIMELINE
Old Testament Timeline, Part 2: write *Joshua* on line 1 and *Rahab* on line 2 in act 2, scene 4.

SMALL-GROUP DISCUSSION QUESTIONS

1. Read Deuteronomy 30. What challenge was Moses setting before the nation? What would happen to Israel in the future? What would some of the consequences (positive and negative) be of worshiping a God who cares whether the people loved Him or ignored Him? What issues of the heart are woven throughout the passage?

2. Read Deuteronomy 30:19-20. What did Moses mean when he said God was their life? How is the Lord your life as a follower of Christ today?

3. What challenges would the people of Israel face in the future that would make it difficult to keep the covenant and obey the Lord? What daily challenges make it difficult for you to serve the Lord and easy to forsake Him?

4. Moses spoke of blessings and curses based on the people's disobedience or obedience. How is this teaching the same for believers under the new covenant? How is this teaching different for believers under the new covenant?

5. Read Joshua 1. What did God tell Joshua to do in verses 1-9? List all of the commands you can find. What did God promise Joshua in these verses? What role would God have in the conquest of the land? What would be Israel's responsibilities in obtaining the land?

6. How did the people respond to Joshua's instructions before entering the land? How was their response different from that of the previous generation?

7. Read Hebrews 3:12–4:11. What rest (or inheritance) has God promised those who have trusted in Christ? What caused the people of Israel to come short of God's rest? What does this mean for us today? How can we avoid this?

8. What role does God play in seeing that we inherit His rest and not fall short? Why is this so important to remember?

9. What role does the body of Christ play in seeing that we inherit God's rest and not fall short? How is this lived out in your church or small group?

10. What does entering God's rest look like in a believer's life today? How does it compare to the rest the Israelites experienced as they entered the promised land?

WEEK 12

This week we will read the remainder of the Book of Joshua. The story takes us from the entrance to the land to the death of Joshua once the land had been settled. Watch especially for God's role in the taking of the land. For God's people the land was a gift, not an achievement.

Joshua 13–21 describes the distribution of the land. Many Bibles have a map at the back that depicts the portions of land assigned to the various tribes. As you read about the distribution, consult this map to keep your bearings.

As you begin this week and as you reach the end of the book, notice the recurrence of themes we have seen so far in the biblical story.

DAY 1 Joshua 3–6

Finally, the Israelites crossed into the promised land. In the reading for today, look for echoes from our reading of the first five books of the Old Testament: the ark of the covenant; the crossing of the Jordan, which echoes the crossing of the Red Sea; the renewal of circumcision; the keeping of Passover; the manna; and Joshua's standing on holy ground, as Moses did at the burning bush. Also notice the central place played by the ark, which represented God's covenant and presence.

How did God keep His covenant with the people of Israel?
How has God kept His covenant with you?

DAY 2 Joshua 7–10

As with the defeat of Jericho and Ai, the campaign against the five kings of the Amorites and the southern cities demonstrated that the battle was the Lord's and not the product of human ability and strategy. Miracles like panic of the enemy, a hailstorm, and the sun and moon's standing still show the victory was God's doing. The last of these supernatural events, which cannot be scientifically explained, is especially significant, since the sun and moon were seen as two of the Canaanites' most powerful gods. Yet God demonstrated they are His creations, and He used them for His purposes. The failure mentioned in this passage came when Joshua did not seek the Lord's counsel about the Gibeonites.

For what or whom are you trusting the Lord to provide guidance and help today?

DAY 3 Joshua 11–14

Joshua 11–12 recounts Joshua's battle campaign against the kings of the north, who were led by the king of Hazor. Notice the Lord's role in the conquest of the land. Chapters 13–21 describe the distribution of the land to the tribes of Israel, fulfilling God's promise to Abraham that his descendants would live in this land.

Today's reading lays a very important foundation for the rest of the biblical story. Notice especially the passage describing Caleb's inheritance and his great courage and loyalty. The passage stands at the beginning of the section on the distribution of the land east of the Jordan, and Joshua's inheritance closes that section (see Josh. 19:49-51). So Caleb and Joshua's loyalty and courage at Kadesh (see Num. 14:5-9) are an important focus in the Book of Joshua.

In what areas do you need to grow in courage or loyalty?

DAY 4 Joshua 15–18

The division of the land continued as God gave His people a place to live. Notice in Joshua 18:1 that the tabernacle was set up at the center of the promised land, and this passage is also near the center of this section on the distribution of the land. God's presence was still to be central for His people.

Judah and Ephraim, the first two tribes to settle Canaan proper (to the west of the Jordan River), would play the most significant roles as the Old Testament story developed.

As you think about the way you live your life, is God at the center of all things for you? Are worship and living by His ways the driving forces of your life? Is He your reference point in all things?

DAY 5 Joshua 19–22

After the remaining tribes of Israel received their divisions of the land in Joshua 19, chapter 20 focuses on the cities of refuge, chapter 21 on cities given to the Levites from among the various tribes, and chapter 22 on the return home of the tribes situated on the eastern side of the Jordan.

At the end of this passage a crisis arose when the eastern tribes of Reuben, Gad, and Manasseh built an altar. The key here is to grasp why this was a crisis and then to understand their motive for building the altar. They were not abandoning the Lord, who was to be worshiped only at the tabernacle in Shiloh, but rather setting up a memorial to remind their descendants to worship the Lord.

What memorials do you have in your life?

How does your church use memorials to remind successive generations of believers to stay true to the Lord?

DAY 6 Joshua 23–24; Judges 1

Joshua 23–24 not only forms a vitally important conclusion to the book but also wraps up much in the biblical story that began with Abraham in Genesis 12. Notice that Joshua 23:6 echoes Joshua 1:8-9.

In chapter 24 Joshua recounted Israel's history and then led the Israelites through a renewal of the covenant, the agreement with God that had been central to the biblical story thus far. Joshua 24:12-13 focuses attention on God's role in taking the land. The land was given by His grace, not by the abilities of the Israelites. On the other hand, Joshua 24:19-20 anticipates a key theme of much of the remainder of the Old Testament: Israel's failure to live up to the covenant.

Judges 1 continues the story told in Joshua, even overlapping it a little.

Spend time thanking God today for all He has given you by His grace.

SMALL-GROUP DISCUSSION QUESTIONS

1. Read Joshua 5:13–6:27. Why was the ground holy where Joshua was standing? What was the man's message from the Lord? What was the significance of this message? What was this encounter meant to teach Joshua? What does it teach us about God and His character?

2. Are you able to submit to God and let Him fight your battles? Give an example of a time when He won the victory for you. How can this portrait of God affect the way you approach the biggest struggles and challenges you face today? What do we communicate to God when we neglect this aspect of His character?

3. Read Joshua 24. What is the significance of Shechem, the geographical location of this meeting? See Genesis 12:1-7; 35:4; Joshua 8:30-35.

4. Note the number of times God used the personal pronoun *I* in Joshua 24:1-13. Why is this significant?

5. Why did God recount the people's history in Joshua 24:1-13? What point was He making to the people?

6. According to Joshua 24:14-15, how should the people respond? In light of what God had done for His people, why was this the appropriate response? What did it mean for the Israelites to serve the Lord? According to verses 16-18, why did the Israelites choose to serve the Lord?

7. Why do you think Joshua responded with the words of Joshua 24:19-20? What challenges would the people of Israel face that would make it difficult to keep the promise they made in Joshua 24:16,24?

8. What present-day idols or gods are you often tempted to serve?

9. In Joshua 24:15 Joshua challenged the people of Israel to make a firm commitment about whom they would serve. How does your life exhibit this commitment?

10. One reason the people were motivated to serve the one true God was remembering His past faithfulness to deliver and fight for them. What motivates you to continue serving God rather than idols?

WEEK 13

This week we will focus on the period of the judges. We are still in act 2, scene 4 in the biblical story, which focuses on settling the land of Canaan. The Israelites would now reap what they sowed in two areas of disobedience:

1. They had not driven the other nations out of the land.
2. They constantly turned to other gods.

The people's disobedience introduced a lot of tension into the story. The narrative takes us from the death of Joshua, the key leader in settling the land, to a time when the Israelites would begin to desire a king to rule over them (see Judg. 21:25).

Unlike the way we use the term in English, the word *judge* referred to an inspired leader, especially one who served as a military leader. As you read, note the disunity of the Israelites. The judges brought together only a few tribes at a time. The spiritual and governmental conditions of the Israelites continued to deteriorate throughout the period, primarily because they refused to acknowledge God as their true King. Yet God showed compassion to His people again and again. His compassion is expressed beautifully in the story of Ruth, with which the week ends.

DAY 1 Judges 2–5

Carefully read Judges 2:11-23, which presents a pattern repeated over and over in Judges:

1. The people sinned, abandoning God's covenant.
2. They suffered as God handed them over to their enemies.
3. God sent salvation in the form of a judge, who delivered them.

Track this pattern as you read about the first four judges.

Have you ever suffered because of the sin in your life?

Do you understand how God has provided salvation for you?

DAY 2 Judges 6–9

The reading for today tells the story of Gideon and his legacy. Notice the reference points in Judges 6:7-10,13, which give a theological perspective on how to understand the trouble the Israelites experienced at the hands of the Midianites. Ironically, Gideon is most often remembered for his request about the fleece in Judges 6:33-40, which expressed a lack of faith on Gideon's part. If we read carefully, we see that Gideon was not very courageous or a great man of faith. Yet God used him anyway, and the story focuses on God's role in the victory. Sadly, the success Gideon experienced turned to distress as he led Israel astray in chapter 8. Thus his legacy, of which we are told in chapter 9, is not a happy one.

Ask God to show you how you can live today for Him as a person of true faith and usefulness in the face of God's enemies in the world.

DAY 3 Judges 10–13

Notice that the cycle of sin, suffering, and salvation is repeated in Judges 10. In chapters 11–12 we are introduced to Jephthah, a gifted outlaw and the son of a prostitute, who led Israel against the Ammonites. Jephthah's story is tragic, illustrating the continuing degeneration of the Israelite people. His rash vow in chapter 11 shows great foolishness. His story and Samson's story in chapters 13–16 portray the sorry state of God's people; even the judges on whom the Spirit of the Lord came were weak, foolish leaders.

If you are in a position of leadership, ask God for wisdom to lead effectively and in a godly fashion. If not, pray for the leaders in your life.

TIMELINE
Old Testament Timeline, Part 2: write *Samson* on line 3 in act 2, scene 4.

DAY 4 Judges 14–18

Samson's story is one of the most expertly crafted and tragic in all of Scripture. Samson was a Nazirite, which meant he was to be set apart as holy to the Lord. Yet he violated his vows of purity (see Num. 5–6) by touching a dead body (the lion), marrying a Philistine, and going to a prostitute. He was downright foolish when it came to women, and it cost him dearly. His story and the one that follows, about Micah's priest, show a culture in great disarray both spiritually and governmentally. Notice especially Judges 17:6, which is repeated in the last verse of the book.

What are the symptoms in your culture of everyone's doing whatever he wants?

Submit yourself in a fresh way to God as your King.

DAY 5 Judges 19–21

The story of the judges comes crashing down in compounding tragedies in the last three chapters. Notice the repetition of the statement "In those days there was no king in Israel" (Judg. 17:6; 21:25; see also 18:1; 19:1). Watch for all the signs of things having gone terribly wrong. The gang rape of the Levite's concubine in chapter 19 echoes the sin of Sodom and Gomorrah in Genesis 19 (think about the great contrast between this story and instructions to husbands concerning their wives in Eph. 5:25-26). Yet this story took place in the heart of the promised land, just north of Jerusalem. Corruption produced chaos when the Israelites almost wiped out the tribe of Benjamin over this affair.

> *Is there chaos in your life or in the lives of those closest to you that has been caused by a disregard for God's commands or principles? Bring the situation to the Lord, asking for His help and guidance.*

DAY 6 Ruth 1–4

Whereas the stories of Judges are appropriately disturbing, Ruth, a story set in the time of the Judges, is encouraging and beautiful, thus presenting a powerful contrast to the Book of Judges. Here we see loyalty to Yahweh and to others, epitomized in the person Ruth. We also see a good man, Boaz, and a village committed to God's ways. As you read, let the beauty of the story wash over you. Notice the parts of the story that speak of faithfulness and compassion. This story is a picture of how well God's ways work when we obey. The Book of Ruth also forms the backdrop for the coming of Israel's greatest king during the time of the old covenant, David.

> *How can you be faithful to God and the people closest to you?*

TIMELINE
Old Testament Timeline, Part 2: write *Ruth* on line 4 in act 2, scene 4.

SMALL-GROUP DISCUSSION QUESTIONS

1. Give examples of the cycle of sin, suffering, and deliverance in the Book of Judges (for example, Judg. 3:6-12). What does this pattern reveal about humanity? What does it reveal about God?

2. The Book of Judges characterizes this period of biblical history by saying, "In those days there was no king in Israel; everyone did whatever he wanted" (17:6). Do people in your culture tend to do whatever they want or obey God as King? Give examples.

3. Evaluate the effectiveness of Gideon and Samson as leaders. How did God use them in spite of their unfaithfulness?

4. In what ways did Ruth demonstrate kindness toward Naomi?

5. What was necessary for Ruth to be redeemed after the deaths of her husband? How do you see God sovereignly working in Ruth's life to bring about redemption?

6. What are the circumstances of our lives that cause us to need a Redeemer? How did God work in your life to bring about redemption?

7. What qualities of Christ did Boaz demonstrate? How did Ruth model the way we should respond to Christ?

8. How does it affect your relationship with Christ to think of Him as your Kinsman-Redeemer?

9. How can you incorporate the understanding you gained from this story into your prayer life?

10. How can you demonstrate Christ's loving-kindness to those around you in order to glorify the Great Redeemer?

WEEK 14

This week we will move into act 2, scene 5 in the biblical story, focusing on kings and prophets. The beginning of 1 Samuel continues the story of ungodliness and chaos we saw in Judges, now epitomized by Eli's sons, who were rogue priests. Yet God was about to do a new thing by raising up Samuel as a leader. Notice the emphasis on "all Israel," first mentioned in 1 Samuel 3:20, as a contrast to the fragmentation we saw in Judges.

The solid foundation laid by Samuel and the anointing of Saul and then David as the first two kings of Israel advance the story from chaos to the time of Israel's greatest ruler. We will also read one of the most loved and recognized of all stories in the Bible, David and Goliath, and one of the most tragic, as Saul's leadership crumbled under the weight of his shallowness and disobedience. These stories give us the characteristics of a great king, personified by David. Eventually, Jesus would come as one of David's descendants to rule over a new kind of kingdom.

 ## SCENE 5: KINGS AND PROPHETS: GOD SHAPES A KINGDOM PEOPLE

DAY 1 | 1 Samuel 1–3

Today we read the beginning of how God would craft a nation for Himself from the chaos of the time when the judges ruled. It started with a barren woman named Hannah. In ancient Israel barrenness was seen as a curse on a married woman since she could not provide children who would help provide for the family and pass on the family name. In Hannah's story and song (see 1 Sam. 2) we see the theme of a powerless person helped by the Lord. From Hannah's anguish and weakness the Lord brought about change in Israel, judging chaotic ungodliness and raising up a godly leader.

As you read today, watch for contrasts between Samuel and Eli's sons. Certain elements also anticipate the coming of Jesus (read 1 Sam. 2:26 in light of Luke 2:52; Heb. 2:17-18).

In what areas do you feel barren or weak today?

Call on the Lord for help and watch for Him to work in your life.

TIMELINE

Old Testament Timeline, Part 2: write *Samuel* on line 1 in act 2, scene 5.

DAY 2 | Samuel 4–8

Today's reading describes a significant time of transition in the history of Israel.

1. In the stories of the capture and return of the ark, notice echoes from the time of the exodus. Israel's God still dwelled among His people and sent plagues on His enemies.
2. You will see the transition from Eli's leadership to Samuel's and from Samuel's leadership to Israel's desire for a king. Watch especially for the people or events that triggered these transitions. With Samuel moving into leadership and the ark of God (representing God's presence) moving back to the heart of the nation, the chaos of the Book of Judges was left behind. Yet in their desire for a king, the people wanted to be like the other nations rather than maintain their distinctiveness.

In what ways are you tempted to follow the ways of the world instead of living distinctly as a follower of God?

DAY 3 | Samuel 9–12

Today we read about "an impressive young man" (1 Sam. 9:2) who served as Israel's first king. Notice elements of the story demonstrating that God works with flawed people (a common theme in the Bible); in Saul's story we see a mix of the Spirit's anointing and human foolishness. The context of the story is Israel's rejection of God as their king, so we anticipate that problems will arise.

Notice passages in which Saul and the people had to wait for Samuel to show up and offer a sacrifice (see 1 Sam. 9:13-14; 10:8). This waiting will play a very important role as Saul's story develops.

Spend time today thanking God that He works in and with flawed people—even you!

TIMELINE
Old Testament Timeline, Part 2: write *Saul* on line 2 in act 2, scene 5.

DAY 4 | Samuel 13–16

Focus on the introduction of the reign of Saul in 1 Samuel 13:1-2 and the conclusion of chapter 15, just before the introduction of David, who would be Israel's second and greatest king. The tragedy of Saul lay in large part in his lack of care in following God's commands. He had a general, surface commitment to the God of Israel but did not concern himself with the details of obedience. He was a good-looking, gifted, but shallow man. Watch for elements of the story that point to Saul's character, especially his lack of patience in waiting on the Lord's timing. As the story shifts to David, notice that the qualification for a king has shifted to an emphasis on heart and character.

> *In what areas of life are you most likely to be careless with the Lord's instruction?*

> *In what areas are you impatient for the Lord to act?*

TIMELINE
Old Testament Timeline, Part 2: write *David* on line 3 in act 2, scene 5.

DAY 5 1 Samuel 17–20; Psalm 59

In today's reading David moved from obscurity to fame as the champion of Saul's army. At the same time, Saul moved from respect for David to being threatened by him and finally to violent attacks on him and his supporters. In the 1 Samuel passage watch for contrasts between David and Saul as God raised up His anointed and prepared Him to be king. As God's person, filled with God's Spirit, David accomplished great things for God's people.

Read Psalm 59 in light of Saul's attacks, noticing how this lament moves from a cry for help to hope to confidence in the future.

> *If you are being unfairly attacked, use Psalm 59 as a prayer. Ask God for courage and effectiveness in a great or small challenge you face.*

DAY 6 1 Samuel 21–24; Psalm 91

A great contrast between David and Saul was their discernment between right and wrong, good and evil. Both used religious language to speak of the circumstances around them. Yet as the passage from 1 Samuel shows, David's conscience was very sensitive to the Lord and to doing what was right in various situations. Saul, on the other hand, was so spiritually insensitive that he could order the execution of the priests of the Lord.

> *On a scale of 1 to 10, how sensitive is your conscience to sin? Are you more like David or Saul in this regard?*

As you read Psalm 91 concerning protection from enemies, think about how we should read such a psalm in light of Scripture as a whole. For example, does Scripture promise that

God will always protect His people from sickness or death? It is interesting that Satan used this psalm to tempt Jesus in the wilderness (see Luke 4:9-12), saying, in effect, "God won't let You get hurt, will He?" Evaluate this idea in light of the cross to which Jesus would eventually be nailed.

Join the psalmist in thanking God for protecting you in many ways and at various times in your life. Trust Him to bring great things from your times of suffering.

SMALL-GROUP DISCUSSION QUESTIONS

1. How did Hannah demonstrate faith in God? How did God show compassion to her? Do you believe God hears your cries for help? How has He responded to a particular need?

2. Read 1 Samuel 8. What reasons did the elders of Israel give for wanting a king? Why did they really want a king? What was wrong with being like other nations? What did God command Samuel to do about the request for a king? How did Israel respond to Samuel's warning?

3. In 1 Samuel 8:7 the Lord told Samuel that the people "have rejected Me from being king over them." In what ways do you fail to treat God as your King? How do you seek other sources of protection? What are the implications of God's being your King?

4. Read God's words in 1 Samuel 16:7. In what ways do Christians today often focus on the outward appearance of others rather than on their hearts? Why does God place an emphasis on the heart throughout Scripture?

5. Read 1 Samuel 17. How was David's response to Goliath's challenge different from everyone else's? How did Eliab, Saul, and Goliath view David? What was it about Goliath that most deeply offended David? What lesson did David say his victory would teach?

6. What does the story of David and Goliath teach us about the character of God?

7. Review the contrasting responses of Saul and David in 1 Samuel 17:32-33. In difficult or seemingly impossible situations, whose response do you most identify with? Do you find it easy to come up with excuses for why something can't be done and trust in your own strength (like Saul) or trust in God and His mighty power (like David)?

8. If you truly believed God was mighty and strong on your behalf, how would this alter your current lifestyle?

WEEK 15

This week's readings might be called "The Rise and Fall of Two Kings." We find a study in contrasts between David, who is the real focus of the story, and several other characters. Watch for these contrasts and notice the picture they paint of David as a superior king. We are at an important turning point in the story of Scripture, where we see Israel's greatest king come into his kingdom. In many ways King David anticipated the coming of King Jesus, one of his descendants, who would establish a very different kind of kingdom.

This week we will also read a number of psalms, many of which are associated with David. Music and worship thrived under David's reign. We will read psalms of lament, which express anguish, cries for help, and hope in God. We will also see imprecatory psalms, which call for God's justice and the fulfillment of His promises.

DAY 1 Psalms 7; 27; 31; 34; 52

We tend to read the psalms as a collection of detached songs that have little to do with the story of Scripture. Yet because they arose from real-life situations, they can speak powerfully to our real-life experiences as we use them to express our own prayers to God. First read these psalms in light of King David's story we have been reading in 1 Samuel (notice the headings in your Bible translation that point to specific moments in that story). Next, enter the emotion of each psalm and notice how it often moves from a cry for help to confident hope in God. Allow yourself to be carried along that same path as you pray the psalms.

If you are not distressed at present, praise God for your current situation and pray for someone you know is struggling under oppression.

DAY 2 Psalms 56; 120; 140–142

The psalms we are reading today continue to express cries to God for help. They also add another element—a cry for judgment on the psalmist's enemies. Such psalms are called imprecatory psalms. How are we to relate to them? Both Old and New Testaments speak of the need to love our enemies. Yet the imprecatory psalms express that God will bring justice and vindication for the one who truly follows Him and judgment for the evil person. Such psalms express confidence that God will fulfill His promises.

Where is great oppression occurring in the world? Think of places where fellow believers are being harshly persecuted for their faith. Cry out to God to judge the evil oppression and to deliver His people.

DAY 3 1 Samuel 25–27; Psalms 17; 73

As you read the stories of 1 Samuel 25–27, notice the contrasts between Abigail and Nabal and between David and Saul.

What do these stories tell us about how to handle conflict?

How do you handle conflict?

In the two psalms notice the emotions expressed through word pictures. Also watch for contrasts between godly and wicked persons. The psalmist was struggling with the fact that the wicked seem to be doing very well in the world. Yet as he concluded each psalm, he realized that God's presence was the only important value in the world. Think of this truth in light of the emphasis in Israel's history and in David's personal history on the presence of the Lord.

List the top five things you value in life at this point.

Did God's presence make the list?

DAY 4 Psalms 18; 35; 54; 63

Today's psalms cry out to God for deliverance and celebrate when God brings the deliverance about. Focus on reading these psalms as songs. Meditate on the word pictures used.

What are the word pictures communicating?

Pay attention to parallelism, the repetition of a thought to emphasize a truth or to express nuances of a thought.

From what do you need deliverance today?

Use these psalms as prayers to God.

DAY 5 | Samuel 28–31; | Chronicles 10

The contrasts between Saul and David continue to heighten in today's passage, and the conclusion of Saul's story is at hand. Saul's consulting of a necromancer (one who calls up the dead) shows how far Saul had fallen, because the practice of consulting the dead or consulting a necromancer was punishable by death (see Lev. 20:6,27), and Saul himself had outlawed the practice. The story also echoes the earlier foolishness of Saul when, facing an impending battle, he panicked and offered a sacrifice himself instead of waiting for Samuel (see 1 Sam. 13). Evidently, the Lord allowed Samuel to return to pronounce judgment on Saul, and that judgment fell at the end of 1 Samuel, when Saul and his sons were killed. David, on the other hand, was protected by the Lord and continued to make wise decisions.

Panic and fear can cause us to do foolish things. Pray for God's wisdom in your decision making, especially in areas that involve great stress.

DAY 6 Psalms 121; 123–125; 128–130

Today's reading is brief, so take your time and carefully pray through these psalms. Notice their Godward bent, focusing your heart on the Lord.

As you pray these psalms, reflect on God as the great center of all life and the provider of all you need. Commit yourself in a fresh way to seeking, trusting, hoping in, and loving Him.

SMALL-GROUP DISCUSSION QUESTIONS

1. In 1 Samuel 25 how did Abigail demonstrate wisdom? How did Nabal demonstrate foolishness?

2. In 1 Samuel 26 what did David's refusal to kill Saul say about his relationship with God?

3. Read Psalm 27:1-6. What did David mean when he said the Lord was his light? How did David see the Lord as his salvation and stronghold in his circumstances? Why were these characteristics of God so important to David? What difference did God's characteristics have on David's perspective in his situation? What did David earnestly desire of the Lord? Why did David desire such fellowship with God? How would David respond to victory over his enemies?

4. What are the greatest sources of fear in your life? What is your normal pattern for responding to fear? How does the fact that the Lord is your light, salvation, and stronghold help you respond to these fears? In what ways have you previously experienced the Lord as your light, salvation, or stronghold?

5. Read Psalm 27:7-10. How does this passage relate to verses 1-6? Why did David hope for the Lord to hear his prayer and have mercy on him? Why do you think David changed his tone from verses 7-9 to verse 10?

6. Can you sympathize with David's frustration in this passage? How? Have you ever felt that God had forsaken you and wasn't answering your prayers? How did you respond?

7. How are you able to maintain trust in God during times when He appears to be silent?

8. Read Psalm 27:11-14. What difficulties was David experiencing in these verses? What did David ask for when enemies and false witnesses rose against him? What prevented David from losing heart?

9. Describe a time in your life in which God brought about deliverance in His timing.

10. Why do you find it difficult to wait for the Lord when you desire immediate deliverance from difficulty?

11. Belief in the Lord's goodness caused David to patiently wait for the Lord even when times were difficult. How has the Lord's goodness helped you patiently wait for Him in similar situations?

WEEK 16

In the story of Scripture we are still in act 2, scene 5. Saul had died, and David had come to the throne. Notice that David's character and zeal for justice asserted themselves in the first chapters of 2 Samuel. The rest of our readings push the pause button on David's story and expose us to psalms and genealogies related to the greatest of Israel's kings. Take time to enjoy the psalms. Use them to deepen your prayer life this week.

The genealogies in 1 Chronicles span from the beginning of creation until after the Babylonian exile, which took place five centuries after the time of David. Yet it is appropriate to anchor these genealogies in the story of David. As the chronicler crafted his genealogies, he was especially interested in the tribes of Judah and Levi, because he was laying the foundation for his narrative about the house of King David and appropriate worship of God through the temple in Jerusalem. See what nuggets of truth you can find in these celebrations of heritage and identity.

DAY 1 2 Samuel 1–4

Second Samuel begins with the transition from Saul's reign to David's long rule over Israel. Watch for details. Joab's revenge and David's very different response to Saul dominate today's story. Notice how countercultural David is in this regard. Saul had pursued and tried to kill him for years; nevertheless, David honored Saul and his family, even crafting a lament for his former master. Certainly, David acted from respect for Saul's position as king. His actions and attitude are instructive for us.

This passage is framed by two stories in which David brought down judgment on the heads of those who acted against Saul. The Amalekite lied about his role in Saul's death (see 1 Sam. 31), hoping to win David's favor; he received wrath instead. David also judged the assassins of Ish-bosheth. Also watch for the way David handled Joab's revenge on Abner.

How do you respond to those who attack you or treat you poorly?

DAY 2 Psalms 6; 9–10; 14; 16; 21

In these Davidic psalms we find a powerful mix of cries to God for help, confidence in God's character, reflections on the wicked, and celebration of God's justice and deliverance. Notice the figurative language used. What might be parallels in our cultural context for words like these:

You will put them to flight
when you aim your bow at their faces (Ps. 21:12)?

Carefully meditate on the use of repetition in these psalms. For instance, each verse in Psalm 6 expresses a thought and then repeats the thought in the second line of the verse.

What does the psalmist's use of repetition add to these psalms?

Choose a passage from these psalms that is most relevant for you at this time.
Turn that psalm into a personal prayer for your need.

DAY 3 | I Chronicles 1–2; Psalms 43–44

First Chronicles 1 focuses on the ancestors of God's people up to the time of Israel (Jacob), and chapter 2 begins the genealogy of the Israelites by focusing especially on the tribe of Judah, the tribe from which the Davidic monarchy came. The genealogies remind God's people that their past as a people—their very identity—had been crafted by God for a purpose. As you read, watch for hints of what the chronicler found especially important.

Psalm 43 records a cry for vindication in the face of great oppression. Psalm 44 is the psalmist's cry for help.

Read Psalm 43 as a personal prayer and reflection and Psalm 44 as a community prayer.
Is there a way Psalm 44 applies to a community in which you are involved?

DAY 4 Psalms 49; 84–85; 87

Psalm 49 offers rich reflections on the limitations of wealth and the importance of placing hope in God.

What is your attitude toward your wealth or lack of it?

Psalms 84–85; 87 focus on the temple, the land, and Zion (Jerusalem), respectively, as places of God's blessing.

Hebrews 12:22-24 says we, as followers of Christ, have come to Mount Zion. This means that through the new covenant we have come to the real place where God lives: He is actively present in our lives.

How does the fact that we are now the temple of God affect your reading of Psalm 84? Praise God for this wonderful truth.

DAY 5 | Chronicles 3–5

The chronicler gave the big picture of Israel's history—its identity as a people. King David, from the tribe of Judah, played a central role in that history, but the history of other tribes was important as well.

What is your identity as God's person in the world?

What is your spiritual heritage? If someone asked you the history of your spiritual ancestors, what would you say?

Thank God for those who blazed the trail of commitment to God for you.

DAY 6 | Chronicles 6; Psalms 36; 39; 77–78

First Chronicles 6 shows the special place the tribe of Levi had in the history of Israel and particularly in temple worship during David's reign. Observe the historical marker in 1 Chronicles 6:31-33.

In reading the psalms for today, focus especially on the character of God, the contrast between His righteousness and the character of the wicked (see Ps. 36), His immortality and power in contrast to the fleeting nature of human life (see Ps. 39), and His greatness as seen in creation (see Ps. 77).

Grasping God's character means recognizing ways He has worked in history in calling a people to Himself. Psalm 78 culminates with a focus on David's special role in that regard.

Worship God today, focusing on various aspects of His character that are reflected in these psalms.

SMALL-GROUP DISCUSSION QUESTIONS

1. Why do you think David was able to mourn over the death of his enemy Saul? How do you respond to people who mistreat you?

2. Read Psalm 10:1. What kind of emotions may have driven David to ask this question? What kind of experiences may have driven David to ask this question? What is the significance of David's addressing God by His covenant name, LORD?

3. Have you ever asked David's question? Have you ever felt abandoned by God in the midst of your affliction? Share your experience with the group.

4. How might recalling the Lord's covenant promises shore up a person's faith when she feels not only afflicted but also abandoned? What are some of His covenant promises?

5. Read Psalm 10:2-11. How did David describe the internal disposition of the wicked? How did David describe the external behavior of the wicked? What do the metaphors suggest about the oppressor's methods?

6. What is the relationship between the condition of one's heart and the confession of one's mouth? Between the condition of one's heart and the conduct of one's hands?

7. How does a disbelief in God contribute to injustice? How does a distorted view of God contribute to oppression?

8. How might an acknowledgment of divine judgment deter wicked ways? How might the reality of divine judgment encourage the oppressed?

9. Read Psalm 10:12-18. What did David ask God to do in verse 12? What does it mean for God not to forget?

10. What truths about God are revealed in David's prayer to God? What is the relationship between prayer and oppression? List all truths about God mentioned in this passage. Discuss the implications of each truth for the way believers should respond to injustice.

11. Why is it important to tell God in our prayers what we believe about Him? How might such a practice strengthen faith and inspire patience in the face of affliction?

12. Do you pray for God to curb injustice and oppression in your town and throughout the world? What might you do individually and together as a group? What does the gospel teach about how God has acted or will act to right all wrongs?

WEEK 17

We are now in the fourth week of act 2, scene 5 in the story of Scripture. This week we will slow down in our reading of David's story, but the narrative passages in days 3–4 are very important because they illustrate that in David's reign the true worship of the Lord took center stage.

This week we will also read a number of psalms and finish the chronicler's genealogies. Allow the psalms to help you settle into a deeper worship of God. Although genealogies are not the most exciting reading in the Bible, continue to think about how they communicate the idea of identity for God's people.

DAY 1 Psalms 81; 88; 92–93

Today we are reading a variety of psalms. Take time to think deeply about these songs.

Read each psalm's main theme as you understand it. Then use them as prayers.

DAY 2 1 Chronicles 7–9

This is the final day when the chronicler shares with us the big picture of Israel's history, which reveals the identity of God's people. Again, notice that David's rule is the point of reference for this history.

Think about your identity in Christ, your role among God's people.

DAY 3 2 Samuel 5:1-10; 1 Chronicles 11–12; Psalm 133

As you read today, notice the unity of Israel under David and the place of covenant, which stands at the heart of the story of the Bible. Also watch for differences between the ways 2 Samuel and 1 Chronicles tell the story. Both accounts emphasize unity, as does Psalm 133, and the taking of Jerusalem, which became the city of David. The chronicler, however, went into great detail in telling about the heroes surrounding David during his reign.

What admirable character qualities are celebrated in the description of David's warriors?

Which of these character qualities do you need as you approach your tasks today?

DAY4 2 Samuel 5:11–6:23; 1 Chronicles 13–16

In the reign of David, we see the worship of the Lord finally take center place among the people of Israel. In these chapters David vanquished the Philistines (notice what happened to their idols) and moved the ark to Jerusalem. True worship of God is now at the center of the story.

At first the narrative about Uzzah's death might be disturbing. However, read this story in light of both Numbers 4:15 and 1 Chronicles 15:11-15. Worship of the Lord must be done on the Lord's terms. One contrast between David and Saul was the care with which David sought the Lord and attempted to follow the Lord's ways. Michal's bitterness toward David when he danced before the Lord reinforces the stark contrast between David's relationship with God and the shallowness of Saul, which was then embodied by his daughter.

Notice the mention of Asaph at 1 Chronicles 16:7. He wrote many psalms in Scripture.

How central in your life is worship? How much time do you give to daily worship?

DAY5 Psalms 15; 23–25; 47

As you read these wonderful psalms today, use them to reflect deeply on your relationship with the Lord. These rich psalms use a powerful mixture of images, figurative language intended to draw us into important truths about God.

How do the images used in these psalms stretch your limited view of God?

DAY6 Psalms 89; 96; 100–101; 107

We end the week as we started it—with psalms. Today's psalms are some of the most powerful songs of praise and thanksgiving in the Bible. Allow the images used in these psalms to stimulate your thinking about how good and powerful God is and about all He has done for you.

As you read, turn these psalms into prayers expressing praise and thanksgiving to the Lord.

SMALL-GROUP DISCUSSION QUESTIONS

1. Read Psalm 23:1-3. David used the images of a shepherd and sheep to describe how the Lord related to him. Jesus also chose this image in John 10:11, describing Himself as the Good Shepherd. What does such an image imply for our relationship with God? What do the images in verse 2 convey? What is the purpose for which the Lord leads us "along the right paths" (v. 3)?

2. Read Psalm 23:4-6. What reasons did David give for his confidence in the Lord? How does God's presence in your life give you confidence? In what ways do you tell others about your confidence in the Lord's provision?

3. What are specific ways you speak or act that fail to acknowledge your need for and dependence on your Shepherd?

4. Read 2 Samuel 6:14-23. What does this incident say about David's priorities?

5. In what ways was David a good shepherd over the people of Israel?

6. If we follow David's pattern of proclamation and praise, what impact should we expect on our lives? On others' lives around us?

7. How can you be more faithful to practice praise in the way you live your life with God and before others?

WEEK 18

The readings for this week take us from the firm establishment of David's kingdom to a major, tragic crack in the bedrock of David's monarchy—the sin involving Bathsheba. The readings of day 1 have special significance for biblical history and theology as a whole. We will read about God's covenant with King David and the promise that one of David's descendants would have an eternal kingdom.

Psalms are interspersed throughout the week, covering a wide variety of topics that correspond thematically to the events in the biblical story. Hear the profound poetry of these psalms. Take time to meditate on them, using them to prompt your own prayers.

DAY 1 2 Samuel 7; 1 Chronicles 17; Psalms 1–2; 33; 127; 132

It would be difficult to overestimate the importance of today's readings in the grand story of biblical history and theology. Keep in mind that God, not David, is the central figure. Here God promised David an enduring kingdom, and the New Testament writers understood several of these passages as being ultimately fulfilled in Jesus. For example, Hebrews 1:5 points to verses from 2 Samuel 7; 1 Chronicles 17; and Psalm 2. As you read the parallel passages from 2 Samuel and 1 Chronicles, take note of the references to the words *name* and *house*, paying attention to the ways they apply to David, David's son, and God.

Notice how today's psalms accent various themes in the promises to David. The promise of an eternal kingdom gives us great hope as Christians.

> *Focus on two key word pictures from these psalms and meditate on the truth communicated by the word pictures.*

> *In whom are you hoping today?*

DAY 2 2 Samuel 8–9; 1 Chronicles 18

A dominant theme in today's readings is God's supporting David against his enemies. As David won victories in war, God's blessing came in the form of stability for the kingdom—secure borders and an administrative structure composed of competent leaders. In many of the psalms we have read, David cried out for vindication and protection for himself and judgment on his enemies. Yet this cry for justice was not a cry for personal revenge but rather for God to fulfill His covenant promises.

Notice the kindness of David's actions towards Mephibosheth. His loyalty to Jonathan overrode a thirst for revenge on the house of Saul.

How does your life exhibit loyalty to God?

How does your loyalty to God's ways override other less noble emotions you might experience?

DAY 3 2 Samuel 10; 1 Chronicles 19; Psalms 20; 53; 60; 75

Today the narrative from 2 Samuel and 1 Chronicles recounts David's war with the Ammonites and illustrates David's continued dominance of the surrounding nations. An important aspect of the plot centers on misjudging the motives of another person, an especially dangerous response when dealing with persons who hold great power. David's motives for sending emissaries to Hanun were noble, but the Ammonites did not read them that way, leading them into a world of trouble.

In what ways are you tempted to misjudge the motives of another person?

Today's psalms offer prayers for help in the face of battles or for the celebration of victory. These psalms point to David's dependence on the Lord as his source of true help. Notice the beauty of parallelism, the repetition of thoughts, in the psalms.

You may not be involved in war today, but you face battles. Are you depending on the Lord for victory?

DAY 4 Psalms 65–67; 69–70

Most of today's powerful, beautiful psalms are attributed to David. As you read, breathe parts of these psalms as your personal prayers to God. Reflect deeply on the words here, meditating on what they reveal about God, especially the greatness of God's works.

What kinds of works are celebrated?

Notice the contrasts assumed in the psalms between God's power or position and human limitations and between God's holiness and our need for forgiveness.

Use Psalms 67 and 70 to pray as you conclude your reading.

DAY 5 2 Samuel 11–12; 1 Chronicles 20; Psalm 51

One powerful clue to the historical accuracy of the Bible is the honesty with which it reveals the great failures of even Israel's greatest leaders. The story of David's adultery with Bathsheba and the murder of Uriah, her husband, provides an example of a biblical character who shows us how not to live. Follow the development of the story: David's callous sin of adultery; his attempt to cover his sin, leading to murder; confrontation of his sin; repentance; and the consequences of his sin.

David's heart had become callous. Why might this have happened? Yet the softness of his heart toward God asserted itself when the prophet confronted him, and he readily repented.

Reflect on the way you process your sin. Do you know how to repent and receive restoration?

Use Psalm 51 to identify essential elements in a prayer of repentance.

TIMELINE
Old Testament Timeline, Part 2: write *Bathsheba* on line 4 in act 2, scene 5.

DAY 6 Psalms 32; 86; 102–103; 122

In several of the psalms for today, the psalmist cried out to God for forgiveness. Meditate deeply on Psalm 32, noticing that it moves from an introduction (vv. 1-2) to a personal testimony (vv. 3-5) and finally to a general exhortation (vv. 6-11). Also notice the figurative language used in verses 3-4 and the emotions communicated by that language.

Is there any sin for which you need to call out to God in repentance?
There is forgiveness in Jesus.

SMALL-GROUP DISCUSSION QUESTIONS

1. Read 2 Samuel 7. How did God advance His covenant in this passage? What did He promise?

2. In 2 Samuel 7:11 God promised to make David a house. What kind of house was God going to build for David? In what ways did Jesus fulfill all of the promises God made to David? Are any of these promises not yet fulfilled?

3. Second Samuel 7:14-15 speaks of the relationship between a father and a son, including discipline. What specific relationship was God referring to? How would discipline be expressed?

4. How did David respond to God's words (see 2 Sam. 7:18-29)? What did his response indicate about his heart? What did David say about God? How did he praise God?

5. What promises has God made to each of us? How often do you praise God for the promises He has made to you? How often do we praise God as a body of believers?

6. Discuss ideas for praising God, based on David's prayer.

7. David was faithful to God during crises and battles but fell to sin in a time of peace. Do you tend to follow the Lord more closely during hard times or peaceful times? Why?

8. Who was Nathan? What role did he play in David's life?

9. How does Psalm 51 provide a pattern for seeking God's forgiveness?

WEEK 19

You are almost halfway through your reading of the Old Testament. Congratulations! We are still in act 2, scene 5, the phase of God's story in which God was transforming His people into a kingdom. This week we will witness the dissolution and then the restoration of David's kingdom. As you read, think about the continuing consequences of David's sin with Bathsheba. Notice how many people's lives were affected. Also observe how the narrative develops in terms of David's responses at various points. God did not abandoned David, but life got much more complex and difficult because of David's sin.

Most of the psalms this week are cries to God in the midst of life's difficulties, especially when dealing with enemies. Think of ways these psalms might apply to you or another believer. Allow the beautiful music of the psalms to wash over you as you read.

DAY 1 2 Samuel 13–15

In Nathan's rebuke of David after his affair with Bathsheba, the Lord said, "I am going to bring disaster on you from your own family" (2 Sam. 12:11). That prophecy unfolded in these three chapters as David reaped the seeds he had sown in the lives of his sons. Track the development of the story step-by-step, noticing especially the deception woven through each stage. Perhaps David's sons had learned from his deception. David is one of the greatest figures in the Bible, but we see in this tragic series of events the cost of lapses in integrity.

> *Are there areas of your life in which you need to shore up your integrity? Ask God to reveal lapses in your use of words, hidden actions or attitudes, work ethic, and similar matters.*

DAY 2 Psalms 3–4; 13; 28; 55

David wrote today's psalms in the face of strong pressure from his enemies; reflect on how David must have felt as his son's forces drove him out of Jerusalem. Notice the potently descriptive language. If you have ever felt that your head was hanging down to the ground, that the light has gone out of your eyes, or that you wished you could escape your situation, you can identify with these psalms.

> *If you are not under attack personally, pray these psalms on behalf of persecuted brothers and sisters around the world.*

DAY3 2 Samuel 16–18

Today we continue to see the consequences of David's sin with Bathsheba. At the end of chapter 16, Absalom slept with his father's concubines on the roof. Occurring in the same place David's sin with Bathsheba started (see 2 Sam. 11:2), this act was a fulfillment of Nathan's prophecy that "another" would "sleep with them publicly" (2 Sam. 12:11-12). The story had a complex cast of characters at this point, some of whom were helping David and others who were opposing him. Notice their actions and the results of their actions. Read for details. Yet at the center stand David and Absalom, because the story really concerns the results of David's sin. David understood this. When Absalom died, David grieved rather than rejoiced.

Are you or those around you facing consequences of sin in your life or in the life of another? Repent and seek the Lord's forgiveness or pray for those around you who are suffering because of sin's consequences.

DAY4 Psalms 26; 40–41; 58; 61–62; 64

Among the psalms for today are a cry for vindication, a plea for help against enemies, a call for justice in the face of injustice, an expression of trust in God, and a prayer for protection. Notice that there are three main actors in these psalms: the one praying, his opponents, and God.

Identify a portion of one of these psalms that seems especially relevant for you today. Meditate on it and pray it to God.

DAY5 2 Samuel 19–21; Psalms 5; 38; 42

The narrative today describes the restoration of David's kingdom and records the outcomes of Absalom's revolt for a number of the characters who played a part. Notice David's response to each. In chapter 21 the author began to offer final reflections on King David's reign. Echoing through this section we still see the implications of David's sin with Bathsheba. He tried to reestablish his own authority, but it seemed a shaky authority. Sin reduces a person, and public sin by a leader reduces that person publicly. Then came Sheba's short-lived revolt, a final chapter in the story of Saul, and fights with Philistine giants, harking back to the beginning of David's career and the victory over Goliath.

In today's beautiful psalms notice the note of longing. For what are you longing in your relationship with God?

DAY 6 2 Samuel 22–23; Psalm 57

In offering final reflections on King David's reign, 2 Samuel weaves into the narrative two songs and then two stories. Today's reading covers the two songs, both of which exalt God as the source of David's success in life and deliverance from his enemies, and the first of the two stories. As you read the songs, focus on God's role. The songs point out that in spite of David's failures, he weathered the failures and lived out an unparalleled reign as king because of God's grace.

The story of 2 Samuel 23:8-39 focuses on David's warriors, a narrative Chronicles places at the beginning of David's reign (see 1 Chron. 11:10-47). This story emphasizes a second reason for David's success: the people surrounding him. Great followers make great leaders.

What success have you had in life?

Do you see your success as a product of God's grace?

Whom has God placed around you for support?

Thank God for His grace, at times expressed through supportive people. Perhaps write one of those supportive people a note of thanks today.

SMALL-GROUP DISCUSSION QUESTIONS

1. How do the events you read in 2 Samuel this week describe the results of David's sin? Think about a time when you experienced God's discipline for a sin you committed. What did He teach you through this experience? How did He show mercy through His discipline?

2. Read Psalm 40:1-5. What two images did David use to describe his time of great difficulty? What do these images communicate about David's situation and what he was experiencing? How did David respond to his circumstances? What image did David use to describe God's deliverance in times of trouble? How is this image significantly different from the image he used to describe his life prior to being delivered?

3. What was David's response to being delivered? What type of song did God put in David's mouth? What does this mean?

4. David praised God for delivering him. When faced with great trouble, do you follow David's example? Why or why not? Share an experience when God delivered you from trouble.

5. In what areas of life are you currently waiting on the Lord? Do you find it difficult to wait on the Lord as David did?

6. As a result of his deliverance, David said:

> Many will see and fear
> and put their trust in the LORD (Ps. 40:3).

What are the implications for us?

7. Read Psalm 40:6-8. What was David's approach to God's will? How would you describe your approach to God's will?

8. David said God's instruction lived within him. What do you do to get God's Word into your heart and life?

9. Read Psalm 40:11-17. Why was David so certain in verse 11 that the Lord would not withhold His mercy from him? What part do verses 1-10 play in that certainty? What gives you certainty that God will pour out compassion on you?

10. How do these verses apply to our ultimate deliverance in Christ?

11. How many times is the word LORD used in this passage? In light of the context, why is this important? What does this reveal about David?

WEEK 20

This week continues our journey through act 2, scene 5, which tells the story of God's building a kingdom people. Here we see the end of King David's story as he prepared for the reign of his son Solomon and Solomon's building of the temple in Jerusalem. Watch for elements of transition at this point, even as you continue to reflect on God as the main hero of the story.

Also reflect this week on the dynamics of David's rule. In what ways was he exemplary as a king? Although he was the greatest of Israel's kings, he also suffered the consequences of his own failures and brought those consequences down on the heads of his people. How would you describe David's character weaknesses?

View the psalms this week as interludes in the story. Enter the story by joining the psalmist as he prayed these songs to God.

DAY 1 Psalms 97–99

Today's reading is brief, so take time to meditate on these psalms. The psalmist celebrated the greatness of God. He is the God of the whole earth—quite a countercultural thought for the time since gods were considered to be limited to a region. God manifests His greatness on the earth through His creation and His people. These psalms also emphasize that people are accountable to God.

Use the words of these psalms to worship the great, awesome God.

DAY 2 2 Samuel 24; 1 Chronicles 21–22; Psalm 30

For a man so blessed with wisdom and discernment, King David had moments when he showed a great lack of discernment. One of the most tragic came toward the end of his life when he commanded a census to be taken of his troops. David's pride in numbers brought great destruction.

Identify the key principles woven into this story.

There are two seeming contradictions between the accounts in 2 Samuel and 1 Chronicles. Samuel says "the LORD's anger" (v. 1) stirred up David to take a census, while Chronicles says Satan did this. Yet two different but compatible perspectives were at work here. Biblically,

God at times permits Satan to do something, as when Job was tested (see Job 1–2). From one perspective it was God's initiative; from another, Satan's. God does not sin, but at times He turns human sinfulness inside out to accomplish His purposes (see Gen. 50:20).

There also seems to be a difference between the numbers counted in the two accounts. Perhaps 300,000 men were in Israel's standing army, and another 800,000 were found in the census, thus bringing Samuel's number in line with Chronicles. Furthermore, the 500,000 from Judah in the Samuel account might be a rounding up of the 470,000 mentioned in the Chronicles account. The key here, however, is that a focus on numbers became a stumbling block.

In what areas are you tempted to take inappropriate pride?

DAY 3 Psalms 108–109

Today we have a plea and praise for victory (see Ps. 108) and one of the harshest imprecatory psalms in the Bible (see Ps. 109). The imprecatory psalms call for God's judgment on the psalmist's enemies, and they can sound jarring to modern readers. Understand that the psalmist was calling for God's judgment on wickedness and for justice for those being oppressed. He appealed to God on the basis of His character as a holy God of justice, asking Him to act on behalf of the person to whom He had made powerful promises.

In what ways do you see horrible injustice toward God's people in the world?
Cry out to God to judge the wickedness and to bring relief to His people.

DAY 4 I Chronicles 23–26

In 1 Chronicles 22 we saw King David's preparations for building the temple. In chapters 23 and following he organized the priests and Levites for service. The Levites were from the tribe of Levi but were not the sons of Aaron, the first high priest. Notice the responsibilities of the Levites (see 1 Chron. 23:28-32) as compared to the responsibilities of the priests (see 23:13). Chapter 25 describes the Levitical musicians, who were to sing to the Lord, proclaiming His messages in song, and chapter 26 describes the gatekeepers and other officials who served in the temple.

Today Christians are the temple of God. What has God done to prepare you for worship?

What can you do to prepare for worship?

DAY 5 Psalms 131; 138–139; 143–145

Among other things, the psalms express emotions with which we can identify as God's people. The psalms for today are highly personal.

Pray this group of psalms from beginning to end, turning each into a prayer. If you would like to focus deeply on one of the psalms, do so with Psalm 139, one of the most beautiful and powerful in Scripture.

DAY 6 1 Chronicles 27–29; Psalm 68

As we finish 1 Chronicles, we find David putting things in order as he prepared for Solomon to take over as king. His preparations included appointing governmental officials and preparing for the building of the temple. From the standpoint of the writer, David's reign ended on a very strong note because of these extensive preparations.

For what transitions in life do you need to make preparations at this time?

What is God's role in these transitions? Is He at the center of your plans? Is His glory your goal?

Psalm 68 praises God for His majestic power. How do you or those around you need to experience God's power?

TIMELINE
Old Testament Timeline, Part 2: write *Solomon* on line 5 in act 2, scene 5.

SMALL-GROUP DISCUSSION QUESTIONS

1. What did you learn about David from the story of the census (see 2 Sam. 24)? What did you learn about God?

2. In what ways did you find Psalm 109 disturbing? What does it teach you about God's justice and righteousness?

3. Read I Chronicles 29:10-22. What works had God accomplished so far in Israel's history?

4. What did David say about God in these verses? Why did he focus on who God was for His people before focusing on what God had done for His people?

5. For what did David express gratitude to God? How does expressing gratitude glorify God?

6. How did David describe the people's giving? With what material resources did God supply the people? Why does God sometimes lavish His people with material resources? How can we use what God gives us to serve Him and accomplish His purposes?

7. What did David pray for the people? What did he mean by the phrase "confirm their hearts toward You" (v. 18)?

8. What did David pray for Solomon?

9. Why is it important to ask God to supply what He requires?

10. How are you depending on God to accomplish His purposes in your life? What about your church?

11. How can we live in such a way as to ensure that people will adore and accredit God for all that takes place in our lives?

12. Read Matthew 6:9-13. What similarities do you find between David's prayer and the prayer Jesus taught His disciples to pray? What elements are necessary for God-centered prayer?

13. How does knowing what God is like affect the way we address Him in prayer? What does adoring God as both eternal Father and universal King do for our faith?

14. Are you quick to credit God for your successes in life? Why or why not? How can you draw public attention to God's worth and work in your life?

WEEK 21

This week we enter the reign of Solomon in the Bible's grand story as we approach the end of act 2, scene 5. Read this section in light of both God's role as the main actor and His faithfulness to His covenant with David. Note again the transitional elements in the story, observing how they establish Solomon's rule as king. Notice especially the key role wisdom plays in the narrative.

We will also read poetic literature on four of six days this week. Psalms 111–119 are somewhat unique, so pick up on the special place these psalms had in ancient Judaism. Song of Songs should be read as love poetry; be sure to note the keys to reading it. At times in the history of the church, the theme of sexual love between a man and a woman caused discomfort, so the church opted to read the Song as allegorical, a word picture of Christ and the church. The Song should be read for what it is: a celebration of God's gift of romantic love.

DAY 1 Psalms 111–118

These are psalms of praise to God. Psalms 113–118 are known as the *Hallel* ("Praise") in Judaism and even today are recited by devout Jews during times of special celebration. This section of the psalms was recited at Passover during the time of Jesus and was sung by Jesus and His disciples on the night before the crucifixion (see Matt. 26:30; Mark 14:26).

> *Identify the verses in Psalm 118 that would have been especially meaningful to Jesus on the night of the Last Supper.*

> *Speak these psalms as prayers to the Lord.*

DAY 2 1 Kings 1–2; Psalms 37; 71; 94

The key to 1 Kings 1–2 is the last sentence in the final verse of chapter 2: "The kingdom was established in Solomon's hand" (2:46). Here David, under the prompting of Nathan the prophet and Bathsheba, subverted a plot by Solomon's older brother, Adonijah, to become king in David's place. Once David named Solomon as king and Solomon was anointed and seated on the throne, Adonijah's plot fell apart.

In David's dying instructions to Solomon, he instructed his son to follow the Lord faithfully and to take revenge on David's enemies, which was a key step in firmly establishing Solomon's reign.

These chapters begin with the young woman Abishag being brought to King David. Her place in the story is significant because Adonijah's ultimate downfall was tied to his desire for her.

As you read the psalms today, reflect on God's judgment on the wicked and His faithfulness to the righteous, though sometimes flawed, person even through old age.

What role does God's covenant play in this part of the story?

DAY 3 Psalm 119:1-88

Psalm 119 celebrates God's Word, expressed variously as His law, His commands, and His precepts. Notice all the benefits the psalmist spoke of in relation to God's amazing Word.

Circle several word pictures (uses of figurative language) that stand out to you most powerfully.

Identify the benefits of God's Word that mean the most to you now.

Thank God for the blessings given by His Word.

DAY 4 1 Kings 3–4; 2 Chronicles 1; Psalm 72

In the two narrative books today we read about the wonderful beginning of King Solomon's reign. Solomon loved the Lord and walked in God's ways. When asked by the Lord, "What should I give you?" (1 Kings 3:5) Solomon answered, in essence, wisdom. God liked that answer, responding that He would give Solomon wisdom, as well as riches, long life, and dominance over his enemies. As 1 Kings 3–4 develops, we first see an example of Solomon's wisdom, then examples of his organizational ability, his great wealth, and even his literary skills. Second Chronicles 1 gives a summary of these chapters.

Psalm 72, labeled as Solomonic, offers a prayer for the king. Notice that the psalm ends with a prayer that God's glory would abound as the result of the king's rule and life.

> *How might you pray for a leader of your church, your government, or the like in ways that parallel the words of this psalm?*

DAY 5 Psalm 119:89-176

Today we read the rest of Psalm 119. As you read, notice how inextricably connected God's Word is to God's character. The psalmist trusted God's Word because he trusted God.

> *In what areas of your life today do you need to draw on God's Word and trust God?*

Also note that the psalmist said he would do certain things to interact with or respond to God's Word.

> *How do you need to respond to the Word today?*

DAY 6 Song of Songs 1:1–5:1

Song of Songs presents us with an extended love poem, containing several episodes and primarily in three voices: the young man, the young woman, and the friends of the young woman ("daughters of Jerusalem"). Often these different speakers are marked with headings in modern Bible versions. Several interpretations of this book have been offered through the ages. An allegorical interpretation sees the Song as depicting the relationship between God and His people; there were Jewish and Christian versions of this interpretation from early on. Other interpretations see the Song as a two-character drama depicting Solomon's love affair with a woman who became his wife or a three-character drama in which the woman, destined for Solomon's harem as a concubine, expressed her love for a shepherd boy from whom she had been separated. Others see it as simply a collection of love poems.

Today we read the first three movements of the book. Song of Songs celebrates appropriate, sexual love between a man and his wife. Thus, it needs to be read as a celebration.

> *If you are married, thank God for romantic love and use the Song to remember that you need to cherish and nurture romantic love with your spouse.*

> *If you are not married, celebrate the depths of God's love for you.*

SMALL-GROUP DISCUSSION QUESTIONS

1. What parallels do you see between Psalm 118 and the life of Jesus?

2. What instructions did David give Solomon about following God as Solomon assumed the throne?

3. What benefits of following God's Word are found in Psalm 119? How have you been blessed by obeying God's Word?

4. What did Solomon ask God for in 1 Kings 3:7-10? Why did this request please God? Why do you think modern-day leaders lack wisdom? In what ways do you need wisdom in your Christian walk today? Do you regularly ask God to give you wisdom?

5. What qualities of leadership did Solomon demonstrate in 1 Kings 3–4?

6. How should the church be different from the world in its approach to sexuality? Do you think God's view of sex is more satisfying and pleasurable than the view of the world?

7. If you are married, discuss ways you can apply Song of Songs to your marriage. How can you show affection to your spouse?

WEEK 22

After finishing Song of Songs this week, we will primarily focus on the Book of Proverbs. These proverbs present guidelines for the way life should be lived. Proverbs should not be read as promises but rather as guidance: this is how life works.

The Book of Proverbs follows this structure:
• Proverbs 1:1-7 is the preamble to the book.
• Proverbs 1:8–9:18 is the prologue, consisting of 10 lessons from a father to a son.
• Chapters 10 and following are an extended collection of wise sayings that deal with a wide range of topics, all of which seek to teach us how to live effectively in the world.

As you read Proverbs, you may be tempted to hurry over these brief, loaded statements. Each day slow down and think deeply about at least a couple of the verses, perhaps even turning them into prayers for wisdom.

DAY 1 Song of Songs 5:2–8:14; Psalm 45

Today we conclude Song of Songs. Continue to follow the conversation between the young man and his lover. Notice especially the powerful figurative language. The images are different than we would use in our culture. Today a young man wouldn't tell his wife, "Your hair looks like a flock of goats, your belly is like a pile of wheat, and your nose is like a tower" (see 6:5; 7:2,4). Yet in that culture these would have been great compliments. The key is to ask how each image communicated a picture of striking beauty.

Psalm 45 is a royal wedding psalm. Interestingly, verses 6-7 are applied in Hebrews 1:8-9 to Jesus' rule of the universe. Notice that the King is addressed as God, and the psalmist says God has anointed Him. This psalm, then, applies ultimately to Jesus, who fulfills the role of the ultimate heir to King David.

What insights does this psalm give you about Jesus as our King?

DAY 2 Proverbs 1–4

Proverbs 1:1-7 is the preamble to the Book of Proverbs, and 1:8–9:18 is the prologue, which consists of 10 lessons from a father to a son. In all of these lessons the father addressed his son and admonished him to pay careful attention to his instructions, teachings, and words. Today we read the first seven of these lessons.

See if you can find the first seven of the father's lessons.

Notice especially how wisdom is personified in these chapters. Meditate on a brief passage from this section, thinking about how you might live more wisely today.

DAY 3 Proverbs 5–8

Today we read lesson 8 through the beginning of lesson 10 in the book's prologue. A large part of this passage deals with the devastating dangers of adultery and seduction. Notice especially the safeguards against falling into temptation that the father offered the son.

By what are you most likely to be seduced this week?

How might you use these safeguards to keep from falling?

DAY 4 Proverbs 9–12

At the end of lesson 10, both wisdom and folly call out to the inexperienced person (see Prov. 9). Both are trying to draw a person in. Wisdom is given more space here, and the result of listening to her is life. The foundation of a life lived wisely is fear—a deep reverence—of the Lord (see Prov. 9:10).

In Proverbs 10–12 we begin a collection of proverbs from Solomon. Read these proverbs as general guidelines for the way life should be lived.

Which of these guidelines do you most need today?

DAY 5 Proverbs 13–16

Notice two things about the proverbs in today's reading.

1. The vast majority of the proverbs in chapters 13–15 are antithetical, first presenting a truth, then a second truth that contrasts with the first in some way. For instance, notice the contrast between the wise son and the mocker in Proverbs 13:1. Both statements are true, but they contrast with each other.

2. Notice that certain themes are treated again and again.

Which of these themes resonates with you at this time in your life?

DAY 6 Proverbs 17–20

Notice that while we still find antithetical proverbs here, most of the proverbs in this section include a double statement of a truth, with both statements making the same point. For example, look at Proverbs 17:2:

> A wise servant will rule over a disgraceful son
> and share an inheritance among brothers.

The ideas that a wise servant will rule and share among the biological children in a home both point to a reward of wisdom. Wisdom elevates a person in status. Also notice that these proverbs speak to a variety of issues: the condition of the heart, wisdom versus foolishness, the power of words, discipline in speech, family relationships, business dealings, conflict, the value of a good spouse, integrity, kindness, and many others.

Choose one of these areas and track it through these chapters.
How might you apply the wisdom of these proverbs today?

SMALL-GROUP DISCUSSION QUESTIONS

1. Identify the ways Psalm 45 magnifies Jesus. What are some characteristics of His rule?

2. What do you think is the purpose of the Book of Proverbs?

3. Read Proverbs 1:2-6 and define *wisdom*. Is it important that Christians live their lives with wisdom? Why?

4. What is the difference between knowledge and wisdom?

5. Notice the occurrences of "fear of the LORD" in the Book of Proverbs. Discuss what it means to fear the Lord. Describe the attributes of a person who fears the Lord compared to one who doesn't. How do we attain fear of God? What is the reward for a person who fears the Lord?

6. Read Proverbs 1:10–2:16 and find the verses that refer to wisdom. What is the difference between the wisdom of the world and wisdom from above? How do we receive wisdom from above? Through whom is wisdom from above imparted?

7. What problems in your life would benefit from the application of godly wisdom? In the church? In the world?

8. How can we pursue a life of wisdom? Will reading the Book of Proverbs make us wise?

9. Read 1 Corinthians 1:18-31. What did Paul mean in saying that Jesus is wisdom? How does it affect your approach to your problems to know that God's wisdom lives in you?

WEEK 23

This week in the story of Scripture we will continue with act 2, scene 5, reading more about Solomon's reign as we come to the pinnacle of his achievements: the building of the temple in Jerusalem. Solomon's rule was marked by the success brought about by wisdom. However, we also see troubling signs that Solomon was not as wholly committed to the Lord as it might seem on the surface. In the life of Solomon, we find both the glory and the shame that mark much of the Old Testament story. God worked gloriously among His people, but they struggled with commitment to God and faced the consequences of their disobedience.

DAY 1 Proverbs 21–24

Again we have a wide range of topics today. Look, for instance, at Proverbs 21:31. You probably do not own a battle horse, but the principle in this passage is that we can have assets that lead to success in life, but we should depend on the Lord for that success. So be prepared, but trust the Lord.

At Proverbs 22:17 we see a shift. Here the verses are not as uniform, varying in the number of poetic lines, and we see topics that were common in the book's prologue.

Do any of these proverbs suggest that you need to shift your way of thinking about life or need to think more carefully about some areas?

DAY 2 I Kings 5–6; 2 Chronicles 2–3

King Solomon gathered building materials for the construction of the temple for the name of the Lord (see 1 Kings 5:5, an allusion to the proclamation of 2 Sam. 7:13). The name of the Lord has to do with both God's character and His fame, and the temple would be Solomon's greatest legacy. In honor of the Lord, Solomon used the highest quality of materials, including gold for overlaying many of the temple's surfaces. These passages emphasize the quality of materials and the care with which the temple was constructed. From a New Testament standpoint, Christ followers are now God's temple, with Christ Himself as the cornerstone (see 1 Pet. 2:5-6).

How might you relate to others in the body of Christ in a way that expresses care and quality this week?

DAY 3 I Kings 7–8; Psalm 11

Today we read about Solomon's palace complex, the crafting of furniture and utensils for the temple, and the dedication of the temple. Bruce Waltke notes that the placing of the account of Solomon's house here in the book's structure is significant. In effect, Solomon interrupted the completion of the temple in order to build his house and the house of one of his wives, Pharaoh's daughter.[1] Although the developing story depicts a glorious dedication ceremony and God's *Shekinah* presence descended on the temple, the passage on Solomon's house reveals that he had a divided heart. This becomes clearer as 1 Kings continues, and it had tragic consequences.

What relationships, projects, or goals threaten to divide your heart spiritually, diverting your attention from God's cause in the world?

DAY 4 2 Chronicles 4–7; Psalms 134; 136

Second Chronicles 4–7 is a parallel passage to the narrative in 1 Kings 7–8 we read yesterday. The prayer at the end of 2 Chronicles differs slightly from the one in 1 Kings. Many ancient speeches were abbreviated or paraphrased by ancient writers, so slight differences are understandable. The writer of Chronicles drew on a tradition that had Solomon quoting Psalm 132:8-10 at the end of his prayer. Notice God's response at the beginning of 2 Chronicles 7. The *Shekinah* glory of the Lord represented God's presence. The presence of the Lord is one of the great themes of Scripture. God wants to live among His people in an active way. He ultimately fulfilled this desire through the coming of the Holy Spirit to indwell the church as the new temple (see Acts 2).

Notice the Lord's response to Solomon.

Praise God today that His eyes are open and His ears are attentive to His people. Ask God to watch over some aspect of your life today.

DAY 5 Psalms 146–150

Sometimes in our relationships we need days to stop and focus on the person we love, telling them all we appreciate about them. Today is such a day in your relationship with God. Fittingly, the Book of Psalms ends with majestic psalms of praise to God. God is praised for His character, compassion, creation, restoration of Jerusalem, and victory. Notice that many verses speak about God ("His name alone is exalted," Ps. 148:13), and many more are exhortations to praise God ("Praise Him, all His angels," Ps. 148:2). Yet these can be turned into personal prayers.

Use these psalms as prayers of praise to God, focusing on His character, compassion, creation, redemption of your soul, and victory.

DAY 6 I Kings 9; 2 Chronicles 8; Proverbs 25–26

Notice two things about God's response to Solomon after the temple and other building programs had been completed.

1. As the main actor of the story, God determined the events in Israel in response to either faithfulness or unfaithfulness.
2. The Israelites were to live their lives with reference to the covenant, so idolatry was a special focus of the warnings here; this will be significant as Solomon's story develops.

Perhaps the king's dealings with Hiram and the mention of the forced labor it took to build Solomon's projects begin to give us glimpses at Solomon's insensitivity to the people he dealt with.

With whom in your life are you most likely to be insensitive?

Pay special attention to Proverbs 26:4-5. These two proverbs, which seem contradictory on the surface, illustrate that the proverbs give guidelines that address various situations in life. Sometimes it is appropriate to respond to a fool one way, and at other times we should respond to a fool differently. Discernment is needed.

SMALL-GROUP DISCUSSION QUESTIONS

1. Read I Kings 8:1-11. Describe the ceremony that preceded the ark as it was transferred from the city of David to the temple (compare to 2 Sam. 6). What did the cloud represent in verse 11? Where have you already seen this cloud in Scripture?

2. Share the way you approach God. What about your church? Do we approach God with a repentant heart that is lifted in praise to God? What can we learn from I Kings 8:1-11 about approaching God?

3. Read I Kings 8:12-21. List ways Solomon said God had been faithful to Israel. Recite ways God has been faithful to you, your family, and your church.

4. Read 1 Kings 8:22-53. List the requests Solomon made of God. What did Solomon ask God to do for foreigners? What did Solomon identify as the purpose of the temple?

5. Read Mark 11:15-19. How does 1 Kings 8 clarify why Jesus was angry about the misuse of the temple?

6. Do you believe God hears all of your prayers? Do you take all of your requests and concerns to God? How can Solomon's prayer guide the way you pray?

7. Read 1 Kings 8:54-61. Why did Solomon ask God to maintain the cause of Israel? Was it for the sake of Israel alone? When God saves people today, is it for their sake alone? What is His purpose for them? When we pray for God to bless us and to maintain our cause, what should be our ultimate purpose in making this request?

8. How are the hearts of God's people turned to Him and enabled to obey His statutes and laws?

9. Read 1 Kings 8:62-66. What was the mood of the people because of the feast? What was their view of God?

10. When is the last time you gave generous freewill offerings to God in praise and thanksgiving for His faithfulness? How can we worship God today in a way that is similar to the picture in 1 Kings 8?

11. Second Chronicles 7:11-14 is God's response to all that happened the day the temple was dedicated. What are the implications of verse 14 for you and your church?

1. George H. Guthrie, *Read the Bible for Life: Your Guide to Understanding and Living God's Word* (Nashville: B&H, 2011), 86–87.

WEEK 24

In the first four days of this week, we will read wisdom literature. Pay special attention to the instructions on how to read Ecclesiastes, one of the most difficult books in the Bible. On day 4 we will also come to the end of Solomon's reign and the end of the united kingdom as we transition to act 2, scene 6 in God's story, "Kings and Prophets: God Divides the Kingdom People." From this point there were two kingdoms, Israel in the north and Judah in the south, and we will read about the kings of each. We will find that all kings of the north were bad, and the kings of the south were a mixed lot, some bad and some good. You will notice that when compared to 1–2 Kings, 2 Chronicles focuses especially on the southern kingdom of Judah and is not as negative about King David's less-than-stellar descendants.

DAY 1 Proverbs 27–29

Many of the proverbs today continue the pattern of giving short pairs of sayings. Chapter 27 offers general statements for wise living. Chapters 28–29 contrast the righteous and the wicked. Yet at times in Proverbs we see longer passages like the one found in 27:23-27. Meditate on this passage. Aspects of life left unattended are eventually unproductive. This applies to business, of course, but analogies can also be drawn to relationships.

> *You may not have a flock, but to what do you need to pay attention so that you are aware of its condition?*

DAY 2 Ecclesiastes 1–6

On its surface Ecclesiastes seems a depressing book and is one of the most difficult to read in the Bible. It was written by an Israelite king who referred to himself as "the Teacher, son of David, king in Jerusalem" (1:1). Ecclesiastes emphasizes that life is a vapor, that is, meaningless in terms of normal human attempts to find fulfillment and happiness (remember that the writer did not have the gift of the gospel, which would come several hundred years later). Death offers perspective. If you think you are wise, rich, or significant in any way, realize that death puts you on the same level with the most common person. Only God matters (see Eccl. 2:25; 5:1-7).

> *In which of your personal gifts or attributes are you tempted to trust instead of trusting God?*

DAY 3 Ecclesiastes 7–12

Begin today's reading with the conclusion, Ecclesiastes 12:12-14. Then go back and read chapters 7–12.

What does this section say about God and how God puts the futility of life in perspective?

How might we read this section in light of the coming of Christ and the resurrection?

DAY 4 1 Kings 10–11; 2 Chronicles 9; Proverbs 30–31

Today we read about both the glory and the disgrace of Solomon. Because of God's gift of wisdom, Solomon attracted attention from the Queen of Sheba. Ironically, Solomon's wisdom did not guard his heart against inappropriate attachment to his many wives and their gods, who had come to him through his interaction with surrounding nations. Notice that his downfall came "when Solomon was old" (1 Kings 11:4) through a violation of the covenant with God, so this part of the story must be read in light of the covenant. In a sense his success, which resulted from the gift of wisdom from God, resulted in his turning away from God.

Proverbs 31, on the other hand, celebrates the gift of a good wife who fears the Lord.

Husband, do you celebrate your wife?

How are you responding to God's gifts today?

Is your heart softening or hardening toward God?

SCENE 6: KINGS AND PROPHETS: GOD DIVIDES THE KINGDOM PEOPLE

DAY 5 1 Kings 12; 2 Chronicles 10

Today we move from the united kingdom under Saul, David, and Solomon to a kingdom divided into north and south. Read today's passages on three levels.

1. Read from the standpoint of God as the main character. Ask yourself what He was accomplishing. He was bringing about judgment on the house of Solomon.

2. Read from the standpoint of the history of the nation of Israel. This was a critical point in its history, when the united kingdom divided into northern and southern kingdoms. Sin has devastating consequences.

3. Read on the level of human interaction. These chapters present a brilliant example of rank foolishness.

To whom do you look for advice? Do you have wise counselors in your life?

Do you grasp how your foolish decisions affect the lives of other people?

DAY 6 | I Kings 13–14; 2 Chronicles 11–12

Both Rehoboam and Jeroboam failed to follow the Lord, and we read about the end of their reigns in today's narratives. First Kings focuses on the judgment against Jeroboam, to whom God said, "You have flung Me behind your back" (14:9) but then concludes with Shishak's coming against Rehoboam and the kingdom of Judah.

When reading the strange story of the man of God's death, found in 1 Kings 13:11-34, keep in mind two things.

1. The man of God, though deceived, chose to disobey the direct command he had received from the Lord.

2. First Kings 14:33 tells us the judgment against the man of God was also meant to be a sign to Jeroboam, but the king ignored it: "After all this Jeroboam did not repent."

Since 2 Chronicles focuses on Judah's kings, Rehoboam is the focus of the 2 Chronicles reading. God softened His judgment against Rehoboam when the king repented.

How do you think about the relationship between sin and its consequences? Is there anything about which you need to humble yourself before the Lord today and ask forgiveness?

SMALL-GROUP DISCUSSION QUESTIONS

1. Identify examples of futility described in Ecclesiastes. Do you agree that everything under the sun is futility?

2. What false hopes are offered by the world today? What things on this earth are you most attracted to and most tempted to believe hold value or meaning? How have you seen these things bring a sense of futility in your life?

3. Read Ecclesiastes 12:13-14. What did the writer of Ecclesiastes conclude was meaningful in life? Why? What is the purpose of life in this world? What are we to live for?

4. What do you fear other than God? What is the relationship between the things we pursue and the things we fear?

5. How does Christ bring meaning and life into a dead and meaningless world?

6. Read 1 Kings 10–11. In what ways did Solomon's life reflect the truths of the Book of Ecclesiastes? What was God's assessment of Solomon's life? What qualities does God desire in a life that is committed to Him?

7. How did the events of 1 Kings 12–14 show God's judgment on the house of Solomon?

8. How far did the northern and southern kingdoms depart from the Lord in only one generation? What does this tell you about the importance of handing down your faith to the next generation? How can you do this?

WEEK 25

The reigns of the kings of Judah and Israel are all evaluated according to the posture of each toward the Lord God. This week, as we continue act 2, scene 6, we encounter three of the most striking characters in this period of Israel's history.

1. Ahab, who married wicked Jezebel, serves as the epitome of an evil king over Israel.
2. Ahab's nemesis, Elijah, served the Lord so impressively that he became the epitome of a true prophet of the Lord and performed some of the greatest miracles in the Old Testament.
3. Jehoshaphat, a king of Judah, although flawed, carried out extensive reforms and led his people to worship the Lord for a time during his reign.

DAY 1 | 1 Kings 15:1-24; 2 Chronicles 13–16

Two kings of Judah are covered today. King Abijah (or Abijam), the son of Rehoboam, reigned for three years. His reign was characterized by not following the Lord, although 2 Chronicles 13 tells of Abijah's one success in battle "because [the Judahites] depended on the LORD" (v. 18). His son Asa, who followed him as king, was a good king who sought the Lord. Yet Asa's treaty with Aram was a failure because it violated the covenant with God and relied on a human solution to the problem with Israel.

Notice the language of wholehearted devotion to the Lord in these stories and think deeply about 2 Chronicles 16:9: "The eyes of Yahweh roam throughout the earth to show Himself strong for those whose hearts are completely His."

Evaluate your heart today. Is your heart completely committed to the Lord?

DAY 2 | 1 Kings 15:25–16:34; 2 Chronicles 17

Read today about the succession of several generations of Israelite kings, all of whom were evil, ignoring the ways of God. Notice that evil escalated in succeeding generations. The Israelite kings stand in contrast to good king Jehoshaphat in 2 Chronicles 17, who emulated his ancestor David and rejoiced in the ways of the Lord.

Also notice in 1 Kings 16:23-24 the origin of the city of Samaria. The area surrounding this city in the center of the land would be an important geographical area in the time of Jesus (the province of Samaria, where the Samaritans lived).

Today emulate King Jehoshaphat, rejoicing in the ways of the Lord.
Extol God's goodness in prayer.

DAY 3 | Kings 17–19

Certainly one of the most dramatic sections in the narrative of 1 Kings concerns the prophetic ministry of Elijah. As you read, ask, "How is God the true hero of these stories?" Here we read the stories of Elijah's performing miracles at the home of the widow of Zarephath, the showdown with the prophets of Baal on Mount Carmel, and God's meeting Elijah on Mount Horeb. Wicked King Ahab had introduced Baal worship into Israel (see 1 Kings 16:31-32). Baal was a pagan fertility god of the crops and rain, and these stories show that God is the one true God, who has power over all things. Enjoy these stories and write down what you learn about God from them.

Also remember that John the Baptist came "in the spirit and power of Elijah" (Luke 1:17), as the forerunner of Jesus, the Messiah.

How was John the Baptist like Elijah?

TIMELINE

Old Testament Timeline, Part 2: write *Elijah* on line 1 in act 2, scene 6.

DAY 4 | Kings 20–21

The story of Ahab gets worse. In 1 Kings 20 notice how the tables were turned on Ben-hadad of Aram. The chapter begins with the king of Aram's clearly having the upper hand and ends with his humiliation. Yet the story is really about Ahab's wickedness. In spite of God's working on behalf of Israel, Ahab paid no attention to the ways of the Lord. God had devoted Ben-hadad to destruction, but Ahab made a treaty with him.

In 1 Kings 21 Ahab's immaturity and wickedness came to a head, spurred on by his evil wife, Jezebel. To satisfy his own desires, Ahab murdered Naboth and stole his vineyard.

As you read, watch for several violations of the covenant and law God had given His people as they came into the land. Ahab's sin was manifested in a lack of attention to God's ways.

In what areas of life do you need to give more attention to the ways of God?

DAY 5 | I Kings 22; 2 Chronicles 18–20

First Kings ends with an alliance between Jehoshaphat and Ahab and its aftermath. These two kings provide a contrast, Ahab serving as the epitome of Israel's bad kings and Jehoshaphat a king of Judah who, for the most part, sought the Lord. As you read the story, notice that Ahab dealt with life strictly from the perspective of human power, failing to take the true prophet's words as from the Lord. Jehoshaphat, on the other hand, sought the Lord.

Notice how God's acts brought about judgment on Ahab, and Ahab's evil son took his place. Because of his alliance with Israel's King Ahab, however, the prophet of the Lord rebuked Jehoshaphat. In response, Jehoshaphat repented and brought about extensive reforms in the land, including setting up a network of sound leadership. Notice that the emphasis in the story is the complete focus and dependence on the Lord during this period.

Praise God that He judges evil in the world, bringing wicked rulers to account.

In prayer express your complete dependence on the Lord today.

DAY 6 | 2 Kings 1–4

Second Kings continues the story of the divided kingdom and the powerful prophets of the ninth century B.C. In today's reading Elijah finished his ministry, and Elisha succeeded him. Elijah foreshadowed the ministry of John the Baptist (see 2 Kings 1:8; Matt. 3:4). Elisha's ministry, however, continued the miracles of Elijah (watch for miracles done by Elijah that are repeated by Elisha) but also foreshadowed the ministry of Jesus. In our reading today, Elisha raised a child from the dead and multiplied bread. The Elijah and Elisha stories are some of the most powerful in Scripture, as God graciously poured out miraculous works.

Praise God that He chooses to manifest His power in the world through miracles.

SMALL-GROUP DISCUSSION QUESTIONS

1. Read 2 Chronicles 16:9. Why is this verse important in its historical context? What does it look like to have a completely committed heart today?

2. How did King Jehoshaphat's leadership differ from that of the other kings in this time period? How did God bless his reign?

3. Read I Kings 18. What is the setting for Elijah's confrontation with Ahab? Why was this significant?

4. Ahab called Elijah the "destroyer of Israel" in verse 17. What was the real reason for the trouble in the land?

5. What accusation did Elijah bring against the people of Israel? How did the people respond?

6. How many prophets opposed Elijah on Mount Carmel? Why was this significant? What did Elijah want to prove to the people?

7. What idols are you susceptible to today? Which of those idols have you worshiped in the past? What is so appealing about those idols? What do they promise? How do they offer hope?

8. What does 1 Kings 18 reveal about God and His character? Why is this important? What does this passage reveal about the god these prophets served?

9. What does 1 Kings 18 reveal about the condition of all humankind? How do people today try to get the attention of their gods? What do they give their gods? What do their sacrifices to their gods say about what they value?

10. Contrast the way Elijah approached the Lord with the prophets' approach to their god. What does this teach us about the God we serve and how we should or should not approach Him? What does this teach about the character of the God we serve?

WEEK 26

This week we will continue to read about the kings of Judah and Israel, most of whom were evil and came to violent ends. This section of Scripture emphasizes God's faithfulness to His covenant and His judgment on sin. We will also read some of the greatest stories in the Old Testament. We will begin with several powerful stories about the prophet Elisha and will end the week with the beautifully crafted story of the prophet Jonah as we move into scene 7, "Kings and Prophets: The Southern Kingdom as God's People." As you read, notice the patterns and details in these stories that underscore various aspects of God's character.

DAY 1 2 Kings 5:1–8:15

This section contains powerful stories in the ministry of Elisha, like the healing of Naaman and the opening of the eyes of Elisha's servant to see the horses and chariots of God surrounding the Aramean army. Jesus, of course, also cured lepers (see Matt. 8:1-4), and He pointed to Naaman's healing as a precedent for outreach to the Gentiles (see Luke 4:27). Second Kings 5:1 refers to Naaman as "a great man." Notice that in his pride Naaman had preconceived ideas about how Elisha would treat him and heal him (see 5:8-12).

Do you ever have preconceived ideas about how God should act on your behalf?

DAY 2 2 Kings 8:16-29; 2 Chronicles 21:1–22:9

Jehoshaphat was succeeded as king by a series of evil rulers in Judah. His son Jehoram led Judah astray, following the evil example of the kings of Israel (Ahab's daughter, Athaliah, was his wife). God's judgment on him, through the prophet Elisha, was severe. Jehoram's son Ahaziah was also influenced by his mother, Athaliah. Thus, Ahaziah also followed the example of Israel's evil kings.

The evil influence of Athaliah on two generations of Judah's kings stems from Jehoshaphat's foolish alliance with Ahab. Although Jehoshaphat was a godly king, his bad relationship with Israel's evil king was costly to the generations that followed. Alliances with evil people have consequences.

Cite a modern-day example of that principle.

DAY 3 2 Kings 9–11; 2 Chronicles 22:10–23:21

God used Jehu to bring about judgment on Joram, the king of Israel, and on Ahaziah, the king of Judah. Jehu also killed Jezebel, those left in the house of Ahab, and the worshipers of Baal. So Jehu became the king of Israel. Because he carried out God's judgment, he was considered better than most of the kings of Israel, but his commitment to the Lord was still mixed with idol worship.

Following the death of Ahaziah of Judah, the evil Athaliah then took the throne herself, thinking she had killed all of the heirs. However, the child Joash was rescued and hidden for six years. Under the leadership of the good priest Jehoiada, Athaliah was overthrown, Joash was put on the throne, and Judah experienced reform. Whereas an evil person like Athaliah caused much harm to God's people, one godly person, Jehoiada, was able to bring about reform.

Pray that God will raise up many Jehoiadas in our day.

DAY 4 2 Kings 12–13; 2 Chronicles 24

King Joash of Judah did well as long as the godly counselor Jehoiada was living, and the work on the temple was done with integrity. But King Joash turned from the Lord when this good man died. The Arameans invaded Judah, and Joash was assassinated.

Today we encounter Israel's evil kings Jehoahaz and Jehoash. Elements of this story remind us of the time of Judges, when God brought judgment on His people but then sent a deliverer for them because of His covenant with them. Notice that the death of Elisha echoed the death of his mentor, Elijah. Recognize the main principles that continue to be underlined: God is faithful to His people, but rebellion brings about consequences.

Thank God today for His faithfulness to His people.

DAY 5 2 Kings 14–15; 2 Chronicles 25–27

King Amaziah of Judah was in some ways a good king, as seen by his commitment to the law of God in 2 Kings 14:5-6, but he ended up turning from the Lord to worship idols. Consequently, he made tactical errors in relating to Israel, which led to defeat and his death.

After King Jehoash of Israel died, Jeroboam II became the king and followed in the footsteps of his namesake. The Lord used this evil king, however, to accomplish good for His people. Recognize that God sometimes "hits straight licks with crooked sticks."

King Azariah was also called Uzziah. A good king of Judah who followed God's ways, Uzziah became arrogant as his kingdom prospered, thinking he was above God's instructions for worship in the temple. Ironically, God's blessings can lead to arrogance and a rejection of God's ways. When God struck Uzziah with a serious skin disease, he was quarantined and could visit the temple no longer. His son, Jotham, was also a good king, further strengthening the kingdom of Judah.

This period in Israel, though prosperous materially, demonstrated political weakness. Notice the succession of five kings in Israel during Uzziah's reign over the southern kingdom.

Thank God for his blessings to you, but also pray for humility.

DAY 6 Jonah 1–4

Jonah is one of the greatest, most beautifully crafted stories in the Old Testament. God is the main character of the story, and it divides nicely into two main movements: chapters 1–2 and 3–4, each section beginning with God's call of Jonah. Each of these main movements also divides into two subdivisions.

- Chapter 1 presents God's call, Jonah's rebellion, and the crisis brought about by his rebellion.
- Chapter 2 gives us Jonah's response, a hymn about God's salvation.
- Chapter 3 presents the reissuing of God's call, Jonah's ministry to Nineveh, and God's compassion on the great city.
- Chapter 4 gives us Jonah's angry response.

The story is beautifully written, so go slowly and enjoy it. Watch for the crises and resolutions in the story. Notice that the non-Jews responded to God appropriately, while God's Jewish prophet responded selfishly. Also notice the emphasis on compassion. God cares about people.

To whom might you show compassion today?

SMALL-GROUP DISCUSSION QUESTIONS

1. In 2 Kings 6:17 Elisha asked the Lord to open his servant's eyes to see the spiritual forces surrounding him. How do you think the Lord's army is fighting around you every day? Read Ephesians 1:18; 6:10-18 and compare this New Testament perspective.

2. Identify some of the good kings you read about this week. How were they faithful to the Lord?

3. Why do you think Jonah refused to go to Nineveh? Is it possible to flee from the presence of the Lord? Why did God relentlessly pursue Jonah in his rebellion?

4. Share a time when you consciously rebelled against God's will for your life. How did God pursue you?

5. In what ways does Jonah's prayer (2:1-9) resemble some of the psalms? What do you think Jonah remembered about the Lord in verse 7? What does it mean to remember the Lord? What did Jonah do after remembering the Lord's salvation? What should we do after receiving the Lord's salvation?

6. What was Jonah's message to Nineveh? Why did God give the people 40 days to repent? How did the people respond? How does God show mercy toward lost people today?

7. How did Jonah respond when the people repented? Why? Why was God gracious to him? Have you ever been angry or rebellious because of God's forgiveness or compassion toward someone? If so, why?

8. How is God's sovereignty portrayed throughout the Jonah narrative?

9. How does knowing that no one is beyond God's redemptive reach shape your confidence in sharing God's love? Is there a particular kind of person that you have trouble loving? Why? How might racism and hatred prevent us from being obedient to the Great Commission?

10. What is keeping us from being obedient to God's command to make disciples of all people? How might we cultivate hearts of compassion like God's rather than emulating the heartlessness of Jonah?

WEEK 27

Congratulations! You are about halfway through reading through the Bible. This week we are still in act 2, scene 6, the divided kingdom. There were still two kingdoms, the northern kingdom of Israel and the southern kingdom of Judah. The middle of the eighth century was a time of great prosperity and seeming safety but also a time of rampant idolatry. Amos and Hosea each prophesied against the northern kingdom, giving us some of the most powerful, penetrating material in the Bible on injustice, lack of concern for the poor, and empty religion. Isaiah's words were directed to Jerusalem and the southern kingdom. The prophets had a threefold message:

1. Return to covenant faithfulness
2. If you don't repent, judgment is coming.
3. God loves His people and has a plan for the future.

The judgment that was on the horizon during this period came in the form of Assyria, a world power that would destroy the northern kingdom of Israel in 722 B.C. As you read this week, think about the peril of presumptuousness. The Israelites of this period presumed that since they were blessed in life, they were acceptable to God.

DAY 1 Amos 1–5

Amos, a sheep breeder from the town of Tekoa in the southern kingdom of Judah, was sent as a prophet to the northern kingdom of Israel in about 760 B.C. This was a time of great prosperity for Israel but also a time of great wickedness. Amos 1:1–2:5 contains pronouncements of judgment against all of the nations surrounding Israel. The Israelites would have cheered these judgments, but they were at the center of the prophetic bulls-eye. Though they were religious, they had forgotten true worship of Yahweh, who delivered their ancestors from Egypt and brought them into the land (see Amos 2:10). Thus, their sacrifices and songs at the false shrine in Bethel (originally built by Jeroboam I) were hollow reflections of the real thing. Having abandoned the true God, they had also abandoned His social values, oppressing the poor and righteous people of the land. Consequently, God was bringing devastating judgment on the land. Read Amos 4–5 very carefully.

Write your understanding of the connection between worship and ethics.

DAY 2 Amos 6–9

There is a pattern in the Prophets.
1. They called the nation to faithfulness to Yahweh's covenant, pointing out violations against it.
2. They pronounced a coming judgment that would result from continued rebellion. This section of Amos contains a series of five visions of coming punishment.
3. They almost always mentioned hope for the future, often related to a righteous remnant God would raise up.

See if you can identify these elements in this section of Amos.

How was Amos 9:11-15 fulfilled by Jesus and the gospel?

DAY 3 Hosea 1–5

Unlike his counterpart, Amos, Hosea was a prophet from the northern kingdom of Israel. His is the first and the longest of what we call the Minor Prophets (referring to their length; they are much shorter than books like Isaiah and Jeremiah). Hosea expressed God's passion for Israel. In fact, in the first two chapters Hosea dramatized God's relationship with Israel by marrying an adulterous woman, or prostitute. Notice the parallels drawn between a faithless wife and Israel's faithlessness to its true God. Also notice both God's passion about His people and His judgment on them for their sin.

Today God continues to be passionate about His people. Thank Him for how much He loves you—so much, in fact, that He will not allow you to live in unfaithfulness.

DAY 4 Hosea 6–9

This section of Scripture contains calls to repentance, laments that Israel was not faithful, and words about judgment that was coming (brought about when Assyria destroyed Israel in 722 B.C.). Notice that Israel's adultery in part had to do with political alliances (trusting other nations rather than trusting God) and in part had to do with religious perversion (worshiping false gods). Also notice that the nation abandoned God in part because they did not remember their own story of the way God delivered them from Egypt.

How might we commit spiritual adultery today, and what spiritual commitments safeguard us from doing so?

How does knowing the story of Scripture well help us remain faithful to God?

DAY 5 Hosea 10–14

Again today we have a mix of passages on God's passion for Israel, a call to repentance, warning of coming judgment, and the hope of restoration. Israel is often called Ephraim, named for a tribe of Israel central to the kingdom.

Watch for figurative language in this section. Israel is called a "lush vine" in Hosea 10:1. The word picture describes the prosperity of the nation, but the result was not positive.

Finally, notice the historical reference to the exodus in Hosea 11:1. The gospel writer Matthew used this verse to refer to Jesus traveling up from Egypt with Mary and Joseph (see Matt. 2:15). God acts in corresponding ways in history. Jesus fulfilled this word from Hosea. Whereas the kingdom of Israel had failed miserably, delivered by God but abandoning Him at every turn, Jesus, whose family was delivered from the wrath of King Herod, lived a life of perfect faithfulness to the Father.

> **Write ways you nurture faithfulness to God in your life.**

DAY 6 Isaiah 1–4

Isaiah the prophet was from Jerusalem in Judah, and he prophesied from 740 B.C. to 687 B.C. The people of Judah had failed to live up to God's desires for them, and judgment was coming. In fact, much of the imagery in the first chapters of the book tells of a time when warfare will have devastated the land. For instance, in Isaiah 4:1 we are told there would be a lack of men to marry in the time of judgment. Judah had failed God primarily by turning to idols and by a lack of social justice. They had failed to keep the covenant, in other words, and judgment was coming.

Yet Isaiah also pointed to a coming time of hope. Read about that time in Isaiah 2:1-4; 4:2-6. Notice in the latter passage the references to the cloud of smoke and glowing flame by night, images representing God's presence that were taken from the period of Israel's wandering in the wilderness.

> **Take time today to evaluate your life. Is there justice? Is your heart committed to the Lord alone as God? Do you know His presence?**

TIMELINE

Old Testament Timeline, Part 2: write *Isaiah* on line 2 in act 2, scene 6.

SMALL-GROUP DISCUSSION QUESTIONS

1. What attributes of God are evident in this week's passages from Amos and Hosea? Which of these traits of God are least likely to be mentioned in the church today? Why do you think that is the case?

2. What was at the root of Israel's sins? What is at the root of the sins you struggle with most? When you struggle with sin, do you focus on its manifestations or its root?

3. Churches often emphasize forgiveness and patience, but these passages emphasize God's wrath. Do you find yourself counting on God's continued patience? Do you think unbelievers take seriously God's inevitable judgment? Why or why not?

4. Read Hosea 14:2-3. What elements should be present in hearts that return to God?

5. How can we seek to be people of faithfulness and steadfast love—the faithful bride of Christ?

6. How can we seek and share knowledge of God?

7. How does the Holy Spirit enable us to remain faithful to God? How does God's Word help us remain faithful?

8. God's love for Israel foreshadows Christ's love for the church. How has God specifically shown you love despite your unfaithfulness?

WEEK 28

We will continue this week with the eighth-century prophets, and in days 1–4 we will still be in act 2, scene 6 of God's story. This week the focus will primarily be on the southern kingdom of Judah and the prophets Isaiah and Micah. We will also read about King Ahaz of Judah, one of the southern kingdom's worst.

In day 5 we will come to another major turning point in the history of God's people: the fall of the northern kingdom to Assyria. This moves us into act 2, scene 7, "Kings and Prophets: The Southern Kingdom as God's People." From this point on, the divided kingdom was no more. Only the southern kingdom of Judah remained.

As you read this week, notice how the prophets mixed calls to repentance, warnings about coming judgment, allusions to the past, hope for a brighter future, and promises concerning a coming One who would lead God's people.

DAY 1 Isaiah 5–8

Chapter 5 presents the Vineyard Song, a dramatic word picture of judgment. As with significant portions of the prophets, this is poetic literature, so parallelism and figurative language are prominent. Parallelism offers the same thought, a contrasting thought, or more information in a parallel form. Isaiah 6 gives the powerful, beautiful call of Isaiah, and words of judgment follow (see 6:9-11; Mark 4:10-12).

In Isaiah 7–8 the prophet mixed words of hope for Judah with warnings about the rise of Assyria. We also see the anticipation of a coming One, words the early church understood to be fulfilled by Jesus (see Isa. 7:14; 8:14-15).

The picture of God presented in these chapters emphasizes God's sovereignty over the nations. Nations may be evil, like Assyria, but they cannot thwart God's plans.

> *Worship God this day as a holy God who moves the political currents of the world toward His desired ends.*

DAY 2 Isaiah 9–12

Look for four elements as you read Isaiah today: a call to repent (for abandoning aspects of the covenant), the coming judgment, echoes of Israel's past (look for allusions to the deliverance from Egypt), and hope for a bright future.

Two aspects of these chapters are especially striking.

1. Assyria would be both God's instrument of judgment and His object for judgment. God would use that nation to punish His wayward people, and then He would judge the Assyrians for their arrogance.
2. This section presents some of the most powerful messianic passages in the Old Testament (for example, see Isa. 9:6-7) and the picture of a future messianic kingdom (see Isa. 11:1-10).

> Isaiah 12 offers a beautiful song of salvation. Sing or speak this as a prayer of praise to the Lord. Meditate on the salvation He has given you or, if you have not experienced salvation, cry out to Him, asking for salvation.

DAY 3 Micah 1–4

Micah was a prophet from Judah to Judah in the eighth century B.C. He was a contemporary of Isaiah, Amos, and Hosea. Micah especially focused on the oppression and injustice of the wealthy and powerful of Jerusalem (carefully read Mic. 2–3).

Notice that Micah equated Mount Zion, on which the city of Jerusalem sits, with a pagan high place, or hill of worship (see Mic. 1:5). As you read Micah, again watch for these main elements found in the Prophets: a call to repentance and covenant faithfulness, the coming judgment, and the hope of a remnant whom God would deliver.

> Where do you see oppression and injustice around you today?

> Pray against injustice, speak out against it, and act against it.

DAY 4 Micah 5–7

Watch today for elements that connect with the broader story of the Bible. There are allusions to God's deliverance of Israel from Egypt and passages that anticipate the coming of the Messiah, Jesus. Micah 5:2 foretells Jesus' birth.

> Read Mark 11:12-14 in light of Micah 7:1-3.

The cursing of the fig tree by Jesus symbolized the judgment that was coming on Jerusalem and echoed the judgment pronounced by Micah.

Meditate deeply on Micah 6:8 and memorize this verse this week.
What does God desire of people?

How might you act justly, faithfully, mercifully, or humbly this week?

SCENE 7: KINGS AND PROPHETS: THE SOUTHERN KINGDOM AS GOD'S PEOPLE

DAY 5 2 Kings 16–17; 2 Chronicles 28

Judah's King Ahaz, who began his reign about 732 B.C., was one of the worst kings of the southern kingdom. Attacked by Aram and Israel, he sought help from King Tiglath-pileser of Assyria. He also imported aspects of Assyrian religion, copying a large altar he saw on a visit to Assyria.

In the 12th year of King Ahaz, Hoshea became the king over Israel in the north. During his reign the northern kingdom was destroyed by Assyria (722 B.C.), now under the rule of King Shalmaneser. Second Kings gives an extensive explanation of why Israel was destroyed. Carefully read 2 Kings 17:14-15. The Lord removed Israel from His presence because it failed to live by His covenant. So now only the kingdom of Judah remained.

What are the worthless things on which you are tempted to focus your life?

How do these things affect your relationship with the Lord?

DAY 6 Isaiah 13–17

Today's reading presents a series of prophecies about coming judgment. It will be important to notice what nation is on the receiving end of each judgment. At the back of your Bible, you probably have a map of the divided kingdom or the kingdoms of Israel and Judah. Use this map to identify the minor kingdoms immediately surrounding Israel and Judah. Babylon and Assyria, on the other hand, were nations hundreds of miles away to the east in the area of the Tigris and Euphrates Rivers and were major players on the world stage in the eighth through the sixth centuries B.C.

Look today for the hope offered by the prophet. What hope was there for a brighter future?

Read Isaiah 13:14 in light of Numbers 27:17; 1 Kings 22:17; and Matthew 9:36.

SMALL-GROUP DISCUSSION QUESTIONS

1. What references to Jesus do you see in Isaiah 8–12? In what ways did He fulfill these prophecies?

2. Read Isaiah 11:1-10. What are some characteristics of the coming Messiah? Of the future messianic kingdom? How does a knowledge of Christ bring these qualities to life in the present day?

3. In Micah 5:15 God stated, "In anger and wrath I will execute vengeance on the nations that did not obey." What had these nations done that was going to bring God's wrath?

4. Do you see God as being both loving and wrathful? How do you hold these two characteristics in tension?

5. Idolatry brought swift and harsh judgment against the nation of Israel. Why does God judge idolatry so harshly? What idols do we worship today? If we sometimes put other things before God, can we lose our salvation? Do people who are saved by grace through faith in Christ ever put things before God in our hearts? Does your security in Christ make you even more appreciative of His work on your behalf?

6. Name ways God has shown His faithfulness to you and your family. Although we know He is always faithful, why do we turn from Him and sin against Him?

7. Read Micah 6:6-8. Does God desire burnt offerings? What does He desire and expect?

8. How can believers continually remind one another of the character and faithfulness of God and stir one another to act justly, love faithfulness, and walk humbly with our God?

9. Read 2 Kings 17:14-15. Why did God bring judgment on the northern kingdom?

WEEK 29

We will still be in act 2, scene 7 this week, which focuses on the southern kingdom of Judah, and we will continue to hear from the prophet Isaiah. As you read the prophet, watch for warnings of coming judgment, as well as the promise of a future for the remnant of God's people. Isaiah spoke to the southern kingdom of Judah, but he also prophesied against various nations in that part of the world. Continue to read the prophet's words carefully, tuning in to the figurative language and references to the various nations. (Use a Bible dictionary or a study Bible for help. Free online resources are available at *www.mystudybible.com.*)

This week we will also meet Hezekiah, the greatest king of Judah after his forefather, King David. Hezekiah brought extensive religious reform, taking God's Word very seriously. He also faced two great crises during his reign, the first of which we will see in day 6 of this week. What in Hezekiah's life might we emulate?

DAY 1 Isaiah 18–22

Today we read oracles against Cush; Egypt; Babylon; Dumah (Edom); Arabia; Jerusalem; and Shebna, a palace administrator in Jerusalem. Cush was a powerful north-African nation, known for their skill with the bow; they were sometimes called Ethiopians or Nubians in the Bible. At the time of Isaiah's writing, Egypt was ruled by a Cushite, Piankhi. Egypt is a special focus here because Jerusalem trusted that nation instead of the Lord for help.

The prophets at times acted out their messages, so Isaiah 20 shows the prophet acting out God's judgment, going naked to make a point! Chapter 22 addresses the Assyrian siege of Jerusalem in 701 B.C., which will be further detailed in chapters 36–37. Shebna represents a self-serving leader deluded by his own power.

Choose two or three verses from today's reading and meditate on them.

DAY 2 Isaiah 23–26

Today's reading begins with a final oracle against Tyre, one of Babylon's allies. As we move to Isaiah 24, however, God brings judgment on the whole earth. Notice the rich figurative language here. God shows Himself to be the King of the whole earth (see Isa. 24:23).

In Isaiah 25 we continue to read words of judgment, but now they are mixed with words of salvation. Carefully read Isaiah 25:6-8, a wonderful promise about the destruction of death. Jesus accomplished this "on this mountain" (Isa. 25:6), in Jerusalem, when He was crucified and resurrected (see Heb. 2:14). This prophecy will be brought to full fruition at the end of the age, when God will "wipe away the tears from every face" (Isa. 25:8; also see Rev. 21:4). Isaiah 26 is a song of blessing for the nation of Judah, since it turned back to the Lord.

Praise God today for the blessings of His salvation and the promise of death's death.

DAY 3 2 Kings 18:1-8; 2 Chronicles 29–31; Psalm 48

Hezekiah, who ruled from about 728 to 686 B.C., was one of the greatest kings of Judah, earning the rare praise "He did what was right in the LORD's sight just as his ancestor David had done" (2 Kings 18:3). In fact, after David he was the epitome of a good king, since he trusted the Lord and kept God's law.

Second Chronicles 29–31 describes Hezekiah's extensive reforms. Notice his detailed attention to covenant and the law given through Moses.

As Psalm 48 celebrates, Zion, the mountain on which the city of Jerusalem sits, is exalted when God rules as the true King of His people.

Identify three aspects of Hezekiah's character or three of his actions that serve as examples for you to follow.

DAY 4 Isaiah 27–30

The image of Leviathan seems to be used in Scripture to represent evil powers. The Vineyard Song of Isaiah 27 presents a beautiful picture of God's reestablishing the nation after it had been punished. Under God's loving care it would thrive like a well-tended vineyard. That time has not yet come.

Isaiah 28–30 offers words of judgment mixed with words of encouragement. Note especially 28:16, which New Testament authors understood as a reference to Jesus (see Rom. 9:33; 1 Cor. 3:11; Eph. 2:20; 1 Pet. 2:4-7), who gives believers an unshakable foundation for life. However, people of both Isaiah's time and Jesus' time tended to use religious words empty of true spiritual commitment (see Isa. 29:13; Mark 7:6-7). Too often people tend to give lip service to the Lord while trusting other things or people to make life work.

123

Pray to the Lord, telling Him that you want to trust Him with your life.
What areas do you need to trust to Him today?

DAY 5 Isaiah 31–35

Isaiah 31 celebrates God as the only true help in life, and chapters 32–33 describe the Lord's deliverance and the establishment of His righteous kingdom. He will bring judgment on the nations (see Isa. 34) and will bring His people to a place of joy (see Isa. 35). Carefully read Isaiah 35 and note the blessings of being in God's kingdom. These realities will be fully experienced when Christ returns and His eternal kingdom is established. Yet as the people of God, we already benefit from these blessings.

Identify and thank God for some blessings of His kingdom that are evident in Isaiah 35.

DAY 6 Isaiah 36–37; 2 Kings 18:9–19:37; 2 Chronicles 32:1-23; Psalm 76

In 2 Kings 18:9-12 the fall of the northern kingdom of Israel is reviewed, in contrast to the reign of Hezekiah in Judah. Generally speaking, among the rulers who had gone before him, Hezekiah was second only to King David as a monarch of Judah. Yet he had challenges, specifically two great crises. We read about the first today: the threat of Assyrian invasion under Sennacherib. Assyria was one of the greatest world powers in the Ancient Near East. It destroyed the northern kingdom of Israel just seven years prior, and in our passages today it threatened Judah.

As you read, contrast the attitudes and worldview of Hezekiah and the Assyrian leadership. When the king over God's people sought God's face and worked closely with God's prophet, the pagan king, without knowing it, was setting himself against God. From a human perspective the odds were overwhelming in favor of the Assyrians, but the Assyrian threat was no threat to God. He would deal with them according to His will.

Is there a situation that seems overwhelming to you at present? Seek God.
Call on Him for help.

SMALL-GROUP DISCUSSION QUESTIONS

1. Read Isaiah 24. How did Isaiah describe the condition of the earth in the last days? What will cause this condition? Describe the connection between human sin and the earth's curse.

2. What thoughts and feelings came to your mind as you read the descriptions of judgment and destruction? What questions did this chapter provoke? Did anything in Isaiah 24 surprise you?

3. In what ways would the truths of this chapter provide hope and encouragement to the people of Israel? How about you?

4. Isaiah 24 describes the future reality of those apart from Christ. Who in your life doesn't know Christ? How can you begin to share the gospel with them?

5. Read Isaiah 25. What were the reasons the people were thankful and sang praise to God in verses 1-5? What are the wonders planned by God?

6. What picture is used to describe God's deliverance of His people in the kingdom? Who is included at this event? What will God do there?

7. List the attributes of God that are evident in Isaiah 25.

8. How does Isaiah 25 give you hope? How does it affect your present choices and attitudes?

9. What is the source of peace in our lives?

10. Isaiah 26:8 says the people's desire is for God's "name and renown." Can you make the same claim about God? What do you desire more than God and His glory?

11. In what ways do you take credit for what God alone deserves the credit?

12. What does Isaiah 26 teach us about people's need for Christ?

13. Examine Hezekiah's prayer in 2 Kings 19:15-19. Was his concern for himself or for God's glory? How would your prayers be different if you always sought the glory of God's name?

WEEK 30

Week 30 will walk us through the end of Hezekiah's reign as we continue act 2, scene 7. We will especially concentrate on the latter half of the majestic prophet Isaiah, with a couple of psalms accenting the themes of Isaiah. Day 1 will wrap up the first half of Isaiah, which, as we have seen, focuses a great deal on judgment.

As we transition to chapters 40 and following, the prophet's words sound a different note, and these are some of the most beautiful and powerful chapters in all Scripture. Here we find words of comfort, hope, salvation, and a promised future. We will also read about God's Servant, a theme that refers variously to God's people as a whole, an earthly ruler, or the coming Messiah.

We will still have words of warning and judgment in this section, and the idiocy of idolatry especially comes under blistering attack. But the overwhelming message delivers promises of God's salvation. Enjoy and meditate deeply on these chapters.

DAY 1 Isaiah 38–39; 2 Kings 20; 2 Chronicles 32:24-33

When Hezekiah was about 40 years of age, he experienced a life-threatening illness, the second major crisis in his life. As we read in these parallel passages, Hezekiah called to the Lord, who granted him another 15 years of life. Then because of his pride Hezekiah foolishly showed off the riches of his kingdom to foreign ambassadors, which eventually had devastating results.

When you read parallel passages like the ones before us today, look for the unique emphasis of each writer. For instance, 2 Chronicles, the account written last, attributes Hezekiah's folly to his pride, pointing out that he did not spiritually benefit as he should have from his miraculous healing. Pride causes us to do foolish things.

Examine your heart. Is there pride there for which you need to repent?

How are you taking or embracing credit for the blessings of God?

DAY 2 Isaiah 40–42; Psalm 46

Today we come to a turning point in Isaiah. The messages of chapters 40–55 are among the most beautiful and powerful in all Scripture. Here God both comforted and confronted His people. In Isaiah 40:18 the prophet asked, "Who will you compare God with?" Then in

40:25 God posed a similar question: "Who will you compare Me to, or who is My equal?" The repetition magnifies the uniqueness of the one true God, a key theme of Isaiah 40. The idols of the nations could not compare to Him (see Isa. 41). Only God could foretell the future deliverance of His people from their punishment, exile from the promised land. God's Servant would bring righteousness to the earth (see Isa. 42).

As you read these chapters, watch for the themes of comfort, God's character and abilities, deliverance, and encouragement to turn away from idols. Also notice that Isaiah 40:3-5 was fulfilled in the ministry of John the Baptist hundreds of years later (see Matt. 3:1-3; Luke 3:1-6). In these and the following chapters of Isaiah, we see glimpses into the ministry of God's ultimate Servant, Jesus.

Praise God today that no one can compare to Him. Slowly read Isaiah 40 again, voicing your praise to God.

DAY 3 Isaiah 43–45; Psalm 80

Isaiah now looks to the future restoration of Israel. Key themes in this section are God as the Savior of His people, the return of God's people from exile, the uniqueness of the one true God and the stupidity of idol worship, and God's anointed deliverer. Cyrus, mentioned in Isaiah 44:28; 45:1, released the Jewish people from exile in Babylon in 538 B.C., almost two centuries after Isaiah's time. Cyrus is the only foreign king to be called anointed, the designation normally referring to King David or the Messiah.

Read Isaiah 45:18-25 very carefully. Do the words of 45:23 sound familiar? Compare them with Philippians 2:5-11. These words, with which God described the submission of the nations to Himself, the early church used to describe the submission of all things to Jesus. God is the only true Savior, and salvation is found in submitting to Him.

Pray today for a person you know who is lost, exiled—distant from God in their sin. Pray that they will come to know God's salvation, to experience the outpouring of His Spirit and His blessings.

DAY 4 Isaiah 46–49; Psalm 135

There are three main messages in this section of Isaiah. Notice how God-centered they are.

1. The prophet continued the idea that no one can compare to God, and those who worship idols are foolish.

2. Only God could tell the future, and the prophet looked into the future to see the fall of the great nation of Babylon. Babylon thought it was untouchable, but God brought its pride crashing down.

3. Corresponding to Babylon's fall, God's people would be delivered from exile. Salvation would come. The Servant seemed to be a representative of the people of Israel, who ministered on their behalf. He was used by God to proclaim that God was Israel's Savior and Redeemer.

> *In Isaiah's day people needed to be saved from their sin and the consequences of their sin. God's ultimate Servant, Jesus, brought about salvation, liberating us from our sin and the consequences of our sins. Praise Him for His salvation.*

DAY 5 Isaiah 50–53

Notice several things about the powerful chapters we read today. God was not willing to let His covenant people fade into oblivion. In spite of their sinfulness and the devastation they had experienced because of their sin, God had a vision for them and was still committed to them. He pointed them back to the history of their relationship with Him (see Isa. 51:1-6).

Also notice the repeated call to wake up. God's people need to respond to God's grace, rising from their spiritual sluggishness.

Finally, the New Testament echoes several of these passages. For instance, Isaiah 52:7 and 53:1 are quoted in Romans 10:15-16, and words from the section on the Suffering Servant, found in Isaiah 52:13–53:12, were explained by Philip, when talking to an Ethiopian eunuch, as speaking of Jesus and the gospel (see Acts 8:32-33). Isn't it amazing that God, hundreds of years before the time of Christ, foretold Christ's sufferings?

> *Isaiah emphasized that God's ability to foretell the future showed Him to be the one true God. Meditate on this aspect of God's person today.*

DAY 6 Isaiah 54–58

Enjoy the section of Isaiah, which expresses God's grace and vision for His people in eloquent ways. Notice echoes of the grand story of God's people (for example, see Isa. 54:9). Also notice the foreshadowing of things to come. Read Isaiah 54:11-12 in light of Revelation 21. Read Isaiah 56:7 in light of Jesus' words when He cleansed the temple (see Matt. 21:13). Focus on the important place of God's Word and instruction in His vision for His people. In chapter 58 identify the nature of true fasting and observance of the Sabbath. This section is rich in theology.

Take time today to think deeply about God's vision for you as His person. How will you let these words affect and shape you today?

SMALL-GROUP DISCUSSION QUESTIONS

1. How does 2 Kings 20 illustrate both Hezekiah's humility and his pride? How does pride lead an otherwise godly person to act foolishly?

2. Read Isaiah 40–42. How did God contrast Himself to the idols of the other nations?

3. What is said about the coming Messiah in Isaiah 40–42? What would He do for His people?

4. Read Isaiah 52:13–53:12. How is Jesus' suffering described in this passage? How is Jesus' glory described? What is the relationship between suffering and glory in Jesus' life? What is the relationship between suffering and glory in a believer's life?

5. What does it mean for the Servant to bear our sicknesses and carry our pains?

6. What benefits did we receive because He was pierced for our transgressions and crushed for our iniquities?

7. What does it mean for us to turn to our own way? Why is this dangerous?

8. How did Christ fulfill the role of the Lamb of God?

9. What language is used in Isaiah 52:13–53:12 to describe Jesus' innocence? Why was this important for our salvation?

10. Was Jesus a victim or a volunteer? What language is used to describe Jesus' compliance? What does that teach us about the nature of grace?

11. How does Isaiah 53:10 affect your understanding of God's will?

12. How did Christ's death remove our guilt? How does knowing Christ removed our guilt enable us to move forward from past disobedience? How does knowing Christ removed our guilt empower future obedience? How does knowing Christ removed our guilt encourage us to repent of sins committed in the future?

13. Read Isaiah 54:9-10. How would God keep His covenant with His people?

WEEK 31

This week we are squarely in act 2, scene 7, "Kings and Prophets: The Southern Kingdom as God's People." We will begin the week by finishing the majestic work of the prophet Isaiah. Watch for passages that anticipate New Testament writings. In the balance of the week, we will read about contrasting kings and two prophets. On the one hand, we read about the evil king Manasseh and his son, Amon, two of the worst kings in Judah's history. On the other hand, we will read about Amon's son, Josiah, who, along with Hezekiah and their ancestor King David, was an outstanding king. Josiah brought about extensive reforms and turned the heart of the nation back to the Lord. Watch for the key to Josiah's spiritual sensitivity.

Finally, we will read two of the Minor Prophets, Nahum and Zephaniah. The former prophesied about the powerful nation of Assyria and proclaimed God's sovereignty over the nations. The latter, probably written prior to Josiah's reforms, offered a powerful message of God's judgment. As you read these prophets, you will see striking parallels to our world situation today. Arrogance, sin, and the need for salvation among the nations are never out of date.

DAY 1 Isaiah 59–63

Isaiah 59 begins with the topic of sin, which builds barriers between God and His people. In Romans 3:15-17 Paul quoted Isaiah 59:7-8 to describe our sinfulness as human beings. Thankfully, as seen in Isaiah 59:15b-21, God is a God of salvation.

Isaiah 60:1–63:6 points to the future glory of Jerusalem, which sits on Mount Zion. Although the words were given to comfort people of Isaiah's time, this section hints that Isaiah prophesied about God's people in the future. The complete eradication of violence and God's serving as Jerusalem's light, without need of the sun, anticipate Revelation 21:3-4, 22-27.

In Luke 4:18-19 Jesus used the words of Isaiah 61:1-2 to characterize His ministry, and Isaiah predicted a time when all of God's people would be called priests (see 1 Pet. 2:9). In short, these chapters speak of God's faithful love being poured out on His people.

How does God pour out His love on you?

Thank Him for His faithful love.

DAY 2 Isaiah 64–66

These final chapters of Isaiah present a striking contrast between judgment on the rebellious and the great blessings to be poured out on the righteous. Notice that judgment comes on those who violate God's law at numerous points, while the righteous tremble at God's Word. God's great desire is to bless His people by blessing Jerusalem.

Again we see in these chapters a strong eschatological bent, relating to the age to come, when Christ will rule over the new heavens and earth (see Isa. 65:17; 66:22; Rev. 21:1).

Think about the great blessings God desires for His people, as described in these chapters. Thank God that He desires your good. Thank Him for the good things He has given you. Thank Him for the good He has planned for His people in the creation of the new heavens and earth at the end of the age.

DAY 3 2 Kings 21; 2 Chronicles 33

The reign of King Manasseh and his son, Amon, formed a dark chapter in the history of Judah. The account in Chronicles differs from that in 2 Kings in that the former includes Manasseh's repentance, a point 2 Kings does not include. Maybe the writer of 2 Chronicles had a historical source or sources to which the author of 2 Kings did not have access, or the writer of 2 Kings may have wanted to emphasize the pervasive evil of Manasseh's reign. In any case the evil of these two kings had serious consequences, and they formed a great contrast with Amon's son, Josiah.

What consequences of evil regimes do you see in the world today? Pray against that evil.

DAY 4 Nahum 1–3

Nahum presents wonderfully crafted prophetic poetry that conveys a powerful message about the fall of the Assyrian Empire and its main city, Nineveh. At the time Nahum wrote, Assyria, a cruel and brutal nation, was at the height of its power, and Judah was its vassal. In the words against Assyria, Nahum proclaimed God as sovereign over the nations and the Savior of His covenant people.

As you read, watch for parallelism and powerful figurative language (ask, "What truth does this image communicate?"). Nahum begins with God as warrior (see 1:2-8), followed by a proclamation of Nineveh's ruin and Judah's salvation (see 1:9–2:2). The visions and taunts that follow in Nahum 2:3–3:7 tell of Nineveh's fall.

Think about oppressive governments in the world today. Praise God that in His timing He will bring those governments to justice. Celebrate God's victory over evil in the world through the cross and the resurrection of Christ.

DAY 5 Zephaniah 1–3

Remember that the key parts of the prophets' message were a call to covenant faithfulness and the need for repentance, impending judgment if there was no repentance, and the hope of renewal or a remnant. The Book of Zephaniah has all of these elements. Written in the time of King Josiah, perhaps prior to the good king's extensive reforms, Zephaniah used powerful language in anticipating the Day of the Lord, a time of devastating judgment, both on Judah and the surrounding nations.

Zephaniah was also fond of hyperbole, strategic exaggeration. Notice, for instance, that in 1:2-3 he alluded to the flood story of Genesis 6 to say that everything on earth would be wiped out. Yet there was hope of renewal (see Zeph. 3:9-20).

Judgment is not a popular topic today. Meditate on the importance of judgment in a biblical view of the world. How do you think God's judgment relates to His love and justice and the renewal He desires to bring in the lives of people?

DAY 6 2 Kings 22–23; 2 Chronicles 34–35

Good King Josiah ruled from 640 to 609 B.C. He started his reign at 8 years of age, became serious about following the God of Israel at age 16, and initiated religious reforms at 20 years of age. When Josiah was 26, the law of God was found in the temple, and 2 Kings especially emphasizes this event as the impetus for radical reforms throughout the land. Notice in 2 Kings the extent to which pagan religions had permeated the culture and the extent to which Josiah went to remove their presence, even desecrating those religious places by placing human bones on the pagan altars.

Josiah was characterized by a Deuteronomy 6:5 commitment to God, for he loved the Lord his God with all his mind, heart, and strength (see 2 Kings 23:25). He also reinstituted the Passover observance and proper worship in the temple.

Josiah's example raises questions for us: How serious are we about eradicating the idols in our lives that detract from worship of the one true God? Are we humble, and are our hearts tender when we hear the Word of the Lord that we have violated?

SMALL-GROUP DISCUSSION QUESTIONS

1. How do Isaiah 60–63 show God's faithfulness to His people? How would these words encourage the people of Israel at this time? How do they encourage believers today?

2. Read 2 Kings 21 and characterize the reigns of Manasseh and Amon. Verse 16 says Manasseh filled Jerusalem with innocent blood. How is innocent blood being shed by rulers today? How do Christians need to respond?

3. Read Nahum 1:1-8. What descriptions of God evoke fear? What other qualities of God are identified?

4. Do you think God's patience ever runs out for those who continue in rebellion against Him? Explain your position.

5. When a person truly comes to Jesus Christ as Savior and Lord, will they habitually and consistently continue to rebel against God?

6. Read Zephaniah 1. What would happen on the Day of the Lord? What demanded punishment in the eyes of the Lord?

7. Read Zephaniah 3:14-20. What works of restoration and deliverance were foretold? Share ways God has brought restoration and deliverance in your life.

8. In what ways is your fear of circumstances or people different from your fear of God? What encouragement do you find in this passage for dealing with fear? How can a believer develop a healthy fear of God instead of others?

9. How does God's judgment of the wicked contrast with His treatment of His people?

10. Describe Josiah's reforms in 2 Kings 22–23. What did he do to lift up and follow the Word of God? What idols does your church need to tear down? How does your church need to lift up the Word of God?

WEEK 32

Continuing our journey through act 2, scene 7, we come to the time just prior to the Babylonian exile, when many of God's people, as punishment from God, were deported to Babylon, a nation hundreds of miles from the land of Judah. This week we will meet the prophets Habakkuk and Joel. Habakkuk carried on a dialogue with God. Joel had a vision of locusts and, among other things, prophesied about the pouring out of God's Spirit. Next we will meet Jeremiah, known as the weeping prophet because of his many laments to the Lord over the destruction of Jerusalem. A priest from the town of Anathoth, Jeremiah started his ministry in 627 B.C. during the reign of King Josiah. Yet the vast majority of his prophecies date to a 22-year period after Josiah's death, when Judah was caught up in volatile world politics between Egypt and Babylon.

As you read this week, notice that the main themes of prophetic literature are all here: a call for repentance and faithfulness to the covenant, certain judgment, and restoration. But for Judah it was almost too late to turn back the coming destruction.

DAY 1 Habakkuk 1–3

Habakkuk was a prophet from about 630 to 605 B.C., beginning his ministry just prior to the beginning of Josiah's reforms. In Habakkuk the prophet carried on a dialogue with God. In chapter 1 he wondered why God allowed His people to live so violently and contrary to God's ways. God answered that He was going to bring the Babylonians to judge them. This puzzled Habakkuk. Why would God use an even more corrupt nation to punish His people? In Habakkuk 2:2-5 God answered by pointing to His justice in punishing all sinful people. Notice the last line of Habakkuk 2:4, a very important verse in the New Testament (see Rom. 1:17; Gal. 3:11; Heb. 10:38). A series of woes on sinners follows. The book ends with a beautiful plea for mercy, a reflection on God's deliverance of His people from Egypt, and a psalm of praise to God regardless of difficult circumstances.

> *Meditate deeply on Habakkuk 3:17-19. What are difficult circumstances you face today? Praise God in spite of those circumstances.*

DAY 2 Joel 1–3

Since the prophet offers us no historical markers, suggestions on the date of Joel vary widely. However, Joel's treatment of the Day of the Lord, understood as both a day of punishment and salvation, is similar to that of Isaiah and Jeremiah. For this reason we have placed the prophet here in our chronological reading of the Old Testament.

Agriculture is central to the message of Joel; a key theme of the book concerns the plague of locusts first mentioned in chapter 1. Locusts were one of the curses promised if God's people abandoned the covenant (see Deut. 28:22,38-42). This is because locusts could devastate the food supply of a nation and lead to widespread starvation. Joel 2:1-11 describes locusts as an invading army (Joel's vision is later taken up by John in Rev. 9:3-12). Each of Joel's visions of the locusts is followed by a call to repentance (see Joel 1:13-20; 2:12-17).

The balance of the book promises God's future blessings on His people, including the pouring out of the Spirit (see Joel 2:28-32), which Peter said was fulfilled on the day of Pentecost (see Acts 2:17-21). So aspects of the blessings would be fulfilled in a time long after the prophet wrote. Notice again the importance of God's presence among His people.

If you are a follower of Christ, thank God that His pouring out of His Spirit on you means that He is present with you at all times. If you have yet to commit your life to Christ, seek to understand the good news that God wants to be present in your life.

DAY 3 Jeremiah 1–4

In his ministry Jeremiah stood alone against almost all leaders of the land. As you read the first chapters of this intriguing book, watch for several things. The key problem is the nation's abandonment of the Lord. Notice the figurative language that describes this idea. Watch for allusions to God's covenant with His people, along with the blessing of the nations promised to Abraham and the curses on those who abandoned the covenant. Finally, Jeremiah ministered in a very sad time and is called the weeping prophet for good reason. Jeremiah 4 records the prophet's lament, an anguished song that suggests the destruction of Judah was like a reversal of God's good creation (see 4:23).

What things in your life draw you away from the Lord like a faithless lover?

TIMELINE
Old Testament Timeline, Part 2: write *Jeremiah* on line 1 in act 2, scene 7.

DAY 4 Jeremiah 5–8

As you read this passage, sort out the following.

1. How Jeremiah's role is described
2. The pervasiveness of the problem with Jerusalem's people: all of the people and all of their leaders were corrupt, failing to love God and live by His covenant.
3. Their misplaced trust in deceitful words and empty religious practices

4. The consequence of their sin: God was bringing an awesome nation from the north (Babylon) that would destroy them.
5. The inevitability of their punishment

When Jesus cleansed the temple in Jerusalem, He alluded to Jeremiah 7:11: "Has this house ... become a den of robbers?" Jesus was saying the religious leaders of His day were much like those of Jeremiah's day.

> **Do you know someone who is far from God and stubbornly unrepentant? Pray for that person today.**

DAY 5 Jeremiah 9–12

The most dominant theme in the reading today is mourning or lament, in which the prophet honestly poured out his sadness to God. Jeremiah mourned because of the destruction of lives and land, the triumph of the wicked, and betrayal by people in his own town. The weeping prophet deeply grieved over the destruction of his people.

In reading lament, we need to enter that grief, recognizing the devastation that sin causes in peoples' lives. We should be deeply sad as we think of people who suffer the consequences of their sin or the sin of others. God calls His people to boast in Him alone (see Jer. 9:23-24) and to turn back to the covenant (11:1-5). Renewal can come from mourning.

> **Allow yourself to grieve over the devastation of sin as you pray today. Boast in the Lord and His covenant relationship with His people. Allow lament to lead you back to God.**

DAY 6 Jeremiah 13–16

As you read, notice that God's resolve to punish His people for their idolatry was resolute, unwavering. There is barely a word of hope here (except in Jer. 16:14-15 about the eventual return from exile 70 years later). Also notice two things about Jeremiah's ministry.

1. The prophets at times acted out a message from God, as Jeremiah did with the linen underwear in 13:1-11. He traveled hundreds of miles to do a simple act, foretelling the exile and illustrating how worthless God's people had become.
2. Jeremiah's words are wonderfully, tragically personal. He was so honest with God that he almost went too far, calling God unreliable (see 15:18), and God rebuked him. Jeremiah's ministry was very, very hard. He had to stand fast in the ministry God had given him, and this pitted him against everyone in his world. Faithfulness does not always lead to happiness. Yet there is joy in the Lord and His Word (see 15:16).

What difficult thing has God given you to do? How are you responding to the situation? Is faithfulness to God more important to you than comfort?

SMALL-GROUP DISCUSSION QUESTIONS

1. In Habakkuk 1 what question did the prophet pose to God? How did God respond in chapter 2? What situations in the world today await God's justice? In what ways do you sometimes question God's justice about these situations? In what ways could God be at work to bring justice without your realizing it? Do you trust God even when things don't appear to be just? Why or why not?

2. Read Joel 1:13-14. Why was the nation told to begin a fast and hold a sacred assembly?

3. Read Joel 2:1-17. How is the Day of the Lord described?

4. How is repentance described in Joel 2:12-17?

5. God instructed the people in Joel 2:12, "Turn to Me with all your heart." How does a person return to God with all his or her heart? How does a church return to God with all its heart?

6. Read Joel 2:12-13. Why did God want the people to tear their hearts and not their garments? What does that mean?

7. How did Joel describe God in 2:13? How do you reconcile this description with the previous description of the Day of the Lord?

8. Share ways you have seen God's grace, mercy, patience, and steadfast love in the past when you repented of sin.

9. Read Joel 2:18-32. Why would God restore His people (see v. 27)?

10. God said He would pour out His Spirit on His people (see Joel 2:28). How was this prophecy fulfilled?

11. Jeremiah is called the weeping prophet. What caused him to grieve? Are you grief-stricken over sin in your life? In your church? In your country?

WEEK 33

The final days of the southern kingdom of Judah are upon us this week, and the readings in day 6 will take us into act 2, scene 8, "Exile: God Disciplines His People." The prophecies of Jeremiah are not always in chronological order, the book shifting back and forth between the last kings of the southern kingdom. Notice the successive deportations to Babylon, which culminated in the destruction of Jerusalem and the temple, to be told in the reading in day 1 of next week (week 34).

Jeremiah shared with the other prophets key themes like coming judgment, a call to repentance, and the hope of restoration. Yet because of his time in history and the prophet's personality, his book is unique. Notice his brutal honesty and his courage as he stood, almost alone, against the political currents of Judah. Also notice passages that speak of a coming restoration and anticipate what God would ultimately do in Christ.

DAY 1 Jeremiah 17–20

Watch for the following themes.

1. Curse and blessing in chapter 17 echo an important aspect of the covenant as expressed in the whole of Deuteronomy.
2. The lack of Sabbath observance manifests how lightly the people were taking God's law.
3. The condition of the heart was a key message, with Jeremiah using the image of sin being engraved on the heart in Jeremiah 17:1.

God gave Jeremiah a parable involving pottery (see Jer. 18:1-12) and then had Jeremiah act out a message of judgment, shattering a clay jug (see chap. 19).

Continue to recognize the depth of Jeremiah's struggle with his situation. In this section the priest Pashhur had him beaten (see Jer. 20:2), and the lament in the remainder of chapter 20 is heart-wrenching.

Choose one of the images from these chapters and meditate on it deeply.

DAY 2 Jeremiah 21–24

Today's reading focuses on judgment against the evil leaders of Judah, both kings and priests. Three kings are mentioned: Jehoiakim, who ruled from 609 to 598 B.C.; his son Coniah, who ruled for a very brief time in 597 B.C.; and Zedekiah, the king from 597 to

586 B.C. Each was killed or deported. Jeremiah powerfully prophesied against these kings because of their lack of justice and righteousness.

Jeremiah also prophesied against prophets and priests, who committed adultery and spoke their own words instead of God's, prophesying peace as if they were communicating the Lord's words. He called these bad leaders evil shepherds who scattered and neglected God's sheep (see Jer. 23:1-4). The words bring to mind Jesus' words in Matthew 9:36, in which He described the people of His day as "sheep without a shepherd" (also see Num. 27:17; 1 Kings 22:17). Jesus is the Good Shepherd (see John 10:1-21), the coming King, and the Righteous Branch foretold in Jeremiah 23:5-8.

> **Meditate on Jesus as the Good Shepherd, who gathers God's people and cares for them. How can leaders today emulate Jesus' leadership in caring for God's people?**

DAY 3 Jeremiah 25–28

Notice that these chapters fall into three primary movements.

1. In chapter 25 Jeremiah prophesied judgment on the whole world. When God called Nebuchadnezzar his servant, this didn't suggest that the Babylonian king feared and served Yahweh but rather that God is sovereign over even the most powerful nations.
2. Chapter 26 describes Jeremiah's persecution. Notice that much of this portion of Jeremiah's story parallels the story of Jesus, who also prophesied the coming destruction of the temple. Yet unlike Jesus, Jeremiah was released.
3. In chapters 27–28 Jeremiah put on a yoke, which was normally used when plowing with an animal. Jeremiah used the yoke to act out the need to submit to the king of Babylon. When the false prophet Hananiah broke Jeremiah's yoke, falsely prophesying that the dominion of Babylon would be short-lived, Jeremiah in turn prophesied that the yoke would be of iron (unbreakable) and that Hananiah would die that year.

> **Who are the false prophets of our day, offering sugarcoated words rather than God's Word?**

DAY 4 Jeremiah 29–32

There were three main deportations of the Israelites from the land of Judah to Babylon, the final one culminating in the destruction of the city and the temple in 586 B.C. Jeremiah, still in Judah, sent a letter to those who had already been exiled, telling them to build homes, raise families, and seek the welfare of the city to which they had been sent by God; the exile was not going to be short-lived, as a false prophecy claimed, giving false hope.

Yet notice that today's reading is permeated with hope. God promised a bright future. He would make a new covenant with people (see Jer. 31:31-34) by which people would know God, have God's laws written on their hearts and minds, and be decisively forgiven for every sin they would ever commit. This prophecy foretells the gospel, which Jesus would establish through His death (see Luke 22:20; Heb. 8:7-13).

Praise God for hope, a hope that has the gospel as its foundation.
Allow the gospel to speak hope into your life today.

DAY 5 Jeremiah 33–37

Today's reading expresses the main messages of the prophets. Jeremiah proclaimed that the people had not followed God's words of covenant (see Jer. 34:8-16 about the freeing of Hebrew slaves and the good example of the Rechabites in Jer. 35). The people had not listened to the warnings given by the Lord through His prophet; therefore, judgment was coming. Yet God had a plan for restoration, which in part had to do with the Righteous Branch, a King who would come from the line of King David (see Jer. 33:1-22). King Jesus would fulfill that prophecy.

Notice the continued persecution of Jeremiah. King Jehoiachin defiantly burned the scroll Jeremiah dictated to Baruch, and while Zedekiah was king, Jeremiah was put in prison.

Meditate on Jeremiah's faithfulness and perseverance in the face of persecution.

 # SCENE 8: EXILE: GOD DISCIPLINES HIS PEOPLE

DAY 6 Jeremiah 38–40; Psalms 74; 79

As we move to act 2, scene 8, we come to a key, infamous moment in the history of God's people: the fall and destruction of Jerusalem. These chapters portray the continued persecution of the prophet; his final meeting with King Zedekiah; and his ultimate vindication and release by the Babylonian king, Nebuchadnezzar. Tragically, Jeremiah's words came true.

Psalms 74 and 79 lament the state of God's people. Their land having been invaded and destroyed, they cried out to God for help. This is a good point in the story to think about the consequences of sin. Even covenant people can suffer as a result of their sin against God.

We need to take sin very seriously and keep our hearts soft before the Lord.
What is the state of your heart today?

SMALL-GROUP DISCUSSION QUESTIONS

1. What message did God illustrate through the pottery in Jeremiah 18–19?

2. Read Jeremiah 23. What was God's judgment on the false prophets and priests? Who is the Righteous Branch in verse 5? How would His reign be different from these evil shepherds of God's people? Who are false prophets today? How does Jesus show Himself as the Good Shepherd to you?

3. Read Jeremiah 31:31-40. How would the new covenant be different from the old? How would God put His law in His children? How do believers seek the power of the Holy Spirit?

4. What role does the old covenant play in our life as Christians? Are the Ten Commandments important to us?

5. Read Jeremiah 33:14-16. What parts of this prophecy have been fulfilled? What parts have not?

6. Read the account of the burning of Jeremiah's scroll and Jeremiah's rewriting it in 36:14-32. What does this incident tell you about God's preservation of His written Word?

7. Identify ways Jeremiah was persecuted in this week's readings. In what ways do you suffer for your stand as a Christ follower? How is it possible to have joy in the midst of suffering?

8. What happened in Jeremiah 39? Do you think God had given fair warning? Why do you think the nation never repented in spite of God's patience and warnings?

WEEK 34

We will begin this week with additional accounts of the fall of Jerusalem. These accounts make it clear that Jerusalem's destruction came about because the people of Judah had abandoned the law of the Lord and their covenant commitments. Even after their defeat, destruction, and deportation, many of the leaders continued to follow the counsel of their own wicked hearts rather than trusting the word of the Lord through Jeremiah.

Much of the rest of the week will concern God's judgments on the nations of the Ancient Near East. These judgments will culminate in an extensive word of prophecy against Babylon, the great nation that dominated this part of the world in Jeremiah's day. Notice important key themes as you read. God is the true God, in contrast to the idols of the nations. As the Creator of all people and nations, He is sovereign over the nations, having the ability and righteous perspective to bring them to judgment for their wickedness.

DAY 1 2 Kings 24–25; 2 Chronicles 36:1-21; Jeremiah 52

Second Kings ends with a helpful overview of the reigns of Judah's last few kings, summing up this critical moment in the nation's history with "Judah went into exile from its land" (25:21). We find the fall of Jerusalem repeated at the end of Jeremiah, in chapter 52, to underscore that Jeremiah was a real prophet, and his prophecies came true.

Second Chronicles offers a poignant interpretation of what happened when Jerusalem fell in 586 B.C.: "The land enjoyed its Sabbath rest all the days of the desolation until 70 years were fulfilled" (36:21). In the law God had commanded that His people allow the land to rest from farming one year out of every seven (see Lev. 25:1-4). He also said if this law was ignored, the land would be given rest by the Lord Himself, who would remove His people to the land of their enemies (see Lev. 26:34-35,43). This is what happened with the exile. God's Word is not to be trifled with! The neglect of the Sabbath laws was one manifestation of the neglect of God's law in general.

> *The exile presents us with a picture of the consequences of sin. Allow that picture to sink into your heart today.*

DAY 2 Jeremiah 41–44

In the chaos following the Babylonians' destruction of Judah, several groups of leaders emerged. Nebuchadnezzar had appointed Gedaliah to govern the land of Judah under the rule of the Babylonians. But Ishmael, who was of the royal family of the kings of Judah, assassinated Gedaliah and, with his followers, captured many of the remnant of God's people. Johanan and the commanders of the army, who had escaped the Babylonians, rescued these people. Johanan and company planned to flee to Egypt, reasoning that Nebuchadnezzar would retaliate against the remaining Judeans for the assassination of Gedaliah.

This remnant and their leaders asked Jeremiah what they should do, promising to follow the Lord's words. Jeremiah told them to settle in the land and not to fear the king of Babylon. Having already made up their minds, they arrogantly rejected the prophet's words, fleeing to Egypt and taking Jeremiah with them. In Egypt Jeremiah prophesied about the destruction of that nation as well by the king of Babylon.

At times people say they are committed to the Lord's words, only to reject those words when circumstances dictate. How deep is your commitment to God's Word? To what extent do your circumstances govern your spiritual walk?

DAY 3 Obadiah; Psalms 82–83

Blink and you might miss the little book of Obadiah, situated between Amos and Jonah among the prophets. Yet this small book, written about 586 B.C., shortly after the Babylonians had destroyed the land of Judah, carries a powerful punch. Obadiah proclaimed judgment against the Edomites, the descendants of Esau, the brother of Jacob. Edom, instead of supporting their relatives, had gloated over Judah's demise and had even taken advantage of it. God proclaimed that Edom, therefore, would be judged and Judah restored. When God is shown to be King, the evil will face consequences for their sin, and the righteous will be saved.

Psalms 82–83 plead with God to bring about justice on earth, to manifest His rule on earth by rising up and judging those who are evil.

Pray, asking God to bring justice to places in the world where evil and oppression reign.

DAY 4 Jeremiah 45–48

In Jeremiah 45 we have an unusual glimpse into the ministry of the prophet: a word from the Lord to Jeremiah's secretary, Baruch. In the ancient world professional scribes were employed to do the tedious work of writing clearly on a scroll. Like Jeremiah, Baruch was devastated by the destruction of the nation. God's Word to Baruch was essentially "Things are going to get worse." Yet God would reward Baruch's faithfulness by sparing his life.

Some people are born into very hard times, and the key for those people is to be faithful to the Lord in the midst of great challenges.

Notice that Jeremiah 46–48 begins a series of prophecies against the nations surrounding Judah. Here we have successive prophecies against Egypt, Philistia, and Moab. Find these nations on a map at the back of your Bible. The central message is that God works behind the scenes of world events.

In our world today there is turmoil among the nations. What is your understanding of ways God might be working to bring about His glory among the nations?

What role does the gospel play in God's plans for the nations?

DAY 5 Jeremiah 49–50

The judgments against the nations surrounding Judah continue in our reading today, culminating in an extensive prophecy against Babylon. Notice the reasons for their downfall. It is also interesting to note the nations the Lord would restore and those that would be utterly devastated, never to rise again. Watch for the use of figurative language, graphic word pictures that add emotional punch to the words of woe.

At the back of your Bible you can probably find Ammon, Edom, and Damascus on a map of the Old Testament era. The people of Kedar and Hazor were nomads who lived in the desert. Elam was a fierce nation located to the east of Babylon. Their warriors were famous for their skill in archery.

Meditate again today on God's power over the nations. When His time of judgment arrives, no evil nation will be able to stand against Him. What nations today are aligned against God?

DAY 6 Jeremiah 51; Psalm 137

Jeremiah 51 continues Jeremiah's extensive prophecies against the nation of Babylon. The length of this discourse is in proportion to the importance of Babylon on the world stage and the massive destruction God would bring on the Babylonians at the hands of the Persians. God, the true Creator of the whole earth (see Jer. 51:15-16), would judge Babylon for its wickedness.

Jeremiah wrote these words on a scroll and commanded Seraiah, who was about to travel to Babylon in the last of the deportations, to read these words in Babylon, tie a rock to the scroll, and then throw the scroll into the Euphrates River. This action symbolized that Babylon would sink and never rise again (see Jer. 51:59-64).

Think today about God as judge. What national sins today will merit His judgment?

SMALL-GROUP DISCUSSION QUESTIONS

1. Read 2 Kings 24–25. In what ways did Jeremiah's prophecies come true? How accurately are you representing God and His ways to the world around you? What opportunities do you have to tell about His judgment? To tell about His salvation in Jesus?

2. What did Jeremiah instruct the remnant in Babylon to do? What did it do instead? Why do you think the people were still being disobedient? How do people follow this pattern today?

3. What nation is judged in the Book of Obadiah? What did it do to earn God's judgment? What does this say about God's jealousy for His people? In what ways does that hold true today?

4. What nations are warned of judgment in Jeremiah 46–50? Why would they be judged? What are modern-day nations doing that will bring God's judgment?

5. In what ways do people today shake their fists at God, refusing to repent? Do you think they will do this even in the end times? Why?

WEEK 35

Continuing with act 2, scene 8, we will begin the week with Lamentations, which is set just after the destruction of Jerusalem and was written by Jeremiah, perhaps with the help of his secretary, Baruch. Each of the first four chapters of the book is divided according to the 22 letters of the Hebrew alphabet, each verse beginning with a succeeding letter. Chapters 1, 2, 4, and 5 each has 22 verses; chapter 3, the climactic chapter describing Jerusalem's destroyers and God's compassion, has three times as many verses.

Lament is a form of poetry often consisting of prayers and hard conversations with God in which gut-wrenching honesty is the norm. Yet lament is intended to lead the mourner back to God, giving clarity to the situation and pointing to hope in God's faithful love.

The week will continue with the first chapters of Ezekiel, a 30-year-old priest taken into exile by the Babylonians in one of the first waves of deportation from Jerusalem. Ezekiel, a contemporary of Jeremiah and Daniel, ministered from 593 to 571 B.C. Unlike most of the prophets, his book is not poetic. However, it is filled with symbolic imagery and dramatic enactments of God's Word.

DAY 1 Lamentations 1:1–3:36

As you read today, watch for figures of speech, such as personification. For example, Jerusalem is spoken of as a person (see Lam. 1). The writer's words express personal anguish; he couldn't stop crying, and his emotions were churning (see 1:12,16,20). Nevertheless, he acknowledged the rightness of God's judgment.

Track all of God's actions recorded in chapter 2 and notice the word pictures in verses 1-9.

The writer became very personal in chapter 3, using metaphors to describe God as a wild bear, a lion, and an archer. A metaphor is a word picture comparing two things by saying one thing is the other: "He is a bear waiting in ambush" (v. 10). (In contrast, a simile compares two things by using the word *like* or *as*.)

The biggest word in this first half of the book is *yet* in Lamentations 3:21, designating a turning to hope. The writer focused on God's character as the source of hope.

What are you lamenting at this point in your life? Lament is ultimately meant to lead us back to God. Turn to God in hope today.

DAY 2 Lamentations 3:37–5:22

Lamentations continues with an exhortation to repent and turn to God (see 3:37-42). That adversity comes from God's mouth (see v. 38) should be read in the context of verse 39: the author was speaking about punishment for sins.

Chapter 4 offers a heart-wrenching description of Jerusalem's devastation. Notice that the verses here are shorter and more terse than those in chapters 1–2. The book ends with somewhat of a whimper, a plea to God for help. Hope seemed hard for the writer to grasp. Most of us have times of profound discouragement in life, tempting us to turn inward and away from the Lord during those times. Yet lament gives us a voice of prayer during those times, and God invites such prayers.

Call to God this day, whatever your situation in life.

DAY 3 Ezekiel 1–4

The first three chapters of Ezekiel recount the prophet's call from God. Priests started their ministry in the temple at age 30, but Ezekiel was hundreds of miles from Jerusalem, exiled in the land of Babylon. Chapter 1 presents a dramatic vision of God, surrounded by cherubim, angelic beings, riding on the clouds. The vision of the four living creatures represents the created order: the lion is the greatest of wild beasts, the ox the greatest of domestic beasts, the eagle greatest of birds, and human beings the pinnacle of God's creation.

God was surrounded by His glory. The rainbow (see Ezek. 1:28) calls to mind the flood, when God displayed His judgment and mercy (see Gen. 9:12-17). Ezekiel was to speak God's Word regardless of the response and was accountable for doing so (see Ezek. 2–3). In chapter 4 the prophet acted out the siege of Jerusalem, dramatizing what it would be like for those in Jerusalem as God's judgment fell.

God has also given His Word to us. We are to speak it to those who are far away from God and need repentance. Will you be faithful in speaking the Word today?

TIMELINE

Old Testament Timeline, Part 2: write *Ezekiel* on line 1 in act 2, scene 8.

DAY 4 Ezekiel 5–8

The focus today is on God's severe judgment on Jerusalem for its practice of idolatry. The day begins with another dramatization, Ezekiel shaving his head and beard. The prophet burned a third of the hair, slashed a third of it with a sword, and scattered a third to the wind. His actions dramatized God's punishment of the Israelites. Yet the prophet was to tuck a few strands of hair into the fold of his robe, showing that God would keep a remnant of the people for Himself.

Ezekiel 8 relates a vision given to Ezekiel about 14 months after the vision of Ezekiel 1. As the elders of Judah gathered in Ezekiel's home in Babylon, a heavenly being took Ezekiel by the hair and flew him to Jerusalem. Then the being took the prophet to four different places in Jerusalem, showing him the horrible abominations being committed there. The vision drove home the reason God was bringing such severe devastation to the land.

> *Severity of judgment is in proportion to the depth of sinfulness. The punishment fits. Think about the fact that we struggle with God's judgment, questioning its "fairness," because we do not understand the seriousness, darkness, and destructiveness of sin.*

DAY 5 Ezekiel 9–12

The first three chapters continue an extended vision in which the Spirit of God had transported Ezekiel to Jerusalem. Watch for the theme of the remnant in these chapters. Chapter 9 presents a vision of slaughter in Jerusalem. The wicked people in Jerusalem had murdered lots of people and worshiped other gods, so they would be destroyed.

We have seen the centrality of God's presence as a key theme in the Old Testament. In Ezekiel 10 God left the temple. The cherubim in this chapter were angelic beings around God's throne. Chapter 11 speaks of judgment on the corrupt leaders of Jerusalem but also promises restoration (read Ezek. 11:19 in light of 2 Cor. 3:3). In chapter 12 the prophet dramatized the exile from Jerusalem in two ways. The dramas served as prophecies of what was about to happen to the people in Jerusalem and the land of Israel.

> *Meditate on Ezekiel 11:19-21. The condition of the heart is central to the prophets' message. What is the condition of your heart today?*

DAY 6 Ezekiel 13–16

Notice several things about our reading today. False prophets, who prophesied from their own imaginations, were condemned in chapter 13. The sin of idolatry is a primary focus in these chapters, and God is deeply concerned about the condition of the heart.

The readings for the week end with two parables, one short and the other rather long. The parable of the vine depicts the uselessness of Jerusalem; it was good only for burning (see

Ezek. 15:1-8). The parable of the adulterous wife presents, perhaps, the most graphic word picture of idolatry and unfaithfulness in all Scripture (see Ezek. 16). Jerusalem, rescued by God and adorned in beauty, had become a lustful, brazenly promiscuous woman. She used God's gifts to attract her adulterous lovers. Unlike a prostitute, she paid others to have sex with her and spread her sexual favors far and wide. God would punish her. Amazingly, the section ends with the hope of a new covenant God would establish.

Faithfulness begins with the condition of the heart. Examine your heart today. Is it soft toward God, or is it soft toward sin and unfaithfulness?

SMALL-GROUP DISCUSSION QUESTIONS

1. How did the writer of Lamentations describe his own struggle? What metaphors and images did he use?

2. List some of the consequences of Jerusalem's sinfulness. Do you feel that Judah's punishment outweighed its offense? Why or why not?

3. In what ways had the people failed to believe God would do what He said He would do? How might our lives better reflect that we believe God will do as He says?

4. How had the people presumed on the Lord? How can we guard ourselves from the sin of presumption?

5. Read Lamentations 3:22-26. How are God's mercies new every morning? How does this affect our lives?

6. What does it mean to wait for the Lord? Why is it important for God to be the object and source of our hope?

7. Why does God willingly restore His people? What does restoration look like? Share ways you have experienced divine restoration.

8. What did the vision in Ezekiel 1 teach you about God?

9. How did Ezekiel's vision in chapters 8–11 reinforce God's judgment of His people? In what ways are believers today lax about the severity of sin?

10. How did the drama in Ezekiel 16 illustrate Judah's unfaithfulness to the covenant? What did God's promise at the end of the chapter indicate about His character?

WEEK 36

We are still in act 2, scene 8, which deals with the exile of Judah in Babylon. Ezekiel the prophet is in Babylon, and two great themes dominate the remainder of the book:

1. God would judge the evil nations that had acted against Israel.
2. God would restore His people.

As you read this week, you will see a rich blend of communication devices used by the prophet. There are illustrations, drama, lament, visions, and direct messages. Here we have wonderfully graphic images like the valley of dry bones in chapter 37. Enjoy these word pictures as you would enjoy a good painting.

Notice nuances. Look for threads, recurring themes. Hear Ezekiel's words as a profound, timeless message about the greatness of God and His vision of restoration for His people.

DAY 1 Ezekiel 17–20

Chapter 17 begins with a parable about covenant breaking, God's judgment, and God's plan for restoring His people. In chapter 18 we find a theological shift from what had been previously taught among God's people. No longer would a child die for the sins of the father. Now everyone would be responsible for his or her own sins. Notice the details of what God considers sinful and the details of God's response. For instance, Ezekiel 18:32 tells us God, though He judges, does not take pleasure in anyone's death.

Chapter 19, two extended word pictures, laments the judgment brought against Jerusalem and Israel. Finally, chapter 20 offers an extensive explanation of why judgment had come. How are we to read these prophecies, with their extensive words of judgment and doom?

Read for the details. Learn more about God. Notice His compassion and plans for restoration. Look for insights into human sinfulness. Examine your own life and attitudes toward God.

DAY 2 Ezekiel 21–24

Notice today the varied images used to communicate that judgment was falling on Jerusalem. God's judgment was like a sharpened, polished, slashing sword (see Ezek. 21). His judgment was like a fire that melts metal, burning away impurities (see chap. 22). Jerusalem had been immoral like her sister Samaria (see chap. 23), so judgment was coming like a boiling pot (see chap. 24). Then Ezekiel himself, on the death of his much-loved wife, became a picture of those who groan in their mourning but are not allowed to mourn normally or openly; rather, they waste away in their grief (see chap. 24:15-27).

God's judgment looms large in the biblical story. Christ has borne our punishment so that we can escape God's wrath. Yet judgment will come on the world at the end.

Others need the gospel we have to share. Are you open in sharing the gospel?

DAY 3 Ezekiel 25–28

Ezekiel 25–32 presents words of judgment against the nations surrounding Judah. Chapter 25 focuses on historic enemies of Judah. These nations had become allies in a stand against Babylon, but they had abandoned Judah at the time of Babylon's siege of Jerusalem.

The remainder of today's reading focuses on Tyre, a small coastal island northwest of Judah. Ezekiel 26–28 present three oracles of woe against Tyre, the first against the city of Tyre, the second lamenting Tyre's destruction, and the third focusing on Tyre's arrogant king. As you can see from chapter 27, Tyre was a thriving business and trade center for that part of the world (think of New York or San Francisco), and God's judgment fell in part because of Tyre's arrogance over its accumulated wealth. In a parallel fashion Revelation 18 borrows heavily from Ezekiel 27 in describing the coming downfall of Rome ("Babylon").

Do we have a false sense of security and arrogance over our wealth?

All nations are answerable to God. How do you understand God's rightful sovereignty over the nations today?

DAY 4 Ezekiel 29–32

The extensive seventh oracle in this series of prophecies against the nations focuses on Egypt. Egypt had played major roles in the Bible's story. It was the powerful nation from which God delivered His people. Egypt had also been a major source of temptation for the Israelites, in terms of both idolatry and politics. Too often the Israelites had chosen to trust Egypt's power rather than the Lord's (see Ezek. 29:6-7).

The prophecies of chapters 29–32 took place over a period of several years, beginning in 587 B.C., at which point the siege against Jerusalem had been going on for about a year. As you read, notice the rich imagery used to describe Egypt and its fall. For instance, the king of Egypt, who arrogantly said he made and owned the Nile River, would be dragged out of that river like a big crocodile and killed.

Notice that this passage calls God the Lord God, emphasizing His ultimate control over the nations. Worship the sovereign Lord today.

DAY 5 Ezekiel 33–36

Notice the rich imagery used in the readings today. Chapter 33 focuses on Ezekiel as Israel's watchman and the continued rebellion of the people. Chapter 34 calls the leaders of Israel self-centered shepherds. Jesus borrowed the imagery here to speak of the judgment (read Matt. 25:32-33 in light of Ezek. 34:17). Jesus also fulfilled the vision of God as the Good Shepherd, who would care for His people (see John 10:7-18).

After a prophecy of judgment against Edom's Mount Seir, the central mountain of the nation that celebrated Israel's downfall (see Ezek. 35), God spoke of the future restoration of Israel's mountains (see chap. 36). For the sake of His holy name, the Lord would restore His people and cleanse them, giving them a new heart and spirit. God would put His Spirit in them and turn their hearts to His ways. This was ultimately fulfilled in the giving of the Holy Spirit, who cleanses us from sin, transforms our hearts, and teaches us God's ways.

Has God's Spirit restored your life from the devastation of sin? If so, rejoice. If not, cry out to God for salvation.

DAY 6 Ezekiel 37–40

The theme of restoration continues today: the restoration of God's people (see Ezek. 37), the restoration of God's rule over His people (see chaps. 38–39), and the restoration of the temple (see chap. 40). Notice the wonderful, unique vision of the dry bones in chapter 37. God brings life from death. Then Ezekiel carved words on two sticks, held the sticks together, and presented them as a picture of God's people being brought back together (remember that the southern kingdom of Judah and the northern kingdom of Israel had been split since 922 B.C.—about 3½ centuries). When Ezekiel spoke of a new king and a new covenant, the words anticipated the coming of Jesus.

Gog and Magog, in chapters 38–39, represented the nations of the world who opposed God. Gog and Magog are echoed in Revelation 20:7-9, in the climactic battle at the end of the age when Satan will suffer his final defeat. So Gog and Magog were an international coalition of nations from all over the world. Yet they were no match for God, who would defend His people.

Finally, chapter 40 deals with the rebuilding of the temple. Don't get lost in the exact measurements, which point to the care God was taking in the building and the grandeur of the new temple. This will lead to a focus on God's renewed presence among His people in our next reading.

Celebrate today that God brings renewal from hardship and devastation.

SMALL-GROUP DISCUSSION QUESTIONS

1. How do you think the judgments you read about this week foretell the judgment coming in the end times? How are believers protected from God's wrath?

2. Read Ezekiel 34:1-10. Who were the shepherds of Israel? What were the specific sins God held against the shepherds of Israel? What were the consequences of the shepherds' sin and failure to care for the people of Israel? What did God mean when He said the people had been scattered and became food for wild animals (see. 34:5)?

3. What does Ezekiel 34:1-10 teach us about the responsibility held by those who lead others spiritually?

4. What aspects of God's character shine through in Ezekiel 34:1-10?

5. In what ways does your life reflect the sins of the people described in Ezekiel 34:1-4?

6. Read Ezekiel 34:11-31. How did God respond to the shepherds' failure in leading the people of Israel? How would His shepherding differ from that of the people's shepherds?

7. Who is the new shepherd God would appoint over His people? How is this new shepherd described? What title would be given to this new shepherd? Do you believe this new shepherd is a reference to Christ? Why or why not?

8. Describe the covenant of peace that would result from the rule of the new shepherd. What are the implications of the Lord's being the Shepherd of your life? How do you see the Lord as the Shepherd of your life?

9. What promises of restoration did God make in Ezekiel 36?

10. What did God mean when He said, "I will remove your heart of stone and give you a heart of flesh" (36:26)? How does He accomplish this in the lives of His people?

11. Read Ezekiel 37:26-27. How has God established a covenant of peace with His people? In what ways is this covenant still to be fulfilled?

WEEK 37

This week we are still in act 2, scene 8. As we complete the Book of Ezekiel in the first two days, we will continue focusing on restoration. The messages here—the building of the temple and the division of the land—are theological in nature. They are true but are not to be taken literally. These images communicated a message of perfect restoration, which would be fulfilled in a new kind of kingdom inaugurated by the Messiah.

The Book of Daniel, which we will begin in day 3, is divided into two main movements. The first six chapters are court stories from the land of Babylon, and stories such as the fiery furnace and Daniel in the lions' den are among the most loved in the Bible. Chapters 7–12 are a series of apocalyptic visions. *Apocalyptic* means *revelation* or *unveiling*. The cosmic curtain is pulled back, revealing God's purpose in the world. Apocalyptic literature, often written in times of persecution, involves visions; symbolic language; and a focus on the real, heavenly perspective behind earthly events. Daniel's visions revealed stages of world history from his day to the time when the Greeks ruled over Palestine, around three centuries after Daniel's time. His visions also pointed beyond these political eras to the eternal kingdom of the Messiah. Because of the symbolic nature of this section of the Bible, this week's reading can be difficult at times. Look for key themes emphasizing God's ultimate control even in the midst of disturbing world events.

DAY 1 Ezekiel 41–44

Today we continue to focus on the perfect temple, which God showed to Ezekiel. God gave Ezekiel the vision so that the Israelites would be "ashamed of their iniquities" (43:10). What God gave Ezekiel was perfect, and it communicated a very special, perfectly organized place of worship, set apart for God's people to approach God. All of the measurements communicated the precision with which God had conceived the way He is to be approached. No haphazard, cavalier approach to God will suffice.

The climax of the section is found in Ezekiel 43, when the glory of the Lord, representing His presence, filled the temple. God's presence among His people is perhaps the key theme of the Bible. Thus, worship stands at the center of our lives as His people.

The priests in Ezekiel 44 anticipated Jesus, the ultimate High Priest (see Heb. 10:19-22) who would do away with the sacrificial system by His one sacrifice. The priests also anticipated Christ's followers, who would be priests to the Lord (see 1 Pet. 2:9).

Think of yourself as a priest today. For whom do you need to intercede?

DAY 2 Ezekiel 45–48

We wrap up Ezekiel by continuing to read about God's restoration of His people. This is a theological message; the measurements of the temple and the law and the division of the land are not to be taken literally. The pictures here speak of God's full restoration of His people, and the words about the Prince anticipate Christ.

Take time to linger over the words about the life-giving river in Ezekiel 47. This speaks of the effects of God's presence and work. Everything in this vision of restoration speaks of God's perfectly reordering reality. Revelation 22:1-5 echoes Ezekiel's vision, speaking of the river of life. The Book of Ezekiel appropriately ends with the city's being renamed "Yahweh Is There" (48:35; also see Heb. 12:22).

Offer praise to God for His plan to restore the heavens and earth and to provide eternal life for His people.

DAY 3 Daniel 1–3

Today's reading presents wonderful stories of faithfulness to God. In Daniel 1 notice the value placed on faithfulness. Daniel and friends were in a foreign land with alien demands made on them, and yet they continued to live by God's laws. Chapter 2 presents the crisis surrounding Nebuchadnezzar's troubling dreams. Watch how the crisis was resolved. Daniel explained that God would raise up a kingdom that would never be destroyed; this would eventually be fulfilled in Christ and the kingdom of heaven. Daniel's ability to interpret the dream also raised his status and the status of his friends. The third story is one of the most loved in the Bible: the fiery furnace. The message is that God delivers those who are resolutely faithful to Him.

How might you remain faithful today though being pressured to abandon God's ways?

TIMELINE

Old Testament Timeline, Part 2: write *Daniel* on line 2 in act 2, scene 8.

DAY 4 Daniel 4–6

Daniel 4–6 continues the series of court stories, which emphasize God's rule over even the most powerful of earthly kings. Watch especially for the emphasis on the need for humility in an earthly ruler and for an emphasis on God's sovereignty. For instance, Daniel 4:17 gives the reason for Nebuchadnezzar's dream.

We get our saying "The writing is on the wall" from the story of Belshazzar in Daniel 5, which functions also to show the transition from the Babylonian Empire to the Persian Empire (see 5:30). The Persians defeated the Babylonians in 539 B.C.

The story of Daniel's being thrown into the lions' den is one of the most loved in the Bible. It depicts God's rescuing a faithful person who stands firm in the face of persecution. Each of these stories presents a crisis.

> Notice that God was the real hero of today's stories, the One who brought about His desired end. How might God use you in the world, among those who do not know the one true God, as you stand firm in your commitment to Him?

DAY 5 Daniel 7–9

The literature in the latter half of Daniel is called apocalyptic, as explained in this week's introduction. Daniel 7–9 presents two visions and an interpretation of Jeremiah's prophecy about the 70 years of exile. The first vision (see Dan. 7:1-28) involves four beasts, which represent four stages of political history. These echo the four empires of Daniel 2. The first three seem to be Babylon, Persia, and the Greeks. Some interpret the fourth to represent Rome, but others understand the kingdom and the little horn to be a world-dominating, evil kingdom at the end of time. These earthly kingdoms are put in perspective in Daniel 7:13-14 by the eternal kingdom of the Messiah. Jesus' use of the title Son of Man for Himself probably comes from this passage.

In chapter 8 Daniel interpreted the vision of the ram and goat as Persia and Greece. Chapter 9 focuses on a new interpretation of Jeremiah's 70 weeks. These passages are difficult to understand because they combine a rich historical background with apocalyptic imagery. Consult a Bible dictionary or a study Bible for more information; free online resources are available at www.mystudybible.com.

> Reread Daniel 7:13-14 and turn these verses into a prayer of praise to the Son of Man, whose kingdom will never be destroyed.

DAY 6 Daniel 10–12

In Daniel 10:1–12:4 an angel gave Daniel a vision of the future. Chapter 10 describes Daniel's encounter with the angel. Chapter 11 depicts the struggle between two political forces, the Seleucids and the Ptolemies, the heirs of Alexander the Great's conquests, over the land of Israel. This happened three centuries after the time of Daniel. The remainder of chapter 11 seems to focus on Antiochus IV, a Greek king who severely oppressed the Jewish people at the beginning of the second century B.C. Daniel 12:1-4 puts these conflicts in eternal perspective.

The Book of Daniel concludes with the question of when these things will take place and what will be the outcome. The words at the end of the book are meant to encourage those caught up in world conflict to endure in trusting God until the end.

What present conflicts in the world disturb you? Thank God that He is Lord over the world and will bring these conflicts to an end one day.

SMALL-GROUP DISCUSSION QUESTIONS

1. What is the significance of the glory of the Lord's filling the temple in Ezekiel 43:5? How do believers and churches give glory to God? How do we keep His worship at the center of our lives?

2. What pictures of total restoration are provided in Ezekiel 45–48? Who is the Prince? How is God shown as the source of life in this new earth?

3. How did Daniel and his companions show faithfulness to God in Daniel 1? Describe situations in which you must take a stand for Christ in spite of social trends and pressures.

4. What does Daniel's prayer in 2:20-23 indicate about God? About Daniel's relationship with God? What is the source of wisdom in our lives? Why do we usually try handling things in our own limited wisdom?

5. How did Daniel give credit to God for the answer to the king's dream? Are you diligent to give credit to God for the things He teaches you and does for you?

6. This story emphasizes that Daniel's God reigns supreme and is sovereign over all earthly kings and kingdoms. What are the implications of this truth for your life?

7. Read Daniel 3:16-18. How did Daniel's friends demonstrate faithfulness to God through their ordeal? How did God give them victory? Who was the fourth person in the fire? How does it strengthen your faith to know that God goes with you through the fire?

8. How did Daniel show complete loyalty to God in chapter 6? How are believers today under pressure to bow to false gods and to compromise their faith?

WEEK 38

As we near the end of our reading through the Old Testament, we finally come to act 2 scene 9, "Return: God Delivers His People Again." This week notice the references back to the exodus and the original vision for God's chosen people, as well as to the failures of the Israelites prior to the exile in Babylon. Yet the tone of the writings this week takes a decided turn to hope for the future. Notice the shift to very positive messages from the prophets Haggai and Zechariah. These prophets, along with Ezra, focused on the theme of renewal of God's people and the rebuilding of the temple. As we have seen in earlier prophets and historical writings, God's judgment of His people in part included His departure from the temple in Jerusalem. Now God returned to live among His people as they learned to live in peace, truth, and righteousness.

We will also begin Esther this week, a story from the period of Persian rule, which deals with heroes God used to deliver the Jews from destruction. You will find the readings this week powerful and encouraging. As you read, watch for key themes we have seen earlier in the Old Testament, but whereas the curses of the covenant were in full play prior to and during the exile, blessing now predominates.

SCENE 9: RETURN: GOD DELIVERS HIS PEOPLE AGAIN

DAY 1 2 Chronicles 36:22-23; Ezra 1–3

In 539 B.C. King Cyrus of Persia defeated the Babylonians, and the Persian king proclaimed an edict in 538 B.C. allowing the Israelites to return home to their ancestral land. In the first chapters of Ezra, the focus is on the restoration of the community of God's people. The extensive account of the people's returning in Ezra 2 points to the importance of ancestry, especially for service as a priest in the temple (see 2:62). In fact, the rebuilding of the temple stands at the center of Ezra and thus at the center of the identity of God's people.

Exile had taught the Israelites that a God-centered life is the only viable life for God's people. What in your life communicates to those around you that you have a God-centered life?

How does God's new temple, the church, stand at the center of your identity?

TIMELINE
Old Testament Timeline, Part 2: write *Ezra* on line 1 in act 2, scene 9.

DAY 2 Ezra 4–6

Most of the events in these three chapters took place from the time King Cyrus of Persia allowed the Jews to return home from exile in 538 B.C. to the time when the temple was completely rebuilt under King Darius in 516 B.C. The one passage in our reading today that is chronologically out of place is Ezra 4:6-23, which speaks of opposition to rebuilding Jerusalem during the reign of the Persian king Artaxerxes, who ruled Persia from 465 to 424 B.C. and was the king during the time of Ezra and Nehemiah (see the beginning of Ezra 7). The reason it was included here was for literary effect, to show the parallels between the opposition to building the temple during the time of Darius and the opposition to rebuilding the city during the time of Artaxerxes. In fact, our reading today focuses on perseverance in the face of opposition to a task given by God.

The prophets Haggai and Zechariah enter the story, giving encouragement for the rebuilding. God also used the Persian government in the rebuilding process. The climax of the section focuses on the dedication of the temple and the celebration of Passover. The Jewish people had not only returned to the land but had also fully returned to following the law of God.

Do you ever face opposition in the tasks God has given you to do?
Resolve today to persevere in the power of God.

DAY 3 Haggai 1–2

Our reading for today is unusually short but rich. The word of the Lord came to Haggai in the second year of the reign of the Persian king Darius (520 B.C.), about 18 years after the exile had ended and the Jews had been allowed to return home. Haggai presented four brief sermons. The people had returned to Jerusalem but had gotten caught up in their own needs and neglected the temple, the Lord's house. In essence his message was "Get to work!" Unlike the responses we have seen to the prophets before and during the exile, the people responded positively to Haggai's message. As you read, watch for this response and the results. God would now bless and live among them.

Again we find the centrality of God's presence among His people as a theme. Haggai also emphasized the need for holiness and the importance of God-directed leadership. It is easy for us to get distracted from building up the Lord's house (today God's people), focusing instead on our own homes and lives.

How can you sacrifice your time and resources to build up fellow brothers
and sisters in Christ?

DAY4 Zechariah 1–7

The prophet Zechariah, a contemporary of Haggai, wrote a rich, encouraging book that has several emphases. Those who had returned from exile would be blessed. God's presence was once again with God's people, and God would bless the work of the leaders in rebuilding Jerusalem and the temple. The nation's true King would return to Jerusalem and would be killed for the sins of the people. The events of Zechariah 1–7, which we read today, and of Zechariah 8, which we will read tomorrow, would happen in the near future.

Zechariah had eight night visions (see 1:7–6:15), filled with symbolic language. You will recognize that John used some of the language in Revelation. Symbolic language is not easy to comprehend, but Zechariah often interpreted the symbols for us. Notice that God was reversing much that was broken during Israel's centuries of disobedience and was renewing the covenant with His people. Chapters 7–8 concern true fasting, which in essence is to live righteously and justly.

> *If God is to bring renewal to our lives, He will lead us to live more carefully by His ways and values. How is renewal taking place in you at present?*

DAY5 Zechariah 8–14

Zechariah 8 presents a beautiful picture of renewal. God would return to Jerusalem and build up the city and the nation as the people learned to live in truth and peace. There would be peace and joy, and covenant blessing would cover the land. Israel would also fulfill its destiny in being a blessing to the nations. Do you see how these words fulfill promises made by God early in the Old Testament story (for example, Gen. 12:1-3)?

Zechariah 9–14 focuses on the future renewal that would take place when the true King came. Notice that 9:9 was fulfilled when Jesus rode into Jerusalem in what we call the triumphal entry (see Matt. 21:1-5). As a Shepherd, God provided salvation (see Zech. 11). Notice the foreshadowing of other events in the life of Jesus, seen in Zechariah 11:12; 12:10; 13:7. Ultimately, the prophet anticipated the very end, when "the Lord my God will come" and "will become King over all the earth" (14:5,9), and all families of the earth will worship Him.

> *How might you and I participate in calling the nations to worship the Lord?*

DAY 6 Esther 1–5

Esther presents us with a beautifully crafted court story of a moment in the Persian Empire during the reign of Ahasuerus (also known as Xerxes, 486–465 B.C.). It focuses on four characters: the Persian king; Esther; Esther's relative, Mordecai; and the evil Haman. Watch for rich ironies in the story. For instance, Esther's rise to the position of queen came because Queen Vashti did not obediently come when called by the king (see Esth. 1:12). Esther's dilemma, however, was whether to approach the king without being summoned (see Esth. 4:10-11). Some elements of this story shock modern sensibilities, but enjoy the story as a celebration of God's using unlikely heroes to deliver His people.

TIMELINE
Old Testament Timeline, Part 2: write *Esther* on line 2 in act 2, scene 9.

SMALL-GROUP DISCUSSION QUESTIONS

1. Read Ezra 1–6. Why did Cyrus allow the Judeans to return to Jerusalem and rebuild the temple? How did God use Cyrus for His purposes? How did Cyrus and his kingdom support the Judeans as they returned to Jerusalem?

2. Why was it significant that the returning people built the foundation for the temple first? What did the people do when the foundation was laid? How were the people opposed in their rebuilding efforts? In what ways is your church the communal center of your life?

3. What was Haggai's message to the people of Judah? How can we apply his message to our priorities today? Are we giving top priority to God's work?

4. What messages of hope and restoration did Zechariah deliver for the returning exiles? Read 4:6. How would God's work of renewal be accomplished?

5. Does your church believe it receives an unending supply of the Holy Spirit? Give evidence. How would God use your church if it were continually filled with the Spirit?

6. Read Zechariah 9:9; 11:12; 12:10; 13:7. How do these verses foreshadow the life of Jesus? How does fulfilled prophecy give you confidence in the Word and promises of God?

7. Name characteristics of the Day of the Lord described in Zechariah 14. How is it similar to the descriptions you have read in the other Prophets? What hope would it have held for the returning exiles? For believers today?

8. How do you see God's sovereignty at work in Esther 1–5? How do you live with a constant awareness that God has plans He has strategically positioned you to accomplish?

WEEK 39

This is our last full week in the Old Testament. We are still in act 2, scene 9, which is set in the period after the Israelites returned from exile in Babylon. This week watch for at least four key themes.

1. Esther, Malachi, Nehemiah, and Ezra each in his or her own way illustrates the importance of sound, God-honoring leadership. Watch for characteristics that make a great leader.
2. Malachi, Ezra, and Nehemiah especially emphasize a return to covenant faithfulness and a focus on God's laws.
3. Religious identity as God's special people serves as a prominent theme of each book. Notice the various ways this identity is expressed and guarded.
4. Undergirding each of these stories and Malachi's prophecy is a clear picture of God's sovereign care for His people when they are rightly related to Him. The hand of God was with the main characters of Ezra, Nehemiah, and Esther, and that made all the difference in the outcomes of the stories.

Watch for these themes as you read, reflecting on the implications for our lives today.

DAY 1 Esther 6–10

As you continue to read Esther today, you see more ironies. Mordecai was honored in place of Haman. Haman was killed on the gallows he intended for Mordecai. The edict condemning the Jews was reversed, and they became the victors over those who would have destroyed them. We see here the playing out of a very old holy war, and it helps put the story in a broader old-covenant context. Haman was an Amalekite and was called an Agagite. The Amalekites were the first nation to oppose Israel after its exodus from Egypt. They came to represent arch opponents of Israel. Saul, the son of Kish, a Benjaminite, had failed to execute Agag, the king of the Amalekites. But now Mordecai, the son of Kish, a Benjaminite, succeeded. Esther 8–10 should be read against the backdrop of conquering the land of Canaan (see Josh.). As with that holy war (with a tragic exception, Josh. 7:1), the Israelites of Esther's day did not touch the plunder of their enemies (see Deut. 13:16). Yet those who had planned to devastate them were devastated instead. The heroes of this story are heroes because of their submission to and trust in God, who was the ultimate hero of the story.

Underlying the Book of Esther is a clear picture of God's sovereign protection of His people. From what do you or those in your life need protection at present?

DAY 2 Malachi 1–4; Psalm 50

Malachi is not clearly dated, but the book seems to address the period just prior to the reforms brought by Ezra and Nehemiah (about 460 B.C.). It is organized around six disputes between Yahweh and His people, each of which began with Yahweh's raising an issue. The people then raised a question, challenging Yahweh. Then God showed the people the ways they had abandoned the covenant. God's people had become spiritually lazy, playing fast and loose with the dictates of God's covenant. They accused God of not loving them, but He showed that it was they who had abandoned the love relationship. Watch for the various accusations the people brought against God and how God answered them.

Also look for a call to renewal, warning of coming judgment, and hope for the future, all prominent themes in the Prophets. The statements about God's coming to refine His temple and about the messenger Elijah, who would go before the Lord, anticipated the coming of Jesus. As God's Anointed One, Jesus was preceded by John the Baptist (whom Jesus called Elijah) and also cleansed the temple.

How does spiritual laziness manifest itself in your life? Repent from it today.

DAY 3 Ezra 7–10

Today we read the rest of the Book of Ezra. First notice the descriptions of Ezra himself. He was a scribe and priest, an expert in the law of God, who "had determined in his heart to study the law of the Lord, obey it, and teach its statutes and ordinances in Israel" (7:10). The Persian king commissioned Ezra to go back to Israel and put things right with the temple so that the people could worship God according to the law. However, when Ezra and the other leaders returned, they found that the Israelites in the land had intermarried with the pagans from the surrounding peoples—a direct violation of God's law. The issue was not racial but religious. The conclusion of the book seems radical, as the Israelites determined to send away their foreign wives, but it communicates that nothing is more important than a right relationship with God.

How far will you go to follow the ways of God?

DAY 4 Nehemiah 1–4

Like its sister book, Ezra, which addresses the same time period, the Book of Nehemiah has several key concerns. It begins with the crisis: the disarray of Jerusalem and its people. At the heart of the concern lies their identity as a people. The abandonment of God's law had led to the exile and dispersion of God's people, as the curses of the law had described in Deuteronomy. So watch for an emphasis on returning to God's Word, renewing a commitment to the covenant and law. This commitment to God's Word undergirds virtually all of the key decisions reflected in the book.

Rebuilding the walls was for protection from enemies but also an important identity marker, clearly identifying those within the city as a distinct group of people. The rebuilding also marked Jerusalem as being in a state of renewal and rebuilding.

How much of your identity as a person is grounded in a commitment to God's Word?

TIMELINE
Old Testament Timeline, Part 2: write *Nehemiah* on line 3 in act 2, scene 9.

DAY 5 Nehemiah 5–7

Continue noticing the emphasis on a renewal of commitment to God's law and covenant and on the identity of God's people. The economic and social crisis reflected in Nehemiah 5 was due to neglecting clear prohibition in the law against charging a fellow Israelite interest (see Deut. 23:19-20). In Nehemiah 6 also notice the various types of opposition to the work of rebuilding the wall and Nehemiah's stellar leadership during this time. The opponents tried to distract, intimidate, build coalitions, and ruin Nehemiah's reputation, but all to no avail. The genealogical records of Nehemiah 7 established clear national identity and a pure commitment to the law (since priests had to be clearly identified; see vv. 63-65).

What opposition to God's work do you face? Follow Nehemiah's example in standing against intimidation and discouragement and in trusting the Lord.

DAY 6 Nehemiah 8–10

Nehemiah 8:1-12 presents a pivotal moment in the restoration of God's people as they listened, understood, and responded to the law. This happened in 445 B.C., just five days after the wall had been finished. They rediscovered the practice of the Festival of Booths (see Neh. 8:13-18) and had an extraordinary celebration. In addition, their exposure to God's Word brought about confession of sin, repentance, and renewed worship.

Notice that much of Nehemiah 9 consists of a prayer, a rehearsal of Israel's history, and the recitation of the pattern of God's blessings followed by Israel's rebellion. God was faithful;

Israel's ancestors, wicked. So the people of Nehemiah's day renewed the covenant with God, a covenant involving separation from foreigners, observance of the Sabbath, and giving resources for temple worship, all of which had been prescribed in the law.

At times in our relationship with God we too need renewal, refocusing commitment to God's ways. What areas of your commitment need to be renewed today?

SMALL-GROUP DISCUSSION QUESTIONS

1. What are some ways you see God working in the story of Esther? What does this tell you about how God works in our lives and in the world? Give examples of a time in your life when you can look back and see that God was at work in your circumstances.

2. What accusations did the people bring against God in the Book of Malachi? How did God respond? How had the people failed to keep the covenant? In what ways are commitment and obedience lacking in God's people today?

3. Read Ezra 9:1-2. How had the Israelites been unfaithful to God after returning to the land? From what things and practices do you think God wants His followers to separate themselves today?

4. Read Ezra's prayer in 9:6-9. How do you respond to your own sin and the sins of others in your faith family? Do you grieve over it, or do you take it lightly? Have you ever felt embarrassed to enter the presence of God? What is the solution to this problem?

5. Read Nehemiah's prayer in 1:5-11. What sins of the people did Nehemiah confess to God? How did Nehemiah regard the authority of God's Word, as reflected in his prayer?

6. What happened after the law was read in Nehemiah 8? What effect did it have on the people? Describe a time when you recognized that your life did not line up with God's Word in a particular way. What did you do in response?

7. Why do we offer so little attention to the Word of God? What are some of the things that distract you from reading and listening to the Word? How can we become a people who pay careful attention to the Word of God?

8. What sins did the people confess in Nehemiah 9? How did the people respond in Nehemiah 10:28-29? What commitments need to be renewed in your life? In your church?

God's New-Covenant People

WEEK 40

After a brief wrap-up of the Old Testament story in day 1, we will move into the New Testament, in which Jesus established a new covenant (see Jer. 31:31-34; Heb. 8:7-13) between God and people. We will begin the third and final act of the Bible's grand story, "God's New-Covenant People." As you read this week, think about ways Jesus fulfilled the longing for God's true King that we saw in the Old Testament. From the reactions of those around Him, we will also see that Jesus came as an unexpected Messiah. People of His day did not expect the Messiah to do things the way Jesus did.

It will take us about six weeks to work our way through the four Gospels. Tracking with the parallels in these wonderful books will seem choppy at points as we skip to various passages in Matthew and Luke. We are using Mark as our base, so our trek through the third Gospel will be more orderly. As you read, look for common themes and unique emphases in the different Gospels. Ask God to speak to you through the life of Jesus.

DAY 1 Nehemiah 11–13; Psalm 126

The remainder of Nehemiah tells of the resettling of Jerusalem and further reforms initiated by Nehemiah. Now that the wall was rebuilt, people needed to reoccupy the city. The genealogies in this section built a sense of identity for the Israelites as a distinct people and continued to demonstrate that the priests and Levites, who would serve in temple worship, were legitimate. They dedicated the rebuilt wall in Nehemiah 12:27-43, and 12:44-47 tells how the Levites and priests were provided for.

After being in Jerusalem for 12 years, Nehemiah briefly returned to the court of King Artaxerxes in Babylon. Coming back to Jerusalem, he found that the people were not being careful with the instructions provided in the law. Notice the various ways in Nehemiah 13 that the law was being violated.

Nehemiah concludes the story of Israel's restoration to the land and the renewal of the covenant. Psalm 126 celebrates this restoration and echoes the celebratory atmosphere we have seen at times in Ezra and Nehemiah.

Using Psalm 126, pray a prayer of celebration to God, thanking Him for times of renewal you have experienced in your life.

SCENE 1: CHRIST'S COMING: GOD'S TRUE KING ARRIVES

DAY 2 Psalm 106; John 1:4-14

Today as we move into act 3 of the Bible's grand story, we find ourselves at a pivotal moment in history. The first scene of this act is titled "Christ's Coming: God's True King Arrives." Psalm 106 is a historical psalm that presents an overview of Israel's history from its exodus from Egypt to the dispersion among the nations. The psalm recounts a history of disobedience and consequences. Yet notice the longing for salvation in this psalm.

John 1:4-14 overviews the coming of Christ, who answered the cry for salvation. As you read about Jesus' glory, think about the *Shekinah* glory we saw in the Old Testament story (for example, when God filled the temple in 2 Chron. 7:1). The Greek term translated "took up residence" in John 1:14 means *to pitch a tent*. Think about the presence of the Lord coming on the tabernacle, the holy tent, in the old-covenant story, and about Jesus, the Lord, becoming flesh and dwelling among us. God's presence among His people, such an important theme in the Old Testament, came to a new realization in Christ.

Tell Jesus what His dwelling in you means to you today.

DAY 3 Matthew 1; Luke 1:1–2:38

Matthew's book seems to have been written to communicate the gospel to a Jewish audience. Matthew built on the foundation of the Old Testament, demonstrating that Jesus fulfilled what the Scriptures had promised about the coming of the Messiah. The genealogy of chapter 1 begins with Abraham, the father of the Jewish people. The perfect balance of 14 generations from Abraham to David to the exile to Christ shows that Jesus came at just the right time in God's providence and began a new era in Jewish history. As you read about Jesus' birth in Matthew, observe the way that Gospel focuses on the fulfillment of Scripture.

The virgin birth emphasizes Jesus' divine nature as the Son of God. Joseph, the focus of the birth account in Matthew and Jesus' adoptive father, would have been considered Jesus' legal father through whom Jesus' right to the throne of David was passed to Him.

Luke begins with the birth of John the Baptist, the forerunner of the Messiah. Mary is the focus in the story of Jesus' birth. Luke 1–2 is peppered with angelic proclamations and songs that sound like Old Testament psalms. Notice the focus on salvation in these songs.

Today thank God for the coming of Jesus the Savior.

TIMELINE
New Testament Timeline: write *Mary* on line 1, *Joseph* on line 2, *John the Baptist* on line 3, and *Jesus* on line 4 in act 3, scene 1.

DAY 4 Matthew 2; Luke 2:39-52

As you read Matthew 2, think about the promises of the coming King we saw throughout the Old Testament. Herod was a powerful but paranoid puppet ruler under the governance of the Roman Empire. Of mixed ancestry rather than Jewish, Herod ruled by political force.

The wise men, in following the star, pointed to Someone at work who was bigger than the Roman Empire—the God who rules the stars. The star and the Old Testament Scripture came together to witness to Jesus' birth as Messiah, the true Jewish King.

The reading from Luke focuses on the only recorded event from Jesus' years as a youth. Notice Jesus' awareness of His identity as the Son of God.

Meditate on the amazing fact that God, in the person of Jesus, entered the world as a human.

DAY 5 Matthew 3; Mark 1:1-11; Luke 3; John 1:15-34

The Gospel writers described John the Baptist's ministry as having been foretold in Malachi 3:1 (Mark) and in Isaiah 40 (all four Gospels). John's ministry was one of preparation. When a king came to town in the ancient world, one way to prepare for the arrival was to smooth out the road coming into the town, filling in the holes and smoothing down the bumps. Notice in Luke's fuller quotation of Isaiah 40 that the road John prepared was cosmic in size: valleys were filled in and mountains smoothed down. The Lord of the earth was coming to bring salvation. John's preparation involved calling people to repentance so that their hearts would be ready to receive the Lord's message.

Jesus, though He had not sinned (see Heb. 4:15), was baptized because it was right for Him to stand with this movement of God (see Matt. 3:15). The baptism also placed God's approval on Jesus and the ministry on which He was about to embark (see Matt. 3:17).

As you read Luke 3, notice the tangible social concerns to which John pointed in calling people to repentance. What fruit do you need to produce in keeping with your repentance?

SCENE 2: CHRIST'S MINISTRY: GOD'S TRUE KING MANIFESTS HIS KINGDOM

DAY 6 Matthew 4:1-22; 13:54-58; Mark 1:12-20; 6:1-6; Luke 4:1-30; 5:1-11; John 1:35–2:12

In today's readings we move into act 3, scene 2, which focuses on Jesus' earthly ministry. The passages have three main focuses: Jesus' temptation, the calling of the first disciples, and the beginning of Jesus' ministry in Galilee (locate the province of Galilee on a map at the back of your Bible). As you read the temptation accounts, notice that the Old Testament accounts of the Israelites wandering in the wilderness form the backdrop. In terms of bread (think manna from heaven), worship, and testing God, the Israelites failed miserably. But Jesus overcame temptation and moved into His ministry in the power of the Spirit.

As you read about the first disciples, watch for patterns beginning to develop. The disciples were surprised at Jesus' abilities and were in a process of discovering Jesus' identity.

Early in His ministry in Galilee, Jesus preached in His hometown. Luke's account especially focuses on Jesus' proclaiming His ministry as Messiah through Isaiah 61:1-2, but next He told listeners His ministry would be very different than they expected.

Do your best to read the Gospels with fresh eyes. What surprises you about Jesus?

SMALL-GROUP DISCUSSION QUESTIONS

1. Read Philippians 2:5-11. What did Jesus give up to come to earth in human form?

2. Read John 1:4-5. Describe the time when the light of the gospel freed you from the darkness of this world. What does a life characterized by light look like?

3. What does it mean to "believe in His name" (John 1:12)?

4. In what ways did John prepare for the coming of Jesus? How did he contrast their ministries in Luke 3:16-17?

5. Identify some acts of the Holy Spirit in Luke 1–4. In what ways do you see the Spirit at work today?

6. Why do you think Jesus wanted to be baptized? Why are believers baptized today? What did your baptism mean to you?

7. How was it possible for the Son of God to be tempted in Luke 4? Do you think He was really tempted by the things Satan offered? How was Jesus victorious over temptation? How can we be victorious over temptation in our lives?

WEEK 41

Our readings in the Gospels seem a bit choppy compared to the long stretches of Old Testament texts we have read. As you move from Gospel to Gospel, focus on each particular moment of Jesus' ministry. Watch for overlaps among the accounts as well as the special emphases of each Gospel writer. Also notice the very different approach the Gospel of John takes as compared to the other three Gospels. Notice the variety of people who came to Jesus and His responses.

Begin to grasp general characteristics of Jesus' ministry: the ways he presented Himself as unique, the way He manifested the kingdom of God, the way he presented the law in contrast to the scribes and Pharisees, the power manifested through His miracles, and how His miracles introduced teachings about the Kingdom.

DAY 1 Matthew 4:23-25; 8:14-17; Mark 1:21-39; Luke 4:31-44

These passages summarize the first phase of Jesus' ministry in Galilee, the foundation of which was Jesus' ministry of teaching. He was bringing a message to Israel. His healings and mighty works met the practical needs of people and demonstrated the power of the Kingdom Jesus was proclaiming. The Kingdom was being manifested in both the teaching and the mighty works. It is also clear from these passages that Jesus sensed a call to the whole of Galilee and was laying a foundation for a ministry to all of Israel.

Ask God to open your eyes to fresh insights on the significance of Jesus' ministry for your life and for all humankind.

DAY 2 John 3–5

Today we read about a series of encounters Jesus had with individuals. John's Gospel is more oriented to the province of Judea than the other Gospels, which focus on Jesus' ministry in Galilee (at the back of your Bible or in a Bible dictionary examine a map of Palestine during the time of Jesus' ministry). The stories in John 3–5 began in Judea but then transitioned to Galilee at 4:43.

Notice today the emphasis on believing, a key theme in John's Gospel (you might want to underline every time the word *believe* is used). For John, belief was not merely agreeing with something mentally. It involved active trust, accepting who Jesus is, committing to follow Him, and keeping His commands (see John 15:1-17).

As you read today, also notice how Jesus broke with the accepted practices of the day. For instance, a religious Jewish male would not normally speak with a Samaritan, a woman in public, or an immoral person; the Samaritan woman of John 4 was all three. Jesus inverted accepted practices in order to live out the Father's will.

Finally, in John we find both wonderful word pictures (like being born again and living water) and very straightforward theological truths, such as "He was even calling God His own Father, making Himself equal with God" (John 5:18).

As you read today, what is Jesus calling you to do in response?

DAY 3 Matthew 8:1-4; 9:1-17; 12:1-21; Mark 1:40–3:21; Luke 5:12–6:19

We see in Mark and Luke the formal choosing of the twelve apostles, who would be official representatives of Jesus. Do you remember the twelve tribes of Israel? Jesus was reconstituting true Israel in His ministry, and the choosing of the twelve was highly symbolic.

From the beginning of Jesus' ministry in Galilee, a number of dynamics characterized His ministry. Jesus' ministry was powerful, demonstrating His authority; healings and driving out demons manifested the kingdom of God. Jesus broke with accepted religious practices of the day, eating with sinners, fasting, and ministering on the Sabbath. Jesus also claimed the authority to override such practices, some of which had been in place for hundreds of years. Notice the religious leaders' reactions. A major power struggle was brewing.

How do we react when God's Word confronts us about our comfortable religious practices that are not necessarily biblical?

TIMELINE
New Testament Timeline: write **Simon Peter** on line 1, **James** on line 2, and **John** on line 3 in act 3, scene 2.

DAY 4 Matthew 5–7; Luke 6:20-49; 11:1-13

Matthew was written to communicate the gospel to Jewish people. Notice the parallels between the Sermon on the Mount (see Matt. 5–7) and the Old Testament. This is Jesus' interpretation of the law, given on a mountain, just as Moses had received the law on Mount Sinai. The Beatitudes (see Matt. 5:3-12) focus on the condition of the heart and on how believers are treated by the world. Jesus and His followers were in the tradition of the prophets, who were persecuted, and who, like salt and light, had an effect in God's name.

Jesus' sermon answers the question "How does someone live righteously in God's kingdom, truly fulfilling God's law?" Jesus centered on internal, heart dynamics in dealing with attitudes and actions. The religion of the scribes and Pharisees, which focused on outward show, wasn't sufficient (see Matt. 5:21-48; 6:1-18). Trust God. Treat others well. Live by Jesus' teaching. Luke's version of the sermon is also associated with a mountain, probably a plateau on the mountain. It includes some material Matthew doesn't and, at the same time, is a more condensed version. Like Matthew, it ends with the analogy of two foundations.

How will you lay a foundation of rock in your life today, acting on Jesus' words?

DAY 5 Matthew 8:5-13; 11:1-30; Luke 7:1-50

Jesus' ministry attracted much attention, and today we see several people come to Jesus. Matthew and Luke tell the story of the faith-full centurion of Capernaum a bit differently. A centurion was a Roman officer who commanded approximately one hundred men. Matthew's Gospel says the centurion himself came to Jesus. Luke's version has two different groups of intermediaries come on behalf of the centurion. In the ancient world an intermediary was received as if the sender were present, so the accounts are not contradictory.

Matthew 8:11 shows that Jesus' vision for the Kingdom included non-Jews. John the Baptist, in prison, sent disciples to ask whether Jesus was really the Messiah. Jesus answered by alluding to passages from Isaiah (see Isa. 26:19; 29:18-19; 35:5-6); as Messiah, He did not come to overthrow the Romans but to reverse the ravages of sin and death. Jesus, however, was clear about John's identity: He was the forerunner of the Messiah (see Mal. 3:1).

In Luke 7 a sinful woman came to Jesus as He dined with a Pharisee. Washing feet was a common hospitality. Notice contrasts between the woman and Jesus' host.

With what questions do you come to Jesus today?

DAY 6 Matthew 12:22-50; Mark 3:22-35; Luke 8:19-21; 11:14-54

Notice that all three Gospels today include the story of Jesus' healing a man both blind and mute and the response of the Pharisees: "The man drives out demons only by Beelzebul, the ruler of demons" (Matt 12:24). Jesus' answer was that His driving out demons was a manifestation of God's kingdom (see Matt. 12:28). But then He made a statement that has troubled many Christians through the centuries, speaking of the unpardonable sin. Mark gives the clearest explanation: blasphemy of the Holy Spirit is calling the Spirit unclean (see 3:30), in other words, seeing Jesus' work by the Spirit as demonic.

Today's passages continue to clarify Jesus' uniqueness (see Matt. 12:38-42; Luke 11:30-32). He overturned common understandings of human obligations in favor of the Kingdom, as with His response to the arrival of His mother and brothers. Luke 11:27-28 presents a striking statement. In response to someone's shouting, in effect, "Your mom is blessed to have had You," Jesus said the person who hears the word of God and keeps it is the one who is really blessed. As you listen to what God says to you today and choose to live it, you are more blessed than if you had been Jesus' earthly parent! Finally, watch for the growing tension between Jesus and the Pharisees over how the law was to be lived.

How faithful are you to live Jesus' teaching when it overrides conventional loyalties and obligations?

SMALL-GROUP DISCUSSION QUESTIONS

1. In John 3 what did Jesus say is required to enter the kingdom of God? What does it mean to be born of the Spirit (see v. 5)? What does it mean to believe in Jesus (see v. 16)?

2. Jesus offered the Samaritan woman living water. Who in your life is thirsty for living water?

3. How did Jesus violate the Pharisees' expectations for the observance of the Sabbath? By what authority did He do these things? What are biblical ways believers should observe the Sabbath today?

4. Read the Beatitudes in Matthew 5:3-12. What does it mean to be blessed? Describe the life of someone you think of as blessed. How do Jesus' words affect your definition of *blessed*? What does it mean to be poor in spirit? Has there ever been a time when you thought of yourself as spiritually bankrupt? What does Jesus want His followers to mourn over?

5. Have you ever been persecuted for righteousness' sake? How? How did you respond?

6. Do you view hatred as a form of murder? Do you view lustful thoughts as adultery? How can Christians keep their thoughts and attitudes pure? How does God change our hearts so that we can obey Jesus' teachings?

7. What do someone's spending patterns say about his or her love for God?

8. Do you have a problem with worry? If so, why? Do you trust more in God or your efforts to make a living? How can you develop greater trust in God? What does it mean to "seek first the kingdom of God and His righteousness" (Matt. 6:33)? What distracts you in seeking the kingdom of God?

WEEK 42

This week we will continue to focus on act 3, scene 2, "Christ's Ministry: God's True King Manifests His Kingdom." As you read, think about ways Jesus was making the kingdom clear. He manifested His kingdom in many ways, for instance by various kinds of miracles, revealing His power over nature, the demonic, sickness, and death. As you read each story, ask, *What does this story tell me about Jesus?*

This week we will also read a great deal of Jesus' teaching on the kingdom and will see a variety of His teaching methods. Jesus not only stood against the religious power structures of His day, embodied by the scribes and Pharisees, but also trained His disciples for their future role as the leaders of His movement. The week will climax with the transfiguration account, in which Jesus' identity and the nature of His kingdom became gloriously clear.

DAY 1 Matthew 13:1-53; Mark 4:1-34; Luke 8:1-18

A great deal of Jesus' teaching was in parables, and our reading today focuses primarily on parables having to do with seeds. The parable of the sower in some ways is the foundational parable for all others (see Mark 4:13), for in it Jesus spoke about receptivity to the Word of God. In His explanation of this parable to the disciples, Jesus identified the dual role of parables. A parable is a story placed alongside spiritual truth to elucidate that truth. For those who have spiritual ears, the parables bring greater clarity to spiritual reality. They teach people how to think about God or about a relationship with God and others in the world. Jesus also pointed to Isaiah 6:9-10, saying that parables are a form of judgment on those who are spiritually imperceptive. As you read the parable of the sower and the other parables in these chapters, notice the details as explained by Jesus.

Think about your receptivity to God's Word. Which seed are you?

DAY 2 Matthew 8:18-34; 9:18-38; Mark 4:35–5:43; Luke 8:22-56; 9:57-62

Today we read some of the most striking stories in the Gospels. There are three different kinds of miracles here—power over nature, power over the demonic, and power over sickness and death. As you read each miracle story, ask, *What does this story tell me about Jesus' identity?* Notice the details of Jesus' interaction with people. For example, in Mark's version of the demoniac story, to whom did Jesus say yes, and to whom did He say no when a request was made?

Read these stories in light of Old Testament background. For instance, read the calming of the storm in light of Psalm 107:29-30 and Jonah 1:4-17. In each passage who has the ability to calm a storm? The woman healed of the flow of blood would have been considered ceremonially unclean for those dozen years (see Lev. 15:25-30), and she would have made anyone she touched unclean. But Jesus reversed things, healing her by that touch. In the demoniac story, being in a graveyard would have made the man ceremonially unclean, and pigs show that this was Gentile territory. Yet Jesus' authority knew no bounds.

How is Jesus' authority manifested in your life today?

DAY 3 Matthew 10; 14; Mark 6:7-56; Luke 9:1-17; John 6

Continue to think today in terms of Jesus' mission and identity. The choosing of the twelve disciples symbolized the twelve tribes of Israel; Jesus was reconstituting the nation of Israel in His ministry. The disciples had a ministry to the world, enabled by the Spirit and identified with Jesus. Persecution and division occur because of Jesus' lordship over life. He is a dividing line. One follows Him wholeheartedly or not.

The feeding of the five thousand has strong messianic overtones. Like Moses, Jesus gave bread in the wilderness (see Ex. 16; John 6), showing that He was a prophet like Moses (see Deut. 18:15-16). Walking on water showed Jesus was Lord of the stormy waters. Only the Lord can walk on the seas (see Job 9:8) or give someone else the ability to do so.

What do Jesus' actions say about His identity?

What are the implications of the fact that Jesus is Lord?

DAY 4 Matthew 15; Mark 7:1–8:10

As you read today, think in terms of boundaries. Boundaries can be important in life, but they can also block our relationship with God and others if set up inappropriately. The Pharisees and scribes applied the law in traditional ways, which Jesus said at points violated the law, missing the issues of the heart about which God is most concerned. Their set boundaries, in this case washing hands ritually, were deceptive, leading people to think they were clean, while their hearts remained defiled.

The stories about the Gentile mother and the feeding of the four thousand show that the Kingdom was pushing past traditional boundaries into the world of the Gentiles. Jesus used the metaphor of dogs in contrast to sheep (commonly used of God's people). Jews often referred to Gentiles as dogs, unclean animals, a word picture for those who were not Jewish. Jesus was testing the mother's faith, and she came through with flying colors.

What religious boundaries have you embraced that are not really biblical?

DAY 5 Matthew 16; Mark 8:11–9:1; Luke 9:18-27

Matthew and Mark begin with the demand for a sign from the Pharisees (Matthew adds the Sadducees), an irrefutable sign from heaven to prove Jesus' identity. Jesus, of course, had given lots of signs (the most common word for *miracles* in the Gospels), and Jesus in essence said, "The signs are already there for the spiritually perceptive." The resurrection would be the sign of Jonah (see Matt. 12:38-42)—someone delivered from death.

In the next story Jesus used the word *yeast* metaphorically (a word picture used for comparison) to speak of wrong teaching, but the disciples took it literally. Caught up in a practical need of the moment, they forgot that Jesus, who had multiplied bread for the masses twice, would not have been concerned about a lack of bread. In Mark, Jesus pointed to Jeremiah 5:21 to underline their spiritual dullness.

A breakthrough of perception came from the Spirit while they were at Caesarea Philippi, for Peter confessed that Jesus was the Christ, God's Messiah. This was a turning point in the Gospels; they pointed to Jerusalem and Jesus' death from this moment on. Peter's rebuke of Jesus—a crucified Messiah would not have made sense to him at this point—led to Jesus' rebuke of Peter. Following Jesus would mean a path to death and self-denial.

Taking up your cross means giving your life completely to Jesus. Are you sold out to Him?

DAY 6 Matthew 17–18; Mark 9:2-50; Luke 9:28-56

Yesterday Jesus predicted His death in Jerusalem. When Jesus said some standing there would not die before the kingdom of God arrived in power, He was probably speaking about the transfiguration. Luke gave us the most detailed account of this event; he said Moses and Elijah were speaking to Jesus about His death (see Luke 9:31). So the context of the transfiguration had Jesus setting His face toward Jerusalem, where He would die.

The transfiguration was a moment when heaven broke into earth. Notice parallels with other places in Scripture where clouds covered a mountain, God spoke, and people were afraid (for example, Moses on Mount Sinai). But the glory of Jesus revealed who He was, God's Son (think of the *Shekinah* glory of God in the Old Testament; see 2 Cor. 4:4). Peter's mistake was assuming Moses and Elijah were on the same level with Jesus (see Luke 9:33).

In the teaching portions today notice the variety of methods Jesus used. Hyperbole (purposeful exaggeration; see Mark 9:43-47), illustration, and parables are represented. Also notice the centrality of the Kingdom in these teachings.

Do you recognize the glory of Jesus in these passages of Scripture?
Will you worship Him accordingly today?

SMALL-GROUP DISCUSSION QUESTIONS

1. What is the purpose of parables? Why do you think Jesus used them? Name some of Jesus' parables you read this week. What do they teach about the kingdom of God?

2. What does the parable of the sower in Matthew 13 teach about receptivity to the Word of God? What kind of soil are you today?

3. In John 6 what did the people say about Jesus after He fed the five thousand? What did the miracle reveal about Jesus' identity? What was the difference between Moses' and Jesus' miracles (see vv. 49-50)?

4. What does it mean for Jesus to be the Bread of life? Why did the multitude seek Jesus in John 6:26? In what ways can we be guilty of wanting Jesus' provision more than Himself?

5. Read John 6:39 and apply this verse to your security in Christ.

6. Read John 6:44. How does the Father draw people to the Son? How did you experience the Father drawing you to Jesus?

7. Why did some people turn away from Jesus in John 6:60-70? Why do people turn away from Him today?

8. Read John 6:63. What is the role of the Holy Spirit in producing life-saving faith? Why is the flesh useless in producing faith?

9. Read Matthew 15:1-20. How were the Pharisees missing the true meaning of the law? How do Christians today create barriers to the gospel?

10. In Matthew 16:16 Peter affirmed Jesus' identity as the Messiah but was then rebuked in verse 23. What did the disciples still not understand about Jesus at this point?

11. Read Matthew 16:24. What do Jesus' words mean? In what ways are we called to die to ourselves each day? How completely do most believers live by these words?

WEEK 43

We now come to the final phase of act 3, scene 2, "Christ's Ministry: God's True King Manifests His Kingdom." This week watch for several dynamics in the Gospels.

1. Especially in John symbolic language is used to describe the person and work of Jesus. Notice that these symbols are rooted in the Old Testament story and present Jesus as the climactic fulfillment of that story.
2. Continue to grow in your awareness of the importance of the cultural background behind these stories. For instance, you cannot read the story of the good Samaritan well without understanding something about the racial tension between Jews and Samaritans in first-century Palestine.
3. Watch for Jesus' use of comparison and contrast in His teachings.
4. Notice the introductions and conclusions to Jesus' stories or units of teaching. The introductions might offer the social setting of what is about to be said; for example, Luke 15:1-2 sets the stage for the parables on lost and found in that chapter. Introductions or conclusions can tip us off to the main point of Jesus' teaching.

Keep your heart soft and open to the Lord as you listen to the Gospel stories this week.

DAY 1 John 7–9

John framed His Gospel around the Jewish celebrations of various feasts. The reading for today has the feast of tabernacles as its context. This feast, which celebrated the harvest six months after Passover, was one of three that Jewish men were to attend during the year (see Ex. 23:14-17; Deut. 16:16). The feast also celebrated the deliverance of Israel during the years of the wilderness wanderings, and John's story focuses on three great symbols from that period, showing how Jesus fulfilled all three.

1. Jesus' teaching on living water recalls the water from the rock in the wilderness (see Ex. 17:1-7).
2. The emphasis on Jesus as the Light of the world echoes the story of the pillar of cloud and fire that guided God's people through the wilderness (see Num. 9:15-23).
3. Jesus identified Himself with references to God's name ("I am"), revealed to Moses in the wilderness (see Ex. 3:13-15).

Also in today's reading notice the rich contrasts—between truth and lies, being from the Father and going to the Father, life and death, physical and spiritual blindness, and opposition to Jesus against belief in Jesus. At this point in the story, opposition was heating up. Finally, notice the repetition of the reflection that Jesus' hour had not yet come. This builds tension in the story as we move toward the time when Jesus would go to the Father (see John 13:1).

How do you respond to the opposition you face for identifying with Jesus?

DAY 2 Luke 10; John 10:1–11:54

Jesus' ministry continued to expand and face opposition. The story of the good Samaritan is one of the most familiar of the Gospels, but take time to notice the details. The Jews hated the Samaritans; Jesus' making a Samaritan the hero of the story drove His point home: everyone is your neighbor, even those you consider enemies, and you are to love them.

In the reading from John today, Jesus called Himself the Good Shepherd, an image taken from the Old Testament. God was Israel's true Shepherd (see Ps. 23), and leaders of God's people could also be called shepherds (see Isa. 56:9-12; Jer. 23:1-4). Jesus said He cares for His sheep, and they recognize His voice. Middle Eastern shepherds had an intimate understanding of their sheep and led them with commands or songs. Jesus also loves His sheep to the point of laying down His life for them.

The story of the raising of Lazarus shows not only that Jesus, who was going to Jerusalem to die, was deeply moved by His friend's death and angered by death's ravages but also that Jesus Himself was the key to resurrection and life.

Listen for Jesus' voice today in His Word. How has He been the Good Shepherd to you?

DAY 3 Luke 12:1–13:30

The themes in this section of Jesus' teaching center on orienting life to God and His ways, especially being ready at any moment to give an account of your life. Notice the contrasts and comparisons: the contrast between hidden and public, the comparison of people with sparrows or flowers of the field, the contrast between those who will be approved in the end and those who will not, the contrast between those who are prepared for the Master's coming and those who are not, and the contrast between narrow and broad ways.

The Kingdom is dynamic (see Luke 13:18-21), growing and spreading like a mustard plant or yeast, but as it grows, it unsettles normal relationships. Jesus is a dividing line in life, and this disrupts things. Yet those who know Him are blessed, receiving the Kingdom; valued by God; provided for; and set free.

What tensions has following Christ brought into your life? Have you been shunned or spoken against because of your commitment? Embrace these as normal for a Kingdom person, but also celebrate the gift of being God's person in the world.

DAY4 Luke 14–15

Today we have another section of brilliant teachings by Jesus. We have now seen a pattern of Sabbath-controversy stories, in which Jesus clashed with the religious leaders over whether it was appropriate to heal on the Sabbath. The Old Testament law did not prohibit such healing; the Pharisees had elevated their traditional application of the Sabbath law, reasoning that healing was work that should not be done (notice that they never pointed to a passage of Scripture). Jesus pointed out their hypocrisy.

In Luke 14:7-34 each body of teaching deals with contrasting groups of people. First, Jesus interpreted Proverbs 25:6-7 on humility: the humble are the ones who will be exalted. This concept is illustrated in the parable of the banquet, the poor and outcast being the ones who participated in the banquet.

Who can follow Jesus? Only those who count the cost and give up everything. His statement about hating family members is a use of hyperbole, strategic exaggeration to make a point. Jesus doesn't really want us to hate, but our love for and commitment to Christ will at times look like hate to other people.

Luke 15 has three parables on lostness. Notice that 15:1-2 gives the social setting of this teaching. In the parable of the lost son, the father represents God, the lost son represents sinners, and the brother represents the Pharisees and scribes.

At the end of the parable, who remains outside the Father's house?

With which of the sons do you identify most?

DAY5 Matthew 19; Mark 10:1-31; Luke 16:1–18:30

One of the most difficult things for us to do as we read the Bible is to set aside our own cultural assumptions in order to hear what Jesus was really saying to us. For instance, in Jesus' teaching on divorce, we may have difficulty comprehending His message when we live in a culture that treats divorce lightly; in this way our culture is much like Jesus' culture. It is difficult for us to hear Jesus' teaching about riches when most of us assume we are not rich (if we have multiple sets of clothing, a car, and a home, we are rich by the standards of most of the world).

When we read, we need to keep in mind Jesus' historical moment. For example, in the story of the rich young man, Jesus was speaking to people who already saw themselves as in covenant with God. This was before the cross and resurrection. So Jesus' answer to the young man focused on turning away from what binds you and prevents you from following Jesus. This is a different form of "repent and believe" than we would expect in Paul's writings, but the gospel of the crucified and resurrected Christ was not yet revealed.

Especially in Luke watch for clues to the main purpose of a passage. For instance, in Luke 16 the punch line in the parable of the dishonest manager comes in verses 9-11. Jesus was not endorsing dishonesty. Rather, he was saying we should use our resources wisely, for Kingdom purposes.

Commit yourself today to listening to and living Jesus' teachings in a fresh way.

DAY 6 Matthew 20; Mark 10:32-52; Luke 18:31–19:27

At the end of the story of the rich young man in Matthew, Jesus commented, "Many who are first will be last, and the last first" (Matt. 19:30; Mark 10:31). The rich young man illustrated that the "first will be last." Now the parable of the vineyard workers illustrates that "the last will be first," giving a wonderful picture of God's elaborate grace (and the struggle some have with it).

These inverted values of the kingdom of God are also seen in Jesus' teaching on leadership, shared in response to the request made by the mother of James and John (Mark focused only on James and John, who were standing there with their mother). Kingdom leadership involves service, not domination or rule by authoritative position.

We also see today the third prediction of Jesus' death as the story accelerates to that climax. Now for the first time Matthew included the manner of death and the involvement of the Gentiles. Matthew, Mark, and Luke all share the story of Jesus' healing the blind in Jericho. Matthew has Jesus healing two blind men, while Mark and Luke focus on just one of the men, a man named Bartimaeus, according to Mark. Various explanations have been offered for why Matthew and Mark say the healing took place as Jesus was leaving Jericho, while Luke says Jesus was drawing near to Jericho. The Jewish historian Josephus explained that there were two Jerichos during this time, an older town on a hill about one mile from the main town of Jericho. Jesus could have been leaving one and approaching the other when He met the blind men.

Do you, as a child of your culture, really believe the first will be last and the last first? Do you live as if you believe this?

SMALL-GROUP DISCUSSION QUESTIONS

1. Read John 8. In what way is Jesus the Light of the world? What darkness does He dispel? Why do some people seek darkness instead of light? How does Jesus provide light for your walk in this dark world? How can believers better reflect Jesus' light to the world?

2. Why did the Pharisees react violently in John 8:59? What was Jesus claiming about Himself?

3. How does the story of the good Samaritan (see Luke 10:25-37) summarize the law? Discuss ways you express your love to God. What are some ways we can love our neighbors in a manner similar to the Samaritan?

4. Read John 10:1-18. List ways Jesus is our Good Shepherd. What does that mean to you personally?

5. What did Jesus' raising of Lazarus from death indicate about Jesus?

6. Read Luke 12:8-9. In what ways are you acknowledging Jesus? In what ways are you denying Him?

7. What did Jesus' parable of the banquet in Luke 14:16-24 say to the Pharisees? How were they presuming on their favor with God? How do we presume on our relationship with God today?

8. What did Jesus mean by His words in Luke 14:26?

9. What do the parables of lostness in Luke 15 teach about God's heart? Do you seek the lost and rejoice when they are saved?

10. In the story of the rich young man, how did Jesus show the law to be inadequate for inheriting eternal life? What was necessary? What barriers keep people from coming to Jesus today?

11. Read Matthew 20:25-28. How did Jesus invert the power structure in His kingdom? How did His life illustrate servanthood? How does your life illustrate servanthood in Christ's kingdom?

WEEK 44

This week we enter act 3, scene 3, "Christ's Deliverance of His People: God's Work Through the Death, Resurrection, and Enthronement of His King." The readings this week will take us through much of the last week of Jesus' earthly ministry, from the triumphal entry into Jerusalem through the moment just after the last supper, when Jesus and the disciples were about to leave the city to go to the garden of Gethsemane. Notice especially this week the rising conflict between Jesus and the religious leaders. Jesus confronted them on their own turf. The temple complex was the seat of their power. Also notice that the focus of Jesus' teaching narrowed to the disciples as we move toward the cross. He was preparing them for His leaving.

As always, keep in mind the Old Testament backdrop of the narrative. Feel the tension. Imagine what it would have been like to be in the crowd in Jerusalem during that week.

SCENE 3: CHRIST'S DELIVERANCE OF HIS PEOPLE: GOD'S WORK THROUGH THE DEATH, RESURRECTION, AND ENTHRONEMENT OF HIS KING

DAY 1 Matthew 21:1-22; 26:6-13; Mark 11:1-26; 14:3-9; Luke 19:28-48; John 2:13-25; 11:55-12:36

We read about several turning-point events today, including the triumphal entry of Jesus into Jerusalem, the anointing at Bethany, and the cleansing of the temple. The Gospel writers sometimes arranged their material for emphasis rather than strict chronology. Ask, *Why does this story occur here in this Gospel?* Notice the material around the story for clues.

The Old Testament backdrop is critical to understanding these events. Jesus' triumphal entry to Jerusalem fulfills Zechariah 9:9, which foretells the Messiah's coming to Jerusalem on a donkey. Notice the context of the Old Testament passages behind Jesus' cleansing of the temple (see Isa. 56:7; Jer. 7:11). Both contexts emphasize the corruptness of Jerusalem and its leaders, who clung to the temple rather than God and His ways. The temple was the most important place on earth for a Jewish person. It was the seat of the Sanhedrin's authority, as well as the center of religious life. Jesus' actions would have been seen as outlandish. As with the cursing of the fig tree, Jesus was acting out a message of judgment. In some quarters of Jewish thought, the Messiah was expected to come and set the temple right. The corrupt systems and values of the world came into conflict with God's ways and a commitment to follow Jesus. This would ultimately lead to a cross but also to resurrection.

Notice the dynamics surrounding these events. John tells us that lots of people came out to meet Jesus as He entered Jerusalem because of the raising of Lazarus, and he tells us it was Mary, Lazarus's sister, who anointed Jesus for burial.

What corrupt systems in your world work against God's kingdom?

DAY 2 Matthew 21:23–22:14; Mark 11:27–12:12; Luke 20:1-18; John 12:37-50

Notice that just after the cleansing of the temple, the authorities came to Jesus and challenged His authority. Jesus in essence said, "OK, let's talk about authority. Where did John's baptism come from—from heaven or from men?" Because they could not discern John's authority, which was from God, they would not be able to grasp Jesus' authority. As you read the parables in Matthew, read them with an eye on the question of authority and the conflict between Jesus and the religious leaders.

Mark and Luke also include the parable of the vineyard owner, which is a clear prophetic word against the religious leaders. Notice that Luke ends the telling of that parable with a different response to the observation "He will come and destroy those farmers and give the vineyard to others" (Luke 20:16). Read the response at the end of verse 16 as coming from the religious leaders who were listening to Jesus.

In our reading from John, the Gospel writer quoted two passages from Isaiah, 53:1 and 6:10. The second quotation sounds as if God were keeping the people from coming to Him. Yet in context this Old Testament prophecy was a word of judgment against those who had rejected the ways of the Lord. Spiritual dullness can lead to greater spiritual dullness.

Are you submitted to the Lord's authority today?

DAY 3 Matthew 22:15–23:39; Mark 12:13-44; Luke 20:19–21:4; 13:31-35

As Jesus moved toward the climax of the story, He was in open conflict with the religious leaders. The readings today focus largely on conflict manifested in questions asked and answers given. The question about taxes was meant to put Jesus in a no-win situation. If He said, "Don't pay taxes," the Pharisees could present Him to the Romans as an insurrectionist. If He said, "Pay your taxes," many of the Jews wouldn't like it. Jesus discerned their "malice" (Matt. 22:18) and gave a brilliant answer.

The Sadducees also had ulterior motives when they questioned Jesus about the resurrection. They did not believe in life after death and were trying to frame the doctrine as illogical. When Jesus said they "don't know … the power of God" (Matt. 22:29), He was referring to God's power to raise the dead. He also said they didn't know the Scriptures and pointed to a portion of Scripture they were supposed to believe, Exodus 3:6, since the Sadducees viewed only the first five books of the Old Testament as valid. Jesus' use of the words "I am" showed that Abraham, Isaac, and Jacob, though dead, were still alive in God's presence when these words were spoken to Moses.

Notice how much of the conflict in these passages centers on the religious leaders' lack of integrity. Their motives and inner lives did not line up with their teachings. Evaluate your life and ask God to identify areas of hypocrisy that need attention.

DAY 4 Matthew 24–25; Mark 13; Luke 21:5-38

In today's reading Jesus addressed being ready for His second coming. We need to keep several theological points in mind as we read.

1. This chaotic, violent world as we know it will come to an end when Christ returns. History is not a meaningless series of events. God is going to bring things to a conclusion according to His plan.
2. No one knows when the end is going to take place. There will be difficult times surrounding Christ's coming, but no one will be able to predict the time of the return.
3. Today's teachings and parables emphasize being ready for Christ's return. We should live each day in light of the day Christ returns. In Luke's version Jesus specifically warned against letting our minds be dulled by partying, drunkenness, and worry.
4. There will be accountability in the end. The way we live in this world matters, and we will give an account of how we lived or did not live for the Lord.

Are you living in readiness today for Christ's return?

DAY 5 Matthew 26:1-5,14-35; Mark 14:1-2,10-31; Luke 22:1-38; John 13

Today we read about Judas's betrayal of Jesus and Jesus' celebration of the last supper with the disciples on the night before His crucifixion. The two events are intertwined, and both have their backdrops in the Old Testament. This meal was a Passover meal (see Ex. 12:1-28), which in the first century had to be celebrated within the walls of Jerusalem. It was a way to remember God's deliverance of His people from slavery in Egypt. For devout Jews, a number of traditions surrounded the meal, including an interpretation of the various elements of the meal, eating a sacrificed lamb, giving to the poor, spending the night in prayer, and singing a hymn (they would have sung the *Hallel*, Ps. 113–118; read 118 in light of this moment in Christ's life and ministry). Jesus interpreted the meal in light of His death, which would provide deliverance from spiritual slavery.

John focused on Jesus' washing the disciples' feet as a dramatic way of teaching sacrificial love. As you read, recognize that only Jesus could change a tradition that God had given in the Old Testament, transforming it in light of the new era He was about to inaugurate. Today we take the Lord's Supper to remember that Jesus' death provided our spiritual exodus.

TIMELINE
New Testament Timeline: write *Judas* on line I in act 3, scene 3.

DAY6 John 14–17

Today we come to a great discourse Jesus gave on the last night before His death. The discourse is framed by the theme "going out." In John 13:30 Judas had gone out into the dark night. In 14:31 Jesus and the disciples went out of the room where Jesus had washed their feet. In 18:1 they went out of the city to the garden of Gethsemane. This gives us a beautiful narrative context for Jesus' words, which focus on three themes: Jesus was going out of the world, the disciples were staying in the world to bear witness to Him, and Jesus would send the Spirit to comfort and continue to minister to them.

Other subthemes are also important. Persecution would happen because of the disciples' identification with Jesus, but Jesus would give them peace and victory (see John 16:25-33). Like a vine and branches (see Isa. 5:1-7), they were to remain closely related to Jesus as the key to bearing fruit for Him (see John 15:1-8). They were also to be unified as the Father and Son are unified. In John 17 Jesus prayed for His glorification, for the disciples, and for those of us who have believed because of the disciples' witness in the world.

> *Celebrate that Jesus has prayed for you. Pray for our unity and love for one another as disciples of Christ.*

SMALL-GROUP DISCUSSION QUESTIONS

1. Why did Jesus become angry in Mark 11:15-18? What are churches doing today that keep others from worshiping? Would you call your church a house of prayer? Why or why not?

2. Read Jesus' teachings on prayer and faith in Mark 11:22-24. How can we develop faith that can move mountains? How important is faith to prayer?

3. Read Mark 11:25. How does unwillingness to forgive another person affect your relationship with God?

4. What was the meaning of the parable in Matthew 21:28-43? To whom was the kingdom of God given?

5. When the Pharisees challenged Jesus in the readings this week, were they seeking to trap Him or to learn the truth? What difference does it make whether we approach God with a heart of belief instead of doubt?

6. Read Matthew 24. What signs will signal the end of the world? Can we know the exact date the end will come? Why or why not?

7. What is the message of the parables in Matthew 24:40–25:13? How can we be prepared for Christ's return?

8. What forms of final accountability did Jesus teach us about in Matthew 25:14-46? On what basis will the nations be judged? How is your church caring for the people Jesus identified?

9. Read the account of the last supper in Luke 22:14-23. What did the bread and cup signify? How did Jesus' blood establish the new covenant? What does the Lord's Supper mean to believers today? To you personally?

10. Read about Jesus' demonstration of servanthood in Luke 22:24-27. How can believers today be servants to one another? To lost people?

11. How did Jesus describe the Holy Spirit in John 14? What would the Spirit's roles be in believers' lives?

12. In John 14:21 what did Jesus say is the proof of love for Him? In what areas do you find it difficult to obey Christ?

13. How do we remain in Christ and produce fruit?

14. Do you believe Jesus' words in John 16:23? Give examples of bold requests in your prayer life and ways God has answered.

15. What did Jesus pray for His disciples and later followers in John 17? How did He describe the unity He desired for His followers? What unites believers in their unity with the Trinity? Is your church known as a loving congregation? Give evidence.

WEEK 45

This week we will encounter the most powerful transition in all of Scripture—indeed, the most powerful transitional moment in all of history—as we move from the humiliation to the resurrection and exaltation of Christ. Watch for details, but don't try to work out an exact harmony among the accounts; the authors included or left out various elements for their own purposes. Continue to ask yourself, *What does this story tell me about Jesus?*

Next we will transition to scene 4, "Christ's Church: God's People Advance the Kingdom." Having been delivered by their King, the church now moved the Kingdom forward by proclaiming the good news about Jesus.

DAY 1 Matthew 26:36-75; Mark 14:32-72; Luke 22:39-71; John 18:1-27

The crisis approaches a climax today as we read about Jesus in the garden of Gethsemane, the Sanhedrin taking Him into custody and interrogating Him, and Peter's denial. *Gethsemane* means *olive press*; carefully read the descriptions of Jesus' anguish in the garden. He felt the full force of the moment and chose the path of obedience all the way to the point of death on the cross. Notice also that His disciples abandoned Him, leaving Him to suffer alone.

Matthew says Jesus was taken to Caiaphas, while John notes that He was first taken to Annas. It is quite possible that Annas (a former high priest) and Caiaphas, as relatives, lived in different wings of the same elaborate home, built around a courtyard. Matthew telescopes the story to focus on Caiaphas, who was the ruling high priest at the moment. The turning point of the story is Jesus' agreeing that He was the Messiah, the Son of God. Notice the reactions to Jesus' claim. Peter, on the other hand, denied identification with Jesus. See especially Luke's account of Jesus' response to Peter's denial.

> *We are called to stand with Jesus before a mocking world, "bearing His disgrace" (see Heb. 13:13). Will you do that today?*

DAY 2 Matthew 27:1-31; Mark 15:1-20; Luke 23:1-25; John 18:28–19:16

In today's reading Jesus was handed over to Pilate and mocked by the military. Watch for parts of the story that are unique to each of the Gospel writers. For instance, Matthew includes Judas's fate, and Luke includes Jesus' appearance before King Herod. John shares more dialogue between Jesus and Pilate than the other Gospels.

It helps to understand some of the Roman political structure. The Romans ruled their provinces (think of a state in America today) through either professional Roman politicians or local kings, puppet rulers appointed by the Romans. Pilate served as the governor of Judea and Samaria, and Herod was the king over Galilee. They were to collect taxes, render judgments, and keep the peace (prevent riots and insurrection). The Sanhedrin, on the other hand, was a religious and political body of Jewish rulers who served under Pilate. Yet the Sanhedrin could bypass Pilate and go directly to Caesar if they thought he was not ruling well. So politics was a delicate balancing act in Palestine. Notice the irony that the Sanhedrin, rebelling against God's Messiah and handing Him over to be murdered, asked for the release of an insurrectionist and murderer. Jesus was beaten in preparation for crucifixion and mercilessly mocked by a cohort of soldiers (about six hundred men). Such a beating was brutal and sometimes resulted in death through loss of blood.

Thank Jesus for His courage and willingness to endure humiliation.

TIMELINE
New Testament Timeline: write *Pilate* on line 2 in act 3, scene 3.

DAY 3 Matthew 27:32-66; Mark 15:21-47; Luke 23:26-56; John 19:17-42; Psalm 22

Crucifixion was a means of brutal execution designed to bring about prolonged torture and shame. As you read the accounts of Jesus' crucifixion, watch for the fulfillment of Scripture. Take note of the various characters that surround the story: not only Jesus' disciples but also curious bystanders, the criminals crucified with Him (one of whom came to a point of repentance, according to Luke), the chief priests, women who had followed Jesus from Galilee, and Roman soldiers.

In crucifixion no vital organs were damaged, and sometimes a person could linger for a few days. The legs of crucified criminals were broken to speed death, since the bodies needed to be taken down before the Sabbath started at sundown.

Jesus chose the moment of His death. The phenomena that surrounded Jesus' death also bore witness that this was no ordinary man. Carefully read Jesus' statements from the cross. Joseph of Arimathea took responsibility for Jesus' body, placing it in a new tomb.

As you read Psalm 22, note the prophecies fulfilled on the day of Jesus' crucifixion. Read 22:27-31 in light of Christ's lordship and the advance of the gospel in the world.

Do you grasp the extent to which God went to provide for our salvation?
Worship Christ, who paid such a high price for us.

DAY 4 Matthew 28; Mark 16; Luke 24; John 20–21

The crucifixion of Jesus and His resurrection from the dead in A.D. 30 are the climactic events of the Gospels. In the crucifixion Jesus died to provide forgiveness of sins and to establish the new covenant. By the resurrection God showed that Jesus was really the Messiah (see Acts 2:36) and demonstrated His power over death. The event says much about the value God places on the physical creation: He will reclaim and transform our bodies rather than just disposing of them. The resurrection also foreshadows a believer's resurrection from the dead (see 1 Cor. 15). Watch for hints about the nature of Jesus' resurrection body.

Each Gospel writer told the story in his own way. The writers at points focused on certain elements for emphasis or dramatic effect. For instance, John focused on Mary alone at the tomb; Matthew and Mark each telescoped the story at the tomb, focusing on one angel rather than the two reported in Luke and John. Luke telescoped the events, leaving out any mention of trips to Galilee. The events surrounding the resurrection are difficult to harmonize because the Gospel writers focused on various aspects of the story for their own purposes. Yet together they gave a powerful witness to the fact that, against all expectations of the disciples, Jesus was raised from the dead, appeared to numerous people at various places and times, and commissioned them with His agenda for the world.

What does the resurrection mean for your salvation? Celebrate the resurrection today.

SCENE 4: CHRIST'S CHURCH: GOD'S PEOPLE ADVANCE THE KINGDOM

DAY 5 Acts 1–4; Psalm 110

Today we transition to act 3, scene 4. Notice that in Acts, which Luke authored as a second volume to continue the story of his Gospel, the Kingdom went forward in the hearts of people as they responded to the good news about Jesus. Watch for several themes that will stay with us throughout Acts. The apostles were witnesses to the historical events surrounding Jesus, which culminated in the resurrection and exaltation. They bore witness to the events as they preached the good news of salvation.

Acts could be titled "The Continuing Acts of Jesus by the Holy Spirit Through the Church," for now the role of the Spirit became key. At Pentecost the Spirit was poured out, cleansing from sin and filling the believers with power. As you read, notice the continued crises and conflict with the same Sanhedrin that crucified Jesus. But now the church rapidly expanded as God gave the believers boldness and miraculous works.

These events constituted the fulfillment of prophecy. Psalm 110:1 is the Old Testament verse most frequently quoted and alluded to in the New Testament. The earliest believers understood this passage to be a fulfilled prophecy of Jesus' exaltation to His position as the Ruler of all things. His enemies will all be subjugated at the second coming of Christ. In the meantime sinners can become His brothers and sisters.

God's Messiah now reigns as Lord. Is He the Lord of your life? Worship Him today.

TIMELINE

New Testament Timeline: write *Holy Spirit* on line I in act 3, scene 4.

DAY 6 Acts 5–8

As you read Acts, watch for Luke's summaries, like the one we saw at the end of chapter 4 yesterday. Also watch for the following pattern. A series of crises, such as the incident with Ananias and Sapphira (see Acts 5:1-11), emphasized the need for purity in the church. Crises were normally followed by God's working powerfully and the further expansion of the church. Such expansion, in turn, was often followed by a reaction, such as when the rulers reacted to the apostles' power and witness (see Acts 5:17-21,33-39).

Notice in Stephen's speech in Acts 7 that this godly man addressed the land and circumcision as foundational for the Jewish people. However, the balance of the speech focused a great deal on Moses and the parallels between his ministry and the ministry of Jesus. Stephen compared the religious leaders accusing him to the rebellious wanderers of the wilderness who rejected Moses. The result of Stephen's martyrdom was further expansion. In Acts 8 we see expansion across racial barriers (with the Samaritans) and across geographical barriers as the Ethiopian (from the Cushite people) took the good news back to northern Africa.

How do you see the Kingdom expanding through your life and church?

SMALL-GROUP DISCUSSION QUESTIONS

1. What was the source of Jesus' anguish in the garden of Gethsemane? How was spiritual warfare being waged in this scene? What does it require for believers to genuinely pray for God's will instead of ours?

2. Why did Peter deny knowing Jesus? In what ways have you denied Jesus? How was your relationship with Him restored?

3. In what ways did Jesus suffer at the hands of the Roman authorities? On the cross?

4. Why did Pilate agree to crucify Jesus even though he didn't find grounds for doing so? Why did Jesus willingly submit to crucifixion (see John 19:11)?

5. Identify the words Jesus said from the cross. How did they point to His identity and His redemptive work?

6. Discuss evidence of Jesus' resurrection. How did Jesus' resurrection proclaim His victory over sin and death? How does it give us hope for our resurrection as believers?

7. What instructions did Jesus give to His followers in Matthew 28:19-20? How effective is your church in making disciples? How effective are you?

8. Read Acts 1:6, which reflects the disciples' narrow view of the Kingdom at this point. What are some ways our view of the Kingdom might be too narrow? Read Acts 1:8. What kind of vision is needed to bring salvation to all nations? What are some ways we get distracted from that mission?

9. Read Acts 1:14. Have you ever experienced this kind of desperate, united prayer? Why is this experience so foreign to us in today's churches? What would it take to cultivate this kind of prayer in your life, family, and church?

10. Read Acts 2:1-13. Describe the coming of the Holy Spirit. Why do churches today try to fulfill their missions apart from the power of the Spirit? What do we rely on instead?

11. Read Acts 2:14-40. How do you explain Peter's boldness? What were the emphases in his message? Is this your approach to sharing the gospel? Peter preached judgment before he preached salvation. Do churches today place a proper emphasis on God's judgment? Why or why not?

12. Read Acts 2:41-47. What were the characteristics of this early community of believers? To what practices did the early church devote itself? How does your church carry out these tasks? Should it be more intentional about doing so?

13. How did Peter and John respond to the Sanhedrin when they were ordered to stop preaching in the name of Jesus (see Acts 4:19-20)? What would happen if all believers were this impassioned and bold? Why aren't we?

14. What did Stephen confront the Pharisees about in his speech? Why did the gospel spread more rapidly after Stephen's martyrdom? How does persecution fan the flames of the gospel today?

WEEK 46

This week we will continue our exciting trek through the Book of Acts. We will witness how God continued to surprise the earliest Christians by doing the unexpected. He converted an archenemy of the movement and brought salvation to those who were not Jewish. We will also witness the continuing expansion of Christianity, with the first and second missionary trips of Paul. The church moved across Asia Minor and into what we know today as Europe.

As the gospel moved forward, the churches experienced struggles and theological questions, prompting the apostles to address difficult issues through letters. James and Galatians, for example, addressed the question of faith and work from different vantage points because they were dealing with different problems. James spoke to those who claimed to be Christians but did not grasp that real faith manifests in righteous works. In Galatians, on the other hand, Paul castigated those who suggested that circumcision was necessary for salvation. For Paul, faith alone in Christ alone establishes a relationship with God. This topic would also be central to the Jerusalem Council, recounted in Acts 15. Notice the way the church arrived at a decision in that council. This week imagine both the excitement and the frustrations the earliest Christians must have experienced.

DAY 1 Acts 9–11

We continue today with very significant events outside Jerusalem as the church continued to expand, the gospel breaking down barriers in unexpected ways. Watch for the elements of surprise in these stories as God did the unexpected through the gospel. Paul, as well as the Christians he encountered, was caught completely off guard by his encounter with Christ on the road to Damascus (A.D. 33 or 34).

Peter and the church were shocked that God would save Gentiles (see Acts 10–11). Notice in Acts 10 the sequence of miraculous occurrences one after the other. It is as if God were saying to Peter, "You can't miss this. Salvation is for the Gentiles too!" To this point the Jews thought the Messiah had come only for the Jewish people. That He had come for Gentiles too was so unexpected that Peter had to defend his baptism of Cornelius and his household before those in Jerusalem who stressed circumcision. Yet the conclusion was clear: the baptism of the Spirit, the entrance and cleansing of the Spirit at conversion, had come to Gentiles who had repented. God had cleansed them from sin and had given them spiritual life (see Acts 11:15-18). It is still amazing when this happens.

How have you been surprised lately by the work of the Spirit through the gospel?

TIMELINE

New Testament Timeline: write *Peter* on line 2 and *Paul* on line 3 in act 3, scene 4.

DAY 2 Acts 12–14

At the end of yesterday's reading we were introduced to the multiethnic church in Antioch in Syria (north of Palestine), where believers were first called Christians. That church would be very important as a missions-sending center. In the reading today Peter was miraculously released from prison, and King Herod was judged by God.

Acts 13–14 focuses on the first major missionary trip (A.D. 47–48), when God sent Paul and Barnabas to the island of Cyprus, the home area of Barnabas, and to a region we refer to as south Galatia, just west of Paul's home, Tarsus, in Asia Minor. Notice the mix of reactions to the missionary work. Miracles, mistaken identities, and mean-spirited opposition mixed in fairly equal measures, moving the story along. The big news here is that lots of Gentiles came to faith in Christ. Churches were planted in a context of persecution. The kingdom of God was expanding outward across the Mediterranean world, tracking especially with the mission of Paul.

> *Pray for Christian missionaries today, who carry the gospel and plant churches in contexts of persecution around the world.*

DAY 3 James 1–5

Because of its practical teaching and orientation to wisdom, some have called James the Proverbs of the New Testament. James was probably writing to a number of Jewish-Christian churches in Palestine as early as the mid-40s A.D. He seemed to have Leviticus 19 as a backdrop, as well as the teachings of his half-brother, the Lord Jesus. James was concerned about how we as believers respond to trials in life, and for James, righteous wisdom means living decisively according to God's will, which is revealed in God's Word. Doubters are "like the surging sea" (Jas. 1:6); they cannot make up their minds as to whether they will follow God wholeheartedly. In fact, to have head knowledge about God is worthless apart from being a doer of the Word. Even demons know God exists. Real religion involves practical actions like caring for the poor and vulnerable and controlling the tongue. It also involves right relationships in the church. Such actions are manifestations of real faith.

> *As you read this practical book, allow the words to penetrate your heart, pinpointing areas that need attention.*

DAY 4 Galatians 1–3

As we saw yesterday, James dealt in part with a problem group that thought once they professed Christ, they didn't need to do any good works. Paul, in his letter to the Galatians, addressed those who sought to establish relationships with Christ by works of the law, especially circumcision. After Paul and Barnabas left the churches of south Galatia, false teachers came and taught that to be saved, a person needed to have faith in Christ but also to be circumcised. In no uncertain terms Paul called this a false gospel. He shared the story of how he received the true gospel and then used the story of his confrontation of Peter as a launching point to proclaim faith in Christ alone as the means to salvation. As you read these first three chapters of the book, notice the emphasis on faith and the contrast between faith and law. Paul pointed to God's covenant with Abraham, which came long before the law, as foundational to his understanding of a relationship with God through Christ.

Do you have a clear understanding of the relationship between faith and law?

DAY 5 Galatians 4–6

In the remainder of Galatians, Paul continued to point out the contrasts between the true gospel and the false teaching offered the Galatians by the intruders who had led them astray. As you read today, observe contrasts between sound and false ministry, between the flesh and the Spirit, and between freedom and slavery. Also notice the nuances of Paul's arguments and appeals to the Galatians. Finally, notice that right thinking lays the foundation for right living. Theology is foundational for a Christian life.

How is the fruit of the Spirit being manifested in your life today?

How strong is the root of right theology in your life and in your church?

DAY 6 Acts 15–16

Acts 15 narrates one of the greatest turning points in the history of the church (A.D. 49). It started with those in Antioch, who taught that a person had to be circumcised in order to be saved (see 15:1). Paul and Barnabas argued against this claim and, with others from the church, were sent to Jerusalem to discuss the matter with the apostles and elders there. As you read, notice the various aspects of the discussion. Peter shared about the conversion of Cornelius (a Gentile) and his household, and Paul and Barnabas recounted the great works God had done among the Gentiles. James added passages from Amos and Isaiah, which pointed to God's heart and vision for the Gentiles. The decision of the Jerusalem Council was a resounding yes to the Gentiles and a no to those who wanted to impose Jewish religious rituals on them.

Acts 16 records the beginning of Paul's second mission trip (A.D. 49–51 or 52), as the apostle traveled back through Asia Minor and into Macedonia. As you read about the journeys, it will help if you have a map handy (probably labeled "Paul's Missionary Journeys" at the back of your Bible). Notice that Paul usually went to the Jewish synagogue first—those with whom he had things in common—and then preached to the Gentiles. As he planted churches, he faced persecution along the way.

What religious rituals today can hinder the advance of the gospel?

How does the gospel cross barriers today?

SMALL-GROUP DISCUSSION QUESTIONS

1. In Acts 9:15 what did Jesus identify as His purpose for Paul's life? Why was Paul's conversion such a remarkable event? Have you ever known or heard of someone whose life was radically changed by the gospel? Share this experience.

2. In Acts 10 why was it hard for the Jewish believers to accept the fact that the gospel was also for Gentiles? How did this realization change the course of redemptive history?

3. Trace the spread of the gospel, according to Acts 11:19. The primary objective of the early church was to make the gospel known for the glory of God. Is your church's primary objective to make the gospel known among the people around you? How is your church putting your strength and time into that purpose?

4. How was Paul opposed in Acts 13–14? What successes did he experience in spreading the gospel? Do you encounter mixed reactions when you witness? Is this a reason to be concerned? Why or why not?

5. In the Book of James how did James instruct the early believers to respond to trials (see 1:2-4,12)? Is that the way you respond? Why or why not? What do trials produce in believers who submit them to God?

6. What does it mean to be a doer of the Word (see Jas. 1:22)? How can we do a better job of obeying God's Word? What did James mean when he said faith without works is dead? How do works demonstrate our Christian faith?

7. What misunderstanding was Paul addressing in the Book of Galatians? What did Paul identify as the only way to be saved (see 2:16)? Read Galatians 3:19-24. What is the relationship between faith and law? What is the role of the law in a believer's life today?

8. How did Paul contrast the works of the flesh and the fruit of the Spirit in Galatians 5? Identify the fruit of the Spirit in Galatians 5:22-23. Name persons you know who demonstrate each fruit. How can believers live by the Spirit?

9. In Acts 15 what was the crisis that led to the Jerusalem Council? What was the outcome of this meeting? Identify ways the crisis of Acts 15 parallels Paul's teaching in the Book of Galatians.

10. Where did Paul travel in Acts 16 on his second missionary journey? What mixture of opposition and progress do you observe? How do you see the Holy Spirit at work in Paul's ministry?

11. Pray for the lost persons in your life. Pray that God would make Christ known through the members of your group.

WEEK 47

This week as we continue with act 3, scene 4, we will finish Paul's second missionary journey and transition to the third. Continue to watch for the dynamics surrounding the advance of the gospel across the Mediterranean world. Follow a map at the back of your Bible as you walk with Paul through his mission trips.

This week we will also read Paul's letters to the Thessalonians, which he wrote shortly after founding the congregation in Thessalonica, and we will begin reading 1 Corinthians, written from Ephesus on his third journey. As you read the letters of the New Testament, it will help to have a study Bible or a Bible dictionary. Free online resources are available at *www.mystudybible.com*. Read an introductory article on each letter to get a basic orientation to what is going on.

Recognize that these wonderful letters were written directly to Christians about what it means to live as followers of Christ in the world. We can be encouraged even through their struggles, and we can be grounded by the theology in these books, even as we are exhorted about our behavior. Continually ask yourself, *How will I live differently this week as a result of reading these letters?*

DAY 1 Acts 17:1–18:18

Paul's second missionary journey (A.D. 50–52) continues today. Notice again Paul's pattern of ministry, as well as the combination of success and opposition. Churches were planted, but the mission continued to be opposed. Also watch for the unique dynamics in the various communities in which Paul preached. The Bereans were wonderfully open to search the Scriptures, while the Athenians lived in a context of intellectual arrogance.

Paul spent a lengthy time in Corinth (18 months), the largest city in Greece and a cosmopolitan economic center of commerce. Notice again that the gospel advanced the Kingdom in the hearts of people while drawing a good deal of opposition.

Why do you think this kind of conflict results from the preaching of salvation?

Where do you see conflict over the gospel today?

DAY 2 I Thessalonians I–5

Paul wrote his first letter to the Thessalonians from Corinth while on his second missionary trip (about A.D. 50; see Acts 17:1-9). The city was the capital of the province and a major seaport, as well as a main stop on the *Via Egnatia*, a Roman highway stretching about seven hundred miles from the Adriatic Sea to the city of Byzantium near the Black Sea. The apostle had to leave Thessalonica shortly after establishing the church in that city.

As you read, you will pick up on struggles that church members were having, as well as theological questions. Understand that this was a church of new Christians, many of whom had come from a pagan background (see 1 Thess. 1:9). For instance, it seems they were experiencing continued persecution and had questions about the second coming of Christ. They needed encouragement to live pure lives. Yet they were standing for the Lord and had a strong witness among the churches of the Mediterranean world. Watch for notes of encouragement, instruction, and thanksgiving in this letter.

How does 1 Thessalonians give you encouragement for living the Christian life?

DAY 3 2 Thessalonians I–3

Second Thessalonians continued Paul's correspondence to the young congregation. Paul offered encouragement and instructed them about the coming of the Lord and about appropriate behavior in their community. There are intriguing passages here. For instance, someone seems to have spoken in Paul's name, proclaiming that the Day of the Lord, Jesus' second coming, had already taken place (see 2 Thess. 2:1-2). Paul told the Thessalonians this was not the case and went on to instruct them about Jesus' coming. Paul was clear that believers should stand firm in sound teaching as we await the Lord's coming. Paul also taught that believers should live responsibly, providing for their needs by working.

How do you view work today? Do you see it as a basic component of Christian discipleship?

DAY 4 Acts 18:19–19:41

Today we transition from the second to the third missionary journey of Paul (A.D. 53–57). At the end of the second trip, the apostle briefly visited Ephesus, foreshadowing where he would focus his mission in Asia during the third missionary trip. When Paul went back to Ephesus, having traveled back through the Galatian region, he had a very fruitful ministry there for a period of about 2½ years (see Acts 19:8-9), so that "all the inhabitants of Asia, both Jews and Greeks, heard the message about the Lord" (19:10). As you read about the success of Paul's ministry and the crisis that arose from it, keep the following facts in mind.

1. As the gospel moved into new territory, God powerfully demonstrated the truth of the gospel by the miraculous. Asia Minor was permeated with cultic, pagan practices, and the gospel confronted this superstitious orientation head-on. God directly bore witness to the truth of the gospel, so He is the real hero of the story.
2. The gospel brought about conflict.

What relational turbulence do you see around you that results from the gospel's confronting a different view of the world?

DAY 5 | 1 Corinthians 1–4

Paul wrote 1 Corinthians in about A.D. 54 while in Ephesus on his third missionary journey. He wrote to respond to a letter he had received from the Corinthians (see 1 Cor. 7:1) and to reports from some in that congregation (see 1:11; 5:1). In the letter he dealt with numerous problems and questions about the behavior of believers in the Corinthian church. In these first four chapters of the book, we see the church as horribly divided, in part due to a faulty understanding of spirituality and a deficient view of the gospel.

How does a right view of the gospel aid in building church unity?

DAY 6 | 1 Corinthians 5–8

In 1 Corinthians 5–6 the apostle continued to address troubling information he had received through reports about the situation in Corinth. He dealt with incest (see 5:1-13), Christians who took each other to pagan courts (see 6:1-11), and encounters with prostitutes (see 6:12-20). It will help to have a study Bible handy as you read these sections so that you can understand the cultural backdrop, as well as the detailed, logical development of Paul's arguments. Free online resources are available at www.mystudybible.com.

In chapter 7 Paul began to address issues about which the Corinthians had written him, and he started with the question of whether it was appropriate for believers to marry. Evidently, some in the congregation argued that young women who were betrothed to be married should not marry. Paul argued that singleness can be a good gift for some, but God gives many the gift of marriage.

First Corinthians 8 is the first of a couple of passages in which Paul addressed the topic of idolatry. Here he answered the Corinthians' question about whether it is appropriate to eat food that had been offered to an idol.

Although you may not struggle with the worship of pagan idols, many principles in this passage are very relevant for us today. Which of these principles strike you as powerfully relevant for your life at this time?

SMALL-GROUP DISCUSSION QUESTIONS

1. In Acts 17–18 how did Athens resemble today's culture? How did Paul customize his message to the Athenian philosophers? How do you see Christianity conflicting with philosophies today? How can churches more effectively engage erroneous worldviews?

2. How was Paul's treatment of the Day of the Lord in 1 Thessalonians 4–5 similar to the descriptions you read in the Prophets? How was it different? What role will Jesus play on the Day of the Lord? How did Paul instruct the believers to prepare for that time? What attitude should believers have toward the coming judgment?

3. What emotions do you typically have about the second coming of Christ? What scriptural teachings give you confidence about that day? When we realize that judgment is getting closer, how should we approach our task of sharing the gospel with the lost?

4. What was Paul's instruction in 1 Thessalonians 5:16? Why do believers have trouble obeying this teaching?

5. Paul warned that "the mystery of lawlessness is already at work" (2 Thess. 2:7). How do you see this spirit at work in your society? How does verse 8 put Satan's efforts in perspective?

6. Paul's third missionary journey began in Acts 18:23. Where did he travel? What conflict arose in Asia in Acts 19? How does Christianity cause conflict today when our values run counter to the interests of the world?

7. What issues were dividing the Corinthian church in 1 Corinthians 1–4? Why do you think Paul mentioned the cross of Christ so many times in chapter 1? How do Paul's words in 1 Corinthians 3:11 address the issue of factions in the church? How is Christ's headship of the body of Christ honored in your church? How does this recognition bring unity?

8. What moral problems did Paul identify in 1 Corinthians 6:7-10? Why were these unacceptable for the body of Christ? To what extent do these issues cause problems in today's churches? How do they affect our ability to represent Christ in the world?

9. What issues today compare to the issue of food offered to idols in Paul's day (see 1 Cor. 8)? In what ways might we need to set boundaries for our behavior in order to influence lost people for Christ?

WEEK 48

Continuing in act 3, scene 4 of the Bible's story this week, we will complete 1 Corinthians and then read 2 Corinthians. This is some of the richest material in all of Paul's writings but also some of the most difficult material to interpret. Use good reference tools to help, including a study Bible and a good commentary. Free online tools are available at *www.mystudybible.com*. Some of the concepts here might seem foreign to you, but read carefully to understand the nuances of Paul's arguments.

As you read 1 Corinthians 15, watch for the analogies Paul used to describe the nature of the resurrection body.

Second Corinthians was written during a very difficult time of ministry for Paul, when he was traveling from Ephesus back to Corinth in about A.D. 56. Tune in to his description of authentic Christian ministry.

DAY 1 | Corinthians 9–11

Paul's letters to the Corinthians indicate that Paul had a rocky relationship with this congregation, and 1 Corinthians 9 reflects that tension. As you read, can you pick up on the criticisms some were leveling against Paul?

In 1 Corinthians 10 Paul reintroduced the topic of idolatry and the balance between Christian freedom, based on right theology, and Christian responsibility for the way our actions affect others.

Chapter 11 begins a section in which Paul dealt with several issues surrounding worship. The apostle discussed head coverings and the Lord's Supper. Scholars disagree about what head covering means, whether it was a veil or the woman's hairstyle. But from a cultural standpoint a woman's wearing her hair down or shaving her head sent clear signals. Married women wore their hair up, and single women wore their hair loose and flowing. In a Jewish context free-flowing hair could be a sign that the woman was suspected of adultery. Short hair could indicate that a woman had been convicted of adultery. So Paul seemed concerned about signals sent.

The Lord's Supper was often taken in the context of home meals. Some people were treating the Lord's Supper and other believers insensitively. Read with an eye to that issue.

What are some modern equivalents of the head-covering issue you read about today? Are there areas of worship that Christians might treat with insensitivity?

DAY 2 | Corinthians 12–14

Today we continue with issues related to worship services. Some of the Corinthians were suggesting that everyone should exercise the gift of languages. Paul said this reflects a misunderstanding of the body of Christ, which has variously gifted parts. The supernatural ability to speak in other languages is a gift, but it is of lesser importance and must be kept in perspective and under control. The use of the gifts must be done in love (see 1 Cor. 13), which is the key characteristic of authentic Christianity. In addition, gifts should be exercised in light of their effect on others. Thus, gifts that edify others in the church are more important than other gifts. Paul was especially concerned that worship services be orderly to build up others in the faith.

What is your spiritual gift or gifts?

How are you exercising the abilities God has given you to build up others in the body of Christ?

DAY 3 | Corinthians 15–16

As Paul wrapped up 1 Corinthians, he gave us our richest, most extensive theological reflection on resurrection. As you read, notice several things.

1. Paul appealed to Jesus' resurrection as the basis for his teaching. Broader Judaism in the first century had no explanations of the nature of the resurrection body. But Paul provided that, for the first witnesses had seen Jesus in His resurrection body and had talked to Him.
2. Paul appealed to the historical reality of the resurrection, suggesting that the historicity of Jesus' resurrection was vital to the Christian movement.
3. Notice the hope reflected in this passage. Believers have much to look forward to. This hope gives us a basis for enduring now (see 1 Cor. 15:58).
4. In chapter 16 look for clues about Paul's ministry and dynamics in the early church.

Think about the reality of Jesus' resurrection. In what ways does it give you hope?

DAY 4 2 Corinthians 1–4

None of Paul's letters express the apostle's heart more openly than 2 Corinthians, which the apostle wrote during a very difficult time of ministry. In this letter, written in about A.D. 56 while Paul was traveling from Ephesus back to Corinth, he vied for the affections of this congregation. False teachers had come in and distracted the believers from the true gospel.

Paul seemed emotionally and spiritually bruised, but from his struggle we have a profound reflection on the nature of authentic Christian ministry.

Read 2 Corinthians 1:1–2:13 as the opening of the letter, looking for clues about the situation behind the letter and criticisms that had been leveled at the apostle. Second Corinthians 2:14-17 introduces the great central section of the book on authentic ministry.

How do Paul's reflections affect your understanding of your ministry as a Christian?

DAY 5 2 Corinthians 5–9

Continue to reflect today on the nature of authentic Christian ministry. Notice how Paul appealed to the Corinthians to separate from those who would hurt them spiritually. Also notice that authentic Christian ministry involves suffering. This is normal for the Christian life that is lived for the advancement of the gospel.

In 2 Corinthians 7:5 Paul picked up where he left off at 2:13 in describing his travels.

Second Corinthians 8–9 offers rich, deep reflections on the nature of Christian giving.

What are some expressions of sacrificial generosity in your life?

DAY 6 2 Corinthians 10–13

Paul concluded the book by writing about the false teachers who had infiltrated the Corinthian church. His words were harsh because much was at stake. Although many in this church had responded well to the exhortations of a previous letter—one that has not come down to us—in which the apostle had rebuked them (see 2 Cor. 2:4), a strong pocket of resistance still existed. Notice the various dynamics to which the apostle appealed as he set himself against these false teachers. Watch especially for what Paul understood to be the role of weakness in a powerful ministry.

Do you know true and false ministers today? How do you distinguish between them?

SMALL-GROUP DISCUSSION QUESTIONS

1. Read 1 Corinthians 9:12. Is there something you need to endure to gain the opportunity to witness to someone?

2. Read 1 Corinthians 9:19-23. In what practical ways can you and your church become all things to all people? How would this enable you to relate to lost people and share the gospel with them?

3. What instruction did Paul provide in 1 Corinthians 11:27-34 for taking the Lord's Supper? Give examples of taking it in an unworthy way today. How can we avoid doing so?

4. Read 1 Corinthians 12. Discuss the purpose of spiritual gifts, examples of gifts, and how gifts work together in the body of Christ. What is your gift? How are you using it?

5. In 1 Corinthians 13 why did Paul say love is superior to spiritual gifts? Identify someone who demonstrates the fruit of love.

6. Read 1 Corinthians 15. Why is Jesus' resurrection vital to the Christian faith? How is it related to a believer's resurrection? In what ways do you find chapter 15 encouraging?

7. What insights from Paul's ministry, found in 2 Corinthians 1:1-11, can be applied to all believers and to the church's ministry to people who need comfort? How does suffering equip us for effective ministry to others?

8. Read 2 Corinthians 3:18. What is the goal of the Christian life? How is this accomplished?

9. Read 2 Corinthians 4:10. What did Paul mean by these words? Why is suffering a necessary part of Christian ministry? How have you experienced this truth?

10. Read the profound truths in 2 Corinthians 5:14-21. Does Christ's love compel you to share Jesus? How are you and your church living as ambassadors for Christ?

11. How did Paul characterize the giving of the Macedonian churches in 2 Corinthians 8–9? Could your church be described that way?

12. Read 2 Corinthians 10:3-5. In what ways do you see spiritual warfare in your world? How do believers wage spiritual warfare?

13. What did Paul's thorn teach him (see 2 Cor. 12:7-10)? How have trials in your life taught you to rely on God's strength?

WEEK 49

This week we will continue in act 3, scene 4, "Christ's Church: God's People Advance the Kingdom." Our readings will take us through the wonderful Book of Romans, and in Acts we will follow Paul's ministry from the end of the third missionary journey through his defense before the governor, Festus, and King Agrippa II.

As you read Romans, follow the nuances of Paul's argument. Pay careful attention to what he said about the Spirit, the law, sin, righteousness, justification, grace, and faith. From chapter 12 to the end, meditate on the practical instructions Paul gave the church in Rome and carefully think about how you should apply the Word to your life.

As we continue in Acts, notice the dynamics that were going on surrounding Paul's ministry. He seemed to be heading for trouble but had a strong sense that God wanted him to go back to Jerusalem. He met trouble there, but God delivered him from very violent opposition. As you read, recognize the various groups around Paul: traveling companions, believers he met along the way, the Christian community in Jerusalem, Jewish opponents from across the Mediterranean world, Jewish leaders in Jerusalem, and various Roman authorities. What is God saying to you through this portion of Acts? How does this history instruct you about the Christian life and God's agenda for the world?

DAY 1 Acts 20:1-3; Romans 1–4

During his three months in Corinth, toward the end of the third missionary journey, Paul wrote the Book of Romans. Having never visited that church and seeing that he would be delayed in coming to them, he wanted to send them a summary of the gospel and basic teachings on the Christian life. After an introduction (see Rom. 1:1-17), in which he presented the letter's main topic (see 1:16-17), Paul laid the foundation of the letter in 1:18–3:20, showing that all people are enslaved and condemned by their sin. Whether pagans who give no attention to the one true God or religious persons whose self-righteousness keeps them from God, all are locked in sin's power. This section culminates with a string of Old Testament texts reinforcing that all people have a sin problem (see Rom. 3:9-20). At 3:21, however, the apostle turned to the solution to this devastating problem: God, in His grace, provided a way for people to be declared righteous. The key is faith, as Paul argued in Romans 4.

Do you depend on your own righteousness for a right relationship with God? There is a better way, the way of faith in Christ.

DAY 2 Romans 5–8

Continue to notice the emphasis on a life lived by faith, set against a life lived by works of the law. Romans 5:1-11 wraps up the section on the triumph of faith, proclaiming that those who are declared righteous by faith are in right relationship with God. In Romans 5:12–7:25 Paul treated the universal reach of the righteousness offered through Christ (see 5:12-21), spoke of a Christian's relationship to sin and the law (see 6:1–7:3), and declared the futility of a religious life apart from the life-giving Spirit (see 7:7-25). So the law of God is set against the law, or dynamic, of sin in a person's life. In chapter 8 the apostle turned to the real law by which a believer must live: the law of the Spirit. Take your time in chapter 8. Savor all it says God has done for us in Christ, by the work of the Spirit.

Praise God for your relationship with Him through salvation in Christ and the work of the indwelling Spirit.

DAY 3 Romans 9–12

In Romans 9–11 we hear Paul's deep burden for the Jewish people. Watch for the theme of God's faithfulness to work according to His promise, as contrasted with the unfaithfulness of many Israelites from the Old Testament era to Paul's day. Paul began with a lament (a heartfelt cry) about the current spiritual condition of his fellow Jews (see Rom. 9:1-5). In Romans 9:6-29 he extolled God's faithfulness to His promise. God shows mercy to children of the promise who come to Him by faith rather than to those who approach Him on the basis of religious works.

In Romans 9:30–10:21 Paul turned to the unfaithfulness of Israel, who to a great extent had rejected the gospel. Finally, in Romans 11:1-32 Paul explained that a remnant of Israel (recall that theme in the Prophets) had been saved through the gospel. He pointed to a time when the Jewish people would turn to the gospel. Having laid out his theology of God's gift of righteousness in the previous chapters, Paul then gave a series of exhortations in chapter 12, detailing how believers should live out God's righteousness.

Which of Paul's exhortations in Romans 12 is most pertinent for you today?

DAY 4 Romans 13–16

Paul often began his letters with a theological foundation and then moved to practical exhortation. Yesterday in Romans 12 we encountered the beginning of a section offering practical exhortation. Today the practical encouragement continues as Paul dealt with a Christian's responsibility to the government (see Rom. 13:1-7), the primacy of love and the importance of holy living (see 13:8-14), caution against judgmental attitudes toward other believers (see 14:1-12), and a warning about causing others to stumble and the need to build others up (see 14:13–15:13).

To conclude the letter, the apostle reflected on his ministry (see Rom. 15:14-21); shared his travel plans (see 15:22-33); and offered encouragement, greetings, warnings, and a benediction of glory to God (see 16:1-27). Notice that Paul balanced encouragement with warning, weaving together Scripture and practical insights.

Choose one of Paul's practical exhortations to apply today or choose a theological point on which to meditate.

DAY 5 Acts 20:4–23:35

As you read the narrative of Paul's journeys in Acts, carefully track the characters and the cause-and-effect events. It will also help to keep a map handy (find a map of Paul's journeys at the back of your Bible or in a Bible dictionary; free online resources are available at www. mystudybible.com). As we rejoin Paul in the story today, he was wrapping up his third missionary journey and moving to the climactic events at the conclusion of Acts. In chapters 20–21 notice the elements that indicated life was about to change for Paul. As you read about the controversies that led to Paul's arrest, you will need to make a careful distinction between those in the Christian movement who were concerned about Paul's teaching (see Acts 21:17-25) and Jewish opponents of Paul from the broader Mediterranean world (see 21:26-29). Jewish zealots, in fact, threatened by Paul's effectiveness, bound themselves with an oath to kill the apostle. Paul's Roman citizenship and the role of the Roman military and government were important to the story as things progressed.

How does the reading today affect your perspective on the controversial nature of Christianity in the world?

DAY 6 Acts 24–26

Paul was in the custody of the Roman governor Felix in Caesarea. Roman historians describe Felix as a thug and a poor ruler. Paul remained in custody in Caesarea for two years. Felix, recalled to Rome by the emperor Nero, was replaced by Festus as governor. Festus was a much better ruler of Judea than Felix, but he died in office after about two years.

Intending to do the Jewish leaders a favor, Festus asked Paul whether he was willing to stand trial in Jerusalem. At this point Paul exercised his right as a Roman citizen to appeal to Caesar, a request to go to Rome to stand trial before the emperor himself, thwarting

Festus's intention to send him to Jerusalem. Before he was sent to Rome, however, Paul made a defense speech and shared his testimony before King Agrippa II, a puppet king of the Romans, who ruled over an area in the north and northwest of Palestine. As you read, notice Paul's passionate argument for the gospel, which he saw as both true and reasonable.

Paul shared the gospel with everyone he met, including powerful rulers.
How do you bear witness to your faith?

SMALL-GROUP DISCUSSION QUESTIONS

1. How does Romans 1 show the condition of natural humanity without God? How does this description remind you of the world today? What judgment is identified for all unrepentant people in Romans 2:5-12? Why is God's judgment the same for everyone? What groups today erroneously think they will not fall under God' judgment?

2. Read Romans 3:21-26. How can sinful people be made righteous in God's sight?

3. Read Romans 5:12-21. How did Jesus' blood make salvation available to everyone?

4. Read Romans 6:4-7. What is a believer's relationship to sin?

5. How is the law contrasted with life in the Spirit in Romans 7? If believers are dead to sin, why do we still sin?

6. Read Romans 8. How does the Holy Spirit enable us to overcome sin and live in God's power? Do you ask the Spirit to fill you with His character and power every day? How does it affect you to know that nothing can separate you from the love of Christ?

7. What hope did Paul offer the Jews in Romans 9–11? On what basis could they be grafted into God's kingdom again?

8. Read Romans 10:13. Who in your life needs to hear that message?

9. Read Romans 12:1-2. What does it mean to be a living sacrifice? How does this relate to life in the Spirit? How can we be transformed by the renewing of our minds?

10. In Romans 15:7 Paul said to accept one another. Why is this important? On what basis are we to accept others? Whom do you have difficulty accepting? Why?

11. Did you find yourself smiling at Paul's audacity in sharing his testimony with King Agrippa? How can believers today take an audacious stand for Christ?

WEEK 50

This week we follow Paul's harrowing journey to Rome, where he was imprisoned under house arrest for two years. While there, he ministered to those in Rome, both within and outside the church, and wrote letters. Four of the letters have come down to us as Philippians, Colossians, Philemon, and Ephesians. Tune in to the various concerns of each of these books and notice how Paul's imprisonment affected the themes.

Titus and I Timothy were written after Paul had been released from prison. Evidently, his first meeting with the emperor Nero went well. Both of these letters address the problem of false teaching in the church, but that emphasis is much stronger in I Timothy. Also, whereas Titus instructed the young minister about the establishment of churches on the island of Crete, I Timothy was written about leadership of the church in Ephesus, which had existed for a while and had been led by Paul for three years. There is much food for thought for the modern church in the books we will encounter this week.

DAY 1 Acts 27–28

Today we finish the amazing Book of Acts. Paul was sent to Rome by ship. Sailing was often a calculated risk, and we see two opposing dynamics in Acts 27: the desire of the captain and owner of the ship to get to their destination versus impending weather that could lead to disaster. Notice, however, that the storm and shipwreck gave Paul a platform for the gospel, as God miraculously worked through the apostle in a number of ways.

The storm and shipwreck are vivid narratives given to us by Luke, who was there (for example, *we* is used in Acts 27:29). Once in Italy, as Paul traveled to Rome, he met and was encouraged by fellow believers. There he was placed under house arrest but was given a good deal of freedom. Shared with Jewish leaders, his gospel brought a mixed response, and Paul saw this as another fulfillment of Isaiah 6:9-10. Acts ends with Paul's spending two years in Rome, boldly preaching the gospel.

Paul took every opportunity to share the gospel. What opportunities have you had this week?

DAY 2 Philippians 1–4

Paul wrote this letter from prison, probably when he was under house arrest in Rome in about A.D. 60. The church was only about a decade old, having been founded by Paul on his second missionary trip, and was experiencing both persecution and a struggle with unity. Epaphroditus, a minister from Philippi, had brought Paul the Philippians' monetary gift to help with the apostle's living expenses and had traveled back to Philippi with this letter. Watch for the following key themes.

1. Paul had great joy, even in the face of possible death, and he encouraged the Philippians to choose joy in the face of the persecution they were experiencing.
2. The Philippians needed to choose unity (see 1:27-28; 4:1-2) since some were struggling to walk together in peace.
3. There were good examples to follow as the believers chose joy and unity: Christ (see 2:5-11), ministers like Timothy and Epaphroditus (see 2:19-30), and Paul (see 3:1-21).

Who is an example of joy in your life?

In what do you need to choose joy today?

DAY 3 Philemon 1-25; Colossians 1–4

The letters to Philemon and the Colossians were sent at the same time (see Col. 4:9; Philem. 10), probably during Paul's imprisonment in Rome. Paul had never visited this church (see Col. 2:1), but he had met those from the church during his ministry in Asia.

The letter to Philemon, written to an individual and his household, concerned a runaway slave, Onesimus, who had become a believer in Christ through Paul's ministry. The message highlights the unity and forgiveness brought to relationships through the gospel.

Colossians was written to the church in the city of Colossae, a city located in the Lycus Valley and on a major crossroads 110 miles east of Ephesus. The Colossian believers lived in a culture permeated by superstition; religious influences emphasizing certain rules and rituals were skewing the theological perspective of many in the church. So Colossians is about growing in sound theology—right thinking about Christ and the gospel. Notice especially the apostle's emphasis on the supremacy of Christ.

Meditate on Colossians 1:15-20. How do religious and cultural currents seek to de-emphasize or negate the supremacy and glory of Christ?

DAY 4 Ephesians 1–4

Another book probably written from prison in Rome, Ephesians gives a strong word of encouragement about Christ's love for the church and His victory over the spiritual powers that oppose God and hurt people. The book seems to have originally been written to a group of churches in the area around Ephesus, the capital of Asia.

Notice the theme of blessing with which the book starts. We have much to celebrate as followers of Christ. God's powerful work in the gospel involves deliverance of people from sin and death, and He has broken down the walls that divide people racially and religiously (Jews and Gentiles), making them a new people who experience God's presence.

Watch for the powerful prayers in this book (see Eph. 1:15-19; 3:14-21) and let them express your prayers to God. In chapter 4 we find a beautiful picture of unity in the church and our purpose: the building up of the body of Christ in love and truth.

> *Read the practical instructions of Ephesians 4:25-32, asking how you might apply this truth to your life today.*

DAY 5 Ephesians 5–6; Titus 1–3

In chapters 5–6 of Ephesians you will find a good deal of practical teaching on the Christian life, and the book ends with an emphasis on spiritual warfare as we stand against the Devil.

Paul wrote Titus, sending the letter to his young protégé probably after his first imprisonment in Rome. Titus was in a ministry that needed much work. Part of his task was to establish churches and organize them around new leadership. So Paul dealt with the appointment of church elders and instructed Titus about false teaching. False teachers seem to have been an almost universal reality in the church of the first century, as they are in ours. The book also gives practical instruction for living rightly as believers, including appropriate behavior.

> *Read Ephesians 6:18 and use the verse as an encouragement to pray throughout this day.*

> *What emphases in Titus seem to be needed in your church at present?*

DAY 6 1 Timothy 1–6

Although much longer than Titus, 1 Timothy has a number of similarities to that book but also key differences. Written from Macedonia in about A.D. 62 after Paul's imprisonment in Rome, 1 Timothy addresses a young minister whom Paul had left behind in Ephesus. It seems that some of Paul's concerns, expressed in Acts 20:28-31, had been realized, false teachers having infiltrated the church. Watch for themes such as the true gospel, qualifications for a church leader, characteristics of false teaching and divisiveness, and right character for a leader. The book underscores the value of godly leadership.

> *Pray for and encourage your church's leaders today. Do something to express your love and appreciation for them.*

SMALL-GROUP DISCUSSION QUESTIONS

1. Read Philippians 1:12-13. How did God use Paul's imprisonment for His purposes? How has God used hardship in your life for His purposes?

2. How does Philippians 1:21 summarize Paul's life and ministry? How would you summarize your life purpose?

3. Read Philippians 2:1-5. How do you define *humility?* How important is humility in the life of a follower of Christ?

4. How is Jesus described in Philippians 2:6-8? How can believers follow Christ's example of servanthood and humility?

5. What does it mean to work out your salvation "with fear and trembling" (Phil. 2:12)? How does verse 13 shed light on this admonition?

6. Read Philippians 3:10-14. How is a believer conformed to Christ's death? How do we know the power of His resurrection and the fellowship of His sufferings? How are you pursuing the prize promised by your call in Christ Jesus?

7. Read Colossians 1:15-20. What is revealed about Jesus' identity? In what ways do you acknowledge that Jesus has first place in everything? In what ways does your church acknowledge that?

8. Read Colossians 3:5-14. What are characteristics of the old nature? How do we put these away? What are characteristics of the new nature? How do we put on the new self?

9. Read Ephesians 4:1-6. What are things that unite the body of Christ? What qualities did Paul want the Ephesian church to cultivate? How does your church display these qualities? How does it display unity in Christ?

10. What standard of Christian maturity is set forth in Ephesians 4:11-15? How do believers grow in the likeness of Christ? What does your church do to foster spiritual growth?

11. Read Ephesians 6:10-18. How does the Holy Spirit equip believers for spiritual warfare?

12. What characteristics does Titus 1 give for good leaders? Bad leaders? How do your church's leaders provide valuable leadership for your church?

13. Read 1 Timothy 6:3-6. Why is doctrine important for a believer and a church? What does your church do to teach biblical doctrine?

WEEK 51

First Peter, Hebrews, and 2 Timothy deal with suffering. First Peter was sent to struggling believers in northwest Asia Minor to give them perspective on their troubles. Christ is our role model. We need to stay focused on God, not on ourselves and our struggles.

Hebrews, on the other hand, was probably written to Roman Christians just as persecution against believers was heating up in the mid-60s of the first century. In this early Christian sermon the author challenged the believers to persevere in the faith by embracing a clearer picture of Jesus and the gospel. Theology lays the foundation for Christian living. Notice the emphases on Jesus' exaltation, on Jesus' high priesthood and the decisiveness of His sacrifice for sins, and on responding positively to God's Word.

When Paul wrote 2 Timothy, he was facing execution. He challenged Timothy to stay true to the gospel. Second Peter and Jude address the problem of false teachers in the church.

DAY 1 | 1 Peter 1–5

The letter of 1 Peter was from the apostle Peter in Rome to the churches in northwest Asia Minor (modern-day Turkey). This rich book was written down by Peter's secretary, Silvanus (see 5:12), probably in the mid-60s A.D. but perhaps much earlier. Notice especially three main themes in this book.

1. The believers in these far-flung provinces of the Roman Empire were being persecuted for their faith, and Peter wrote, in part, to put their suffering in perspective. Our rejection by the world follows the pattern of Christ's rejection. So we, as Christ followers, should understand what it means to suffer for His name. Suffering reminds us that this world is not our ultimate home; we are foreigners here.

2. In suffering, we as believers are to be profoundly God-centered, focusing on God, praying to Him, and understanding that He rewards those who suffer for doing what is right. Notice how often Peter referred to God, Christ, and the Holy Spirit.

3. Suffering is not an excuse for sin. We are to live holy lives, loving one another, for we are a holy nation. We, with Christ as the cornerstone, are being built into a spiritual house to live as God's people before the world. In chapters 3–4 Peter gave specific instructions for living well in the face of suffering of various kinds.

Are you suffering for the name of Christ?

Are you responding to suffering in the ways outlined by Peter?

DAY 2 Hebrews 1–4

Rather than a letter, Hebrews seems to have been crafted as an early Christian sermon, to which the author attached a letterlike ending (see 13:22-25) before sending it to this persecuted church. The book was probably written in the mid-60s A.D., just before an escalation of Nero's persecution against believers in Rome. It is a beautiful, powerful book that has much to say to the church today. Notice the focus on Jesus. In the first two chapters the author spoke of Jesus as compared to the angels. Having been exalted to the right hand of God after His resurrection, Jesus is at the highest position in the universe. Both in His person and work, no one can compare to Him (see 1:5-14). Yet He became human to die for us and to become both our High Priest and sin sacrifice (see 2:10-18).

Watch for shifts between passages that teach about Jesus and those that challenge listeners to action (see 2:1-4; 3:1-4). The latter build on the former.

Are you in awe of Jesus today? Does His greatness motivate you to action?

DAY 3 Hebrews 5–8

Hebrews 4:14-16, which we read yesterday, is the opening for the great central section of Hebrews (4:14–10:25) on the high priesthood and superior offering of Jesus. Hebrews 5:1-10; 7:1-28 deals with the appointment of Jesus as a superior High Priest. The argument is a bit difficult to follow at points, but identify specific reasons the author said Jesus is a superior Priest. Notice how much he focused on Psalm 110:4. Hebrews 5:11–6:20 presents us with another section of exhortation by which the author challenged the hearers with their need to respond to God's Word.

Hebrews 8:1-13 is somewhat transitional, turning to the topic of this superior Priest's superior new-covenant offering. As you read the twists and turns of the author's argument, focus on the parts that seem clearest to you. Perhaps use a good study Bible to investigate parts that seem obscure. Free online resources are available at www.mystudybible.com. Keep your focus on Jesus and what He has accomplished on our behalf.

Use Hebrews 8:7-13 to praise Jesus for the great blessings of the new covenant.

DAY 4 Hebrews 9–13

Hebrews 9:1–10:18 shows that Jesus' offering was superior because it involved His death (the shedding of His blood) rather than the deaths of animals, He took His offering into heaven, and His sacrifice had to be made only one time.

Hebrews 10:19-25 both rounds out the central section of the book on the superiority of Jesus' priesthood and launches a series of exhortations. Here we read positive and negative examples, warnings and promises, and straightforward words of encouragement and practical instruction. Chapter 11 is an example list of overwhelming evidence that faith is the right way to live for God. Faith is trust in God based on what He has revealed as true about Himself. The author challenged readers to trust God in the midst of their difficulties, to see who Jesus is and grasp the significance of what He had done on their behalf.

Do you really see who Jesus is? Is He the foundation for your life?

DAY 5 2 Timothy 1–4

The last of Paul's letters, 2 Timothy, was written in about A.D. 64, shortly before Paul was martyred for the faith. As in 1 Timothy, Paul wrote against false teachers, but much of the letter challenged Timothy to stay loyal to the gospel. Notice Paul's concern for Timothy. Paul himself was in prison for the gospel and was expected to face execution. His circumstance shaped aspects of the letter. Watch especially for what he said about life and death.

In the face of difficult situations today, embrace the hope found in Christ's victory.

DAY 6 2 Peter 1–3; Jude

As with Paul in 2 Timothy, 2 Peter presents Peter as anticipating his own death (see 1:14). So the apostle pointed his readers to the true gospel, grounded in what God had revealed in Jesus, and he warned them about false teachers (see chap. 2). A warning against false teachers is also the message of the little Book of Jude.

Notice parallels with false ideas that are very popular today. Peter encouraged believers to live in light of the coming of Christ on the Day of the Lord, a theme we first saw in the Old Testament Prophets. In essence both Peter and Jude encouraged Christ followers to be on guard against wrong teachings and to grow in the faith.

How are you guarding yourself against wrong teachings? How are you growing in your faith?

SMALL-GROUP DISCUSSION QUESTIONS

1. How did Peter describe the blood of Christ in 1 Peter 1:19? Is Jesus' blood precious to you? Why?

2. Read 1 Peter 2:9. In what way are believers a royal priesthood? What are our responsibilities as priests?

3. What is the difference between suffering for good rather than evil (see 1 Pet. 3:17)? Read 1 Peter 4:12-14. What should a believer's attitude be toward suffering? Why?

4. In Hebrews 1 in what ways is Jesus superior to the angels?

5. Read Hebrews 2:17. How is Jesus our High Priest? Read Hebrews 4:14-16. Why is Jesus able to identify with our weakness? How does He intervene for us before God's throne? What does this mean to you?

6. Read Hebrews 8. How did Jesus bring about a new and better covenant?

7. Why does Hebrews 9 say Jesus' sacrifice was superior to the Old Testament sacrifices? What does this mean for believers today?

8. Read Hebrews 10:19-36. How are we to live in response to what Jesus has done? Define *faith*, according to Hebrews 11:1. What saints were commended in Hebrews 11? Why? Read Hebrews 12:1-2. How is Jesus the source and perfecter of our faith?

9. Read 2 Timothy 1:7-8. How does Christ give you power and boldness for the Christian life and witness?

10. In what ways is Paul's description of the last days in 2 Timothy 3:2-5 similar to the present day? How do you see these godless qualities promoted in our society? How does your church lift up the truth in your community?

11. Read 2 Timothy 3:16-17. How does God's Word equip you for every aspect of the Christian life? What are some ways your church teaches the Word?

12. Paul summarized his legacy in 2 Timothy 4:6-8. What is the spiritual legacy you want to leave? How does living with eternity in view change the way you live now?

13. Read 2 Peter 1:16-21. What evidence did Peter give for the truth of Jesus' identity? How does Jesus' fulfillment of prophecy give you confidence in witnessing? What fulfilled prophecies you can identify?

14. Read 2 Peter 3:9. Why has God delayed the time of judgment?

15. Read Jude 3. What does it mean to contend for the faith? What are some ways you contend for the faith?

WEEK 52

We have come to the final week in our reading plan. This week we will continue in act 3, scene 4, by reading 1–3 John. These letters were written to combat false teachers and to encourage certain basics as central to true Christian living.

On day 2 we will move into act 3, scene 5, which will explore the Book of Revelation. This remarkable book is at once beautiful, powerful, and wonderfully intimidating—perhaps the most difficult book in the Bible to read. It will help greatly if you have a good study Bible in hand as you read. Free online resources are available at *www.mystudybible.com*. Remember that apocalyptic literature is based in symbolism, and the symbols of the book draw heavily from the Old Testament.

Revelation repeatedly returns to the heavenly throne room. One scholar suggested that Revelation is dramatized as a heavenly courtroom scene in which the rebellious nations of the world are on trial and found wanting, and God's people are vindicated.[1] Watch for the gospel and a celebration of Christ as keys to the unfolding of the book. Christ will defeat the wicked forces of the world by His sacrificial death and will bring those forces to judgment in the end. His people will be vindicated and welcomed into God's presence. The end of the book depicts the reversal of the fall (see Gen. 3) and the re-creation of the heavens and the earth—a wonderful resolution to the Bible's grand story.

DAY 1 1 John; 2 John; 3 John

Tradition tells us that the apostle John wrote 1–3 John. With his distinct writing style John confronted false teachers in the community and pointed to the basics of true Christian belief and practice. As you read 1 John, watch for comments about false teaching. For instance, John emphasized that Jesus had really come in the flesh, addressing a wrong teaching that said Jesus was not really human. The false teachers also seemed to proclaim that they don't sin, and yet they also neglected to meet the needs of other believers, for whom they should have been expressing love. As you read, watch for the essentials to which John pointed as basic to Christian life and belief. He used words like *remain, walk, light, confess, love,* and *know,* and he constantly pointed to the Father, Son, and Spirit. Also watch for contrasts in this book between light and darkness, life and death, truth and lies, loving and hating.

Second John also took up the theme of false teachers. Notice repeated words in this book. Third John, the shortest book in the Bible, was addressed to an elder of the church named Gaius, urging him to show hospitality to the itinerant minister Demetrius, the letter carrier.

How will you live the truths of 1–3 John this week?

SCENE 5: CHRIST'S SECOND COMING AND REIGN: GOD'S FUTURE FOR THE KINGDOM

DAY 2 Revelation 1–5

Revelation 1–5 lays the foundation for the book by setting forth a prologue (see 1:1-8); interaction among John, Christ, and a network of churches in ancient Asia (see 1:9–3:22); and twin visions of the heavenly throne room (4:1–5:14). As you read, remember that much of the language in Revelation is symbolic, representing real truths but doing so with word pictures. For instance, in 1:16 Jesus has a sharp sword protruding from His mouth. This is a symbol for the powerful Word of God as a word of judgment. Notice Jesus' centrality to this whole section of Revelation, as He will be in the whole book.

The descriptions of the seven churches in Revelation 2–3 are to be instructive for all churches of all time (see 2:23). Chapter 4 shows us that God is at the center of Revelation, and chapter 5 shows us that Christ is at the center of the purposes of God. Pay particular attention to why the Lamb was praised in chapter 5. The opening of the scroll was the opening of God's purposes for His people and judgment on His enemies.

Praise the Lamb today for the gospel.

TIMELINE
New Testament Timeline: write *Jesus* on line I in act 3, scene 5.

DAY 3 Revelation 6–10

The scroll in Revelation 5 has seven seals, and the vision of the seals will lead to the blowing of seven trumpets, then to seven bowls. The vision of the seals (see 6:1–8:5) provides scenes of judgment (the first four seals); the cry of the martyrs for justice (seal 5); the cry of the wicked to be hidden from God's face (seal 6); and the seventh seal, which after an interlude of silence leads to the seven trumpets. The seven seals thus lay a foundation for the detailed judgment of the wicked and vindication of the righteous that follow.

In Revelation 8:6–9:21 the trumpets blow a warning about God's judgment. The plagues of Egypt (see Ex. 7–10) and Joel's locust plague (see Joel 1:6; 2:1-5) provide the backdrop for these images. Revelation 10 focuses again on John's role in delivering the prophecy. The gospel story, that sin devastates and Christ saves, is depicted on a cosmic scale.

Praise God for His righteousness, even in judgment.

DAY 4 Revelation 11–13

We read more about the conflict between world forces that oppose the church and Christ's followers. Revelation 11 depicts the prophetic role of the church as it stands for the Word of God in the world. Moses and Elijah provide the imagery here. Revelation 12–13 stands at the heart of the book. Chapter 12 gives a picture of the gospel; Christ has already defeated Satan and provided salvation for His people, but Satan attempts to hurt Christ's people.

The beasts of Revelation 13 have their backdrop in Daniel 7. For the churches in Asia during John's time, the beast represented the Roman emperor, and the beast from the earth symbolized the priesthood of his cult. On a grander scale, however, the beasts represent the political forces of all time that oppose Christ and the church. The Scriptures indicate that this opposition will increase at the end of the age before Christ returns.

Pray today for our Christian brothers and sisters facing persecution around the world.

DAY 5 Revelation 14–18

Revelation 14 introduces the remaining visions in the book, anticipating the fall of Babylon (Rome), the harvesting of God's people, and the winepress of God's judgment. In Revelation 15:1–16:21 we read about the seven bowls of God's judgment on Babylon. The bowls echo the plagues proclaimed in the seven trumpets but without the limitation to one-third, and the first five bowls are based on the plagues against Egypt in the exodus. The sixth bowl calls forth the drying of the riverbed of the Euphrates River, bringing to mind the crossing of the Red Sea. But here the river is dried to make way for the kings of the east in preparation for the final battle. The seventh and final bowl echoes the plague of hail in Exodus but also heralds and initiates the judgment of Babylon.

In Revelation 17–18 we see the fall of Babylon. Notice in the final chapters of the book the contrast between the great, wicked city Babylon and the city of God, the heavenly Jerusalem.

Identify world powers and systems that do not follow God. How has God warned them that judgment is coming?

DAY 6 Revelation 19–22

Christ's second coming and reign constitute the glorious end of the story of the Bible, which God will write on our future. Notice the convergence of earlier themes as God re-creates the heavens and the earth and again walks with people (see Gen. 1–2). In Revelation 19 the judgment against Babylon and its downfall are celebrated, and the marriage of the Lamb